60

FARRAR
STRAUS
GIROUX

Praise for *Rumspringa*

"Never sensationalizing, Shachtman lets the teenagers themselves articulate their struggle to choose between a tradition-bound life and the myriad temptations of 'the real world.'"   —*The Washington Post*

"[An] absorbing study of Amish youth . . . Scrupulous and open-minded."   —Karen Karbo, *Newsday*

"[An] even-handed study."   —Emily Bobrow, *Time Out New York*

"A fascinating glimpse into the lives of Amish youth . . . Full of jarring images."   —Harry Merritt, *The Baltimore Sun*

MARK CONNOLLY

Tom Shachtman

RUMSPRINGA

Tom Shachtman is an award-winning documentarian and the author of many books, including *Skyscraper Dreams*, *Around the Block*, and *The Day America Crashed*.

RUMSPRINGA

This book is based, in part, on research done for
the Stick Figure Productions documentary *The Devil's Playground*.

RUMSPRINGA

To Be or Not to Be Amish

TOM SHACHTMAN

NORTH POINT PRESS

A division of Farrar, Straus and Giroux

New York

North Point Press
A division of Farrar, Straus and Giroux
18 West 18th Street, New York 10011

Distributed in Canada by Douglas & McIntyre Ltd.
Printed in the United States of America
Published in 2006 by North Point Press
First paperback edition, 2007

The Library of Congress has cataloged the hardcover edition as follows:
Shachtman, Tom, 1942–
Rumspringa : to be or not to be Amish / Tom Shachtman.— 1st ed.
    p.   cm.
Includes bibliographical references (p.   ).
ISBN-13: 978-0-86547-687-5 (hardcover : alk. paper)
ISBN-10: 0-86547-687-X (hardcover : alk. paper)
    1. Rumspringa.   2. Amish teenagers—Conduct of life.   3. Amish teenagers—
Religious life.   4. Amish teenagers—Social life and customs.   I. Title.

E184.M45S53 2006
305.235088'28973—dc22

                                                          2006004329

Paperback ISBN-13: 978-0-86547-742-1
Paperback ISBN-10: 0-86547-742-6

Designed by Debbie Glasserman

www.fsgbooks.com

5 7 9 10 8 6

For Leon Shachtman, 1913–2004

The majority never *has right on its side.*
Never, I say! That is one of these social lies
against which an independent, intelligent man
must wage war. Who is it that constitute the
majority of the population in a country? Is it the
clever folk, or the stupid? . . . (Uproar and cries.)
Oh, yes—you can shout me down, I know!
But you cannot answer me. The majority has
might *on its side—unfortunately; but* right *it has*
not . . . The minority is always in the right.

—Henrik Ibsen,
An Enemy of the People

Contents

A Note to the Reader   *xi*

1. "Going Away"   3

2. "A Glory Old Time"   34

3. "Straightforward Conversations"   60

4. Education: "Prepare for Usefulness"   91

5. Faith and Doctrine: "Stand Fast and
   Believe the Word as Written"   116

6. Shunning: To Keep the Church "Pure"   148

7. Farming: "The Ideal Occupation"   173

8. "Working Away"   189

9. "Women's Lib Would Have a Field Day
   Among the Amish"   211

10. Seeking Solutions   232

11. "Coming Home"—An Essay   251

   Notes   *273*
   Selected Bibliography   *281*
   Acknowledgments   *285*

A Note to the Reader

The more than four hundred hours of interviews that are the backbone of this book were conducted over a six-year period. They began in 1999 with research for what eventually became the Stick Figure Productions documentary *The Devil's Playground*, broadcast in 2002. The interviewers were the director, Lucy Walker, and the producers, Toby Oppenheimer, Steven Cantor, and Daniel Laikind. I conducted further interviews and some reinterviews between 2002 and 2004.

In accordance with long-standing tradition in writing about the Old Order Amish, in this book interviewees from the sect are referred to by full names only if they have previously been publicly identified in the press. Otherwise, and to preserve their privacy, individuals are identified by first names and initials. For the same purpose, in certain instances some personal details have been altered.

—Tom Shachtman
Salisbury, Connecticut
September 2005

RUMSPRINGA

"Going Away"

In the gathering dusk of a warm, humid summer Friday evening in northern Indiana, small groups of Amish-born girls between the ages of sixteen and nineteen walk along straight country lanes that border flat fields of high cornstalks and alfalfa, dotted here and there with neat, drab houses set back from the roads. One pair of girls walks westward, another pair eastward toward the destination; a threesome travels due south. Although not yet baptized members of the church, these young ladies all wear traditional "plain" Amish garb: solid-colored, long-sleeved dresses with aprons over them, long stockings and black shoes; white bonnets indicative of their status as unmarried cover their long hair, which is parted in the middle and pinned up in the back. A few carry small satchels. Though they are used to exercise and walking strongly, their demeanor is demure, so that they appear younger than non-Amish girls of the same age. The walkers pass homes where the women and children in the yards, taking in the last of the wash off clotheslines, wear no shoes, as though to better sense the warm air, grass, and dirt between their toes. Along these country lanes, while there are a few homes belonging to the "English," the non-Amish, most are owned by Old Order Amish families.

As the shards of sunset fade, electric lights are turned on in the English homes, but only the occasional gas lamp pierces the twilight of the Amish homesteads, illuminating buggies at rest in driveways, silhouetting horses in small pastures against high clouds, and here and there a dog and cat wandering about. No music can be heard coming from the Amish houses as the girls walk past, no faint whisper of broadcast news, no whir of air conditioners. All that disturbs the calm is the occasional animal bark, whinny, snort, or trill, and every few minutes the rapid clop-clop-clop of a horse-drawn vehicle going past; the girls' peals of laughter sound as innocent, as timeless, and as much a part of the natural surround as birds' calls.

From their several directions, the walkers converge on the home of another teenage Amish girl. There they go upstairs to the bedroom shared by the young females of the family, to huddle and giggle in anticipation of what is to happen later that night, after full dark. In a window visible from the lane, they position a lit gas lamp, and they leave open an adjacent side door to the house and stairway. These are signals to male Amish youth out "cruising" that there are young ladies inside who would welcome a visit, and who might agree to go out courting—a part of the rumspringa, *or "running-around," tradition that has been passed down in Amishdom for many generations.*

The setting for this evening's *rumspringa* activities, near the town of Shipshewana and the border between LaGrange and Elkhart counties in north-central Indiana, is similar to those in the other major areas of Old Order Amish population, Holmes and Wayne counties in Ohio, and Lancaster County in Pennsylvania; and similar *rumspringa* preparation scenes at young girls' homes are also enacted regularly in those areas.

Such activities usually go unseen by tourists, despite Shipshewana in Indiana, Berlin in Ohio, and Intercourse in Pennsylvania having become tourist destinations for millions of Americans each year. Shipshe, as the locals call their town, has only a few streets but these are lined with nearly a hundred attractive "specialty" shops that sell merchandise as likely to have been manufactured in China as crafted in Indiana.

East and west of the sales district, the area is rural and mostly Amish. The young ladies gathered in that upstairs bedroom, waiting for young men to come calling, work in Shipshe, Middlebury, Goshen, and other neighboring towns as waitresses, dishwashers, store clerks, seamstresses, bakers, and child-minders. All have been employed since graduating from Amish schools at age fourteen or fifteen, or leaving public schools after the eighth grade, and have been dutifully turning over most of their wages to their families to assist with household expenses. After their full days at work, and before leaving their homes this evening, the young ladies have also performed their chores: feeding the cows they milked earlier in the day, providing fresh bedding for the horses, assisting with housecleaning and laundry, with the preparation, serving, and clearing away of the evening meal, and caring for dozens of younger siblings.

In the upstairs bedroom, the girls play board games and speak of certain "hopelessly uncool" teenagers in their age cohort, girls and boys whom they have known all their lives but who are not going cruising and who seem content to spend their *rumspringa* years attending Sunday sings after church and volleyball games arranged by parents or church officials.

An hour later, when the girls have had their fill of board games, and when the parents of the house are presumed to be asleep, cars and half-trucks are heard pulling into the dirt lane. The battered, secondhand autos and pickups are parked well off the road, to be less visible to passersby in horse-drawn buggies. Out of the vehicles clamber males from sixteen to their early twenties, most of them Amish-born but at this moment trying hard not to appear Amish, wearing T-shirts and jeans, some with long hair or crew cuts instead of Amish bowl cuts. A few English friends accompany them. The young Amish-raised men have day jobs in carpentry shops, in factories that make recreational vehicles and mobile homes, in construction, or at the animal auction and flea market in town; none are farmers, though most still live at home, some on farms and the rest on "farmettes," five- to ten-acre homesteads that have a vegetable garden and areas of pasturage for the horses and the occasional family cow.

The young men shine a flashlight on the upstairs room where

the lamp is lit, and at that countersignal one girl comes downstairs and greets the guys, who then creep up the stairs. After introductory banter in the crowded room, the girls are invited to go with the boys, and they all troop back out to the cars, the Amish girls still in their traditional garb. A few words pass between the daughter of the house and her parents—who have not, after all, been asleep—but while these include admonitions to be careful, they do not specify that she is to come home at a particular hour. If the parents are worried about this pack of teenagers "going away" on a Friday night—perhaps not to return until Sunday evening—they do not overtly display that emotion.

Once the young ladies hit the cars, and the cars have pulled away from the homestead, appearances and behaviors begin to change. While riding along, each Amish girl performs at least one of many actions that have been forbidden to her throughout her childhood: lights up a cigarette, grabs a beer, switches on the rock and rap music on the car radio or CD player, converses loudly and in a flirtatious manner with members of the opposite sex.

Coursing past a small schoolhouse where a few of the riders attended classes in the recent past and into the small, nearly deserted center of Shipshewana—whose restaurants stop serving at 8:00 p.m.—the convoy heads south, past the auction depot, stopping for a while on the outskirts of the business district at a gas station and convenience store. In addition to vehicle parking spaces, the station has a hitching post for horses and buggies. What these Amish teenagers seek on this visit is the convenience store's bathrooms, located next to a side door. In a bunch, the girls head into them, occupying for a while both the Gents' and the Ladies' as their male companions stand guard and graze the aisles, the older ones buying beer for them all, the younger ones springing for jerky, chips, and nuts. There are no sexually explicit magazines here at which the boys might glance, because such magazines are not carried in local stores, in deference to the wishes of the Amish and Mennonites in the area. A few young males shove quarters into a gambling machine, the Pot O Silver, which has the potential of returning them five or ten dollars for every half-dollar they put in. No one wins more than a quarter.

When the girls emerge from the bathrooms, only two of the eight still look Amish; the other six have been transformed. They wear jeans, T-shirts, and other mainstream American teenager outfits, some revealing their navels. Hair coverings have been removed, and a few have also let down their hair, uncut since childhood. "Ready to party," one lady avows. "Cruisin' and boozin'," another responds. The counter clerk, an older woman in Mennonite garb, seems unabashed by the changes in attire.

In the cars once again, cell phones—also forbidden equipment—emerge from hiding places, some from under the girls' clothing. Calls to compatriots in other vehicles, buggies as well as cars, yield the information that many dozens of Amish teenagers are now roaming the roads while trying to ascertain the location of this week's "hoedown." Soon it is identified: closer to Emma, a town three miles south of Shipshewana and not far from Westview High, the public school attended by many of the non-Amish revelers. The cars pass a young woman in a buggy heading in the direction of the party; she is smoking a cigarette and talking on her cell phone; the buggy's window flaps are open, to disperse the tobacco smoke and perhaps to facilitate the cell phone connection.

As they would in similar settings in Holmes or Lancaster County, the young Amish on the road to a party in northern Indiana pass familiar territory composed of quiet Amish homesteads and farms, suburban-looking English homes, a few factories and assembly buildings, and some small workshops. Here is a roadside stand operated by a Yoder family; there is a quilt boutique run by a Miller family; the small-engine repair shop of a member of the Esh family is nestled on a side road but has a sign visible from the main route; over yonder is a Weaver family furniture-making factory.

Around midnight, scores of Amish teenagers and twentysomethings converge on the back acres of a farm south of Shipshewana, several miles from the nearest town, a third of a mile from the farmhouse, and hidden from the nearest road by a forest of cornstalks. A used-car-lot inventory of cars, trucks, buggies, bicycles, and motorcycles is already parked here. Iced coolers of beer are put out; Amish teenagers reach for bottles with both hands. Young, mechanically adept men hook up portable CD players and boom-box speakers to car batteries. Shortly, rock and rap music blasts. Heads nod and bodies sway to the beat.

Many of the Amish kids know the words of the most current rock songs, even of black rap recordings that speak of mayhem in inner-city ghettos and anger against whites, songs they have learned from listening to battery-powered radios that they bought with the first money they earned, and that they have kept hidden at home. "When I'm angry at my bossy brothers," one young lady says, "I play rock on my radio; when I'm happy, I play country."

To have a focus for the party, the participants gather straw and brush for a bonfire. Its bright light and stark shadows crosshatch partygoers at the edges of the center, where various transactions are occurring. Most of the Amish youth are from northern Indiana, but some have come from across the state line in Michigan or from many hours away in Missouri and Ohio. There are about four hundred youth at this almost-deserted site, out of about two thousand adolescent Amish in northern Indiana. Some of the kids are what others refer to as "simmies," literally, foolish in the head, young, naïve, new to *rumspringa*—and, most of them, willing to work hard to lose the label quickly.

Beer is the liquid of choice, but there are also bottles of rum and vodka, used to spike soft drinks. Some of the younger kids do not know the potency of what they are drinking, or what it might do to them. Many will be sick before long. Most guzzle to mimic the others, while gossiping about who is not there or is not drinking. This night, one young woman will wonder why she always seems to drink too much.

In one corner of the party, joints of marijuana are passed around, as are pipes of crank (crystal methamphetamine). Lines of cocaine are exchanged for money. A handful of the partygoers are seriously addicted, while others are trying drugs for the first time. Crank is incredibly and instantly addictive, and it is relatively simple and cheap to make; the only ingredient used that is not available from a local hardware store, anhydrous ammonia, is a gaseous fertilizer easily stolen from tanks on farms. Those few partygoers interested in doing hard drugs gather in a different location than the majority, who prefer drinking beer or smoking pot.

As the party gets into full swing, and beer and pot are making the participants feel no pain, a few Amish girls huddle and make plans to jointly rent an apartment in a nearby town when they turn eighteen, as some older girls have already done. Others shout in Pennsylvania Dutch and in English about how much it will cost to travel to and attend an Indianapolis rock concert, and the possibilities of having a navel pierced or hair cut buzz short. One bunch of teens dances to music videos shown on a laptop computer; a small group of guys, near a barn, distributes condoms.

As such parties wear on, the Amish youth become even less distinguishable from their English peers, shedding their demureness, mimicking the in-your-face postures of the mainstream teen culture, with its arrogance, defiance, raucousness, inner-city-gang hand motions and exaggerated walking stances.

"The English girls prefer us Amish guys because we're stronger and better built and we party harder," insisted one young Amish man at a similar party. Another countered that it is because the Amish guys have more money in their pockets—the result of not having to spend much on food and shelter, since most of them are living at home. The English guys are also partial to the Amish young ladies, this young man added, because Amish girls are "more willing than English girls to get drunk." Of temptation-filled parties like this, one Amish young woman will later comment, "God talks to me in one ear, Satan in the other. Part of me wants to be Amish like my parents, but the other part wants the jeans, the haircut, to do what I want to do."

Couples form and head off into the darkness. Some petting goes further than exploration, and this night one of the girls who earlier walked that country lane loses her virginity. Another partygoer becomes pregnant; several weeks from now, when she realizes it, she will simply advance her wedding date so that her child, as with about 12 percent of first births among the Amish, will be born before her marriage is nine months old. This evening, as well, a few female partygoers will bring boys home, and, with their parents' cognizance, spend the night in "bed courtship," on the girls' beds but "bundled" separately.

During parties like this, as the hours wear on, the boys frequently damage property. There are fistfights; one partygoer recalled a particularly bad incident in which a lad in a fit of bloody rage ripped the earring stud from another young man's ear.

At first light, the farm's owners and their children move about the area, to herd in and milk the cows. One farmer's daughter, spotting a partygoer about to throw up, smilingly hands her an empty pail.

An hour later, the sun is fully up, but most of the exhausted partygoers in various sheltered locations around the back acres are still asleep. Undisturbed, they will wake again near noon. Some have made plans to go to a mall, twenty miles away, to shop and see a movie before continuing the party tomorrow evening in another semideserted location.

Near Shipshe, Berlin, and Intercourse, those Amish youngsters walking on the wild side of *rumspringa* during this weekend will party on until, late on Sunday, they return home to sober up and ready themselves for Monday and the workweek. Most have no plans to tell their parents, upon returning to the family hearth, precisely where they have been for the previous forty-eight hours, or with whom they spent their "going away" time. While the parents may well ask such questions, the children feel little obligation to answer them.

Rumspringa is a Pennsylvania Dutch term, usually translated as "running around" and derived in part from the German word *Raum*, which means "space" in the sense of outside or outdoors space, room to roam. "Running around outside the bounds" is a more complete translation. The *rumspringa* period begins when an Amish youth turns sixteen; at that age, since the youth has not yet been baptized, he or she is not subject to the church's rules about permitted and forbidden behaviors. During *rumspringa*, Amish youth—a large percentage of them for the first time in their lives—go on their own in the outside world. Nearly all continue to live with their families, however, and many, maybe even a majority, do not go to the parties or otherwise engage in behaviors that Amish parents and church officials consider wild. Rather, they attend Sunday singings, occasionally go bowling, take part in structured activities supervised by church elders—tame stuff—but they have license to do things they have never done before. An individual's *rumspringa* ends when he or she agrees to be baptized into the church and to take up the responsibilities attendant on being an adult member of the Amish community.

Rumspringa and the Amish are the subject of this book. Interviews with youth going through *rumspringa*, and with their parents and others in the Amish community concerned with their *rumspringa* activities, constitute the bulk of its pages. Considering that the Amish make up a very small percentage of the country's population, and that not even all Amish teenagers take part in *rumspringa* activities, the question arises: What makes *rumspringa* of interest to readers who are not Amish?

The Amish are more like most mainstream Americans than almost any other minority in our midst. They share with the majority, and with this author, a common heritage: they are of "white" European stock, they embrace the Judeo-Christian ethos, and they come from families that have been in the United States for more than one generation. Also relevant are the ways in which the Amish differ from the majority, namely, in practicing an intense Christian religiosity that suffuses their daily lives, in deliberately attempting to live separately from the larger society, and in refusing to adopt precisely those practices and products of our mainstream society that have come to define and represent America and Americans to the rest of the world—our cars, our entertainment, our consumerism. This combination of shared heritage and deep cultural differences makes the Amish a particularly significant mirror for the rest of us.

The way the Amish practice Christianity may be the most salient facet of that mirror, for the United States of America is a nation whose bedrock precepts, rules of law, and standards of conduct are rooted in a Judeo-Christian, Bible-based ethos. Some of us pay more attention to those roots and text, others less, but they are always there, affecting who we are, what we do, and how we do it. As for mirrors held up by other minority groups, the majority is often able to dismiss the relevance to itself of the ways of life, behaviors, and critiques of American society that come from Asian Buddhists or Arab Muslims on the grounds that their backgrounds, cultures, and practices have so few similarities to the abovementioned majority. One cannot do the same with the Amish.

So: I contend that the adamantine Amish mirror is clearer than other, more shadowed reflective surfaces, and hope that it is also capable of sharper focus.

No images in the Amish mirror may be more illuminating, this father of two grown children has found, than those detailing how the Amish deal with adolescence. As do most parents, I find it important to listen very carefully to children when they are going through stressful events and periods—which is why this book takes a documentary approach to the lives of Amish youngsters in *rumspringa*, quoting them at length, and why it also delves into the activities of their parents and community members in regard to *rumspringa*.

"Adolescents seem to serve as a repository for the conflicts of the culture and as a bearer of its mythic projections. The more complex society becomes, the more perplexing, troubling, and problematic their role appears to be," writes S. C. Feinstein, editor of a scholarly journal on the subject. Adolescence is a journey from childhood to adulthood, and Amish adolescents, as do most Americans of that age, experience joys, ills, temptations, and challenges during their journeys, and face dangers that are far from trivial—addictions, sexually transmitted diseases, criminality, and the failures that may stem from inadequately preparing for assumption of the responsibilities of adult life.

Amish kids encounter those dangers and challenges in more concentrated form than do most of the children of the majority culture, for two reasons. First, they arrive at adolescence after childhoods that are far more sheltered (and structured) than those of our own children, and, second, Amish teens begin the *rumspringa* journey carrying weighty baggage consisting of the moral imperatives, biblical precepts, and complex sets of rules that the sect has imparted to them in their homes, at church, and in school.

Adolescence in America today presents youngsters with the thrill of escaping from parental supervision, with the titillation of closer contact with the opposite sex, with the lure of forbidden substances, the attraction of newness itself, and the heady scent of rebellion. In addition to experiencing these sensations, Amish youth are roiled by powerful emotional currents specific to their situation. As one regular Amish partygoer put it, after highly sheltered childhoods they have been "unleashed . . . All of a sudden you could do something—you could breathe!" Able at last to indulge their curiosity about the world, they do so, to frissons of endangerment and empowerment.

Rumspringa is practiced mostly in the larger and older Amish settlements of LaGrange, Holmes, and Lancaster counties; in many smaller Amish enclaves, while the teenagers may be said to be in *rumspringa* because of their age and unbaptized state, they are not permitted to do a lot of running around. Other Anabaptists, such as the more numerous Mennonites, do not have a *rumspringa* period, although, like the Amish, Mennonites insist that their young people come to the church through a freely chosen, informed, and adult baptismal decision.

"We don't give our young folks leave to go out and sin just to get it out of their system," says Dennis L, an Amish grandfather in Shipshewana. "What we give them is a little space so they can be with people their own age and find a partner." The purpose of *rumspringa*, such elders insist, is to give youngsters leave and ways to find an appropriate mate. The community's expectation is that, upon completion of the courtship task, a young Amish couple will end their *rumspringa* by agreeing to marry and concurrently make the commitment to be baptized—to "join church," in their idiom. The further expectation is that after marriage the pair will settle down, engage in no more experimental behaviors, and live fully Amish lives, under the direction of the church.

At stake for the Amish community in the *rumspringa* process is nothing less than the survival of their sect and way of life. For if the unbaptized children who venture into the world at sixteen do not later return to the fold in sufficient numbers, the sect will dwindle and die out.

What a tremendous risk these Amish parents and communities take in permitting their adolescents a *rumspringa*! The threat is that these children, once let loose, may never return; but that gamble must be chanced by the community because its members sense that the threat of not permitting the children a *rumspringa* is even greater. Absent a *rumspringa* process, there would be a higher probability of loss, of many more Amish youth succumbing to the lure of the forbidden, perhaps even after marriage and baptism, with resultant defections from the sect and havoc within it. The Amish count on the *rumspringa* process to inoculate youth against the strong pull of the forbidden by dosing them with the vaccine of a little worldly experience. Their gamble is also based on the notion that there is no firmer adhesive bond to a faith and way of life than a bond freely chosen, in this case chosen after *rumspringa* and having sampled some of the available alternative ways of living.

Judged by practical results, *rumspringa* must be termed largely successful. According to studies done by Thomas J. Meyers, a sociology professor at Goshen College, more than 80 percent of Amish youth do eventually become Amish church members. In some areas, the "retention rate" exceeds 90 percent.

Still, questions arise about the process. Is the choice of returning to the sect made in an entirely free manner? Have the children really "been there, done that" before they return? When on the loose, did they master the emotional and intellectual tools needed to survive in that world before deciding to give up on it?

Many Amish parents worry about their youth in *rumspringa*, whether or not those youth participate in the party scene, because the adolescents now going through *rumspringa* are significantly different from their forefathers and foremothers. While earlier generations of Amish spent their entire lives on farms, having little interchange with the non-Amish world, today more than 70 percent of male adults do not farm, and if current trends persist, an even larger percentage of their children will spend their lives in nonfarm occupations. The concern among Amish elders is that this nonfarm home and work environment will overexpose the next generation of Amish to the "English" world, and that even if they return to the church after *rumspringa*, their altered outlooks may eventually compromise the church's ability to sustain itself.

"A good party is when there's, like, two hundred kids there—really loud music, and everybody's drinking and smoking and having a great old time. . . . It starts getting really good at, like, twelve o'clock, and the last people don't leave till five. And then, all at once somebody's, like, 'The cops are here! Okay, let's all start running,' And we do," says Joann H of north-central Indiana.

A shy girl, dark-haired, dark-eyed, plain-faced, she had contemplated going out into the world with some trepidation, and not just because she thought herself not particularly good-looking and worried about her ability to attract a future husband; Joann was both intrigued and scared by what might happen to her. She had seen something of English culture at Das Dutchman Essenhaus, the big tourist complex where she waited on tables, but she had not really been beyond the community's borders.

It has taken her a while to get into the swing of partying. When Joann began her *rumspringa*, she would go with other girls to a friend's house and await the guys, but when they came calling in their jalopies, they always seemed to choose other girls as companions. Some Friday nights, Joann did not get asked out; however, when all the girls and guys traveled in a pack, she did go. She would change into jeans as her companions did, but she still felt tentative and "confused" about the scene. The boys drank and carried beer with them, and "if you want some you've got to ask—that's not really cool, asking a guy, 'Hey, can I have a beer?' You know, that's like, 'Hey, what are you after?' " A girl requesting alcohol, she feels, is implying that she wants to get drunk and to have the boy take advantage of her. So Joann never asks for a beer, though she accepts one if it is offered; and if there are beers sitting in the common cooler, she'll take a can.

The oldest girl in her family, Joann has an older brother, who, when she turned sixteen, had been "out there" already for a year, having fun, partying. "I didn't really have a lot of friends," she says, "so I just kind of went out and hung out with my brother and his friends, and before I knew it I was in up to my chin."

Her parents have not dissuaded her, because her father, when young, had "walked on the wild side," and so had his brothers. As Joann grew up, she heard tales of how her father and uncles had guzzled beer and hard stuff, raced hot cars, smoked cigarettes like chimneys, chased women, and run around as though they would never return to the Amish fold. Dad told the stories as cautionaries: though he had come back to the church, his brothers never did. In her father's view, Joann's uncles "got in with the wrong crowd, got in too deep," and went "so far away that they couldn't come back." But Joann knows these uncles—reasonably good guys, even though they have left the Amish faith—and after her first taste of the outside world, she newly empathizes with their unwillingness to decelerate from the "sixty miles an hour they were used to going" in their cars and trucks to the five miles per hour at which they would have to travel in horse-drawn buggies had they become Amish adults. And she is beginning to share her uncles' unease at the prospect of forever wearing only drab Amish clothes and in countless other ways having to "abide by the rules of the church."

She feels this way most keenly when at weekend parties, which to her are wonderfully exciting. In a barn, or in a shop where the machinery is pushed aside to make a dance floor, or at a clearing—wherever—there is lots to drink and smoke, and plenty of darkness if you want to get cozy with a boy, black lights and strobes to add to the exotic, "unreal" feel. The scene is so wild and wacky that, although Joann feels that at heart she is a "good girl," within a few weeks after she began partying in earnest she could hardly wait for weekends to go out and be "bad." "Whenever there is a party, I'm there and I'm drunk . . . just, you know, hanging out with anybody I want to, going out with any guy I want to, just kind of 'Who cares?' " She knows it isn't right but justifies her behavior by reasoning that everybody else is doing it.

Not everyone: about half the Amish Joann's age in this northern Indiana community don't attend the parties, preferring the Sunday sings and volleyball playing; she has known those guys and girls all their lives—they have been her classmates at school, her seatmates at church—but right now Joann feels she has little in common with them. Still, to keep the wild side somewhat at bay, she has made rules about what she will and won't do. Druggies, for instance—she decided not to associate with them at all. One guy, who understood her rule, confessed that he used to smoke pot but insisted he wasn't doing it anymore. Joann recounts, "I'm, like, 'Okay, cool, I'll give you a chance.' " They went around for a few weeks, but then he admitted he was still smoking. They discussed the matter, and he told her, "It's a lot easier for me to talk to people when I'm high," and said that he had been high when he had asked her out. "I'm, like, 'Oh, that makes me feel really good.' " They stopped dating.

Joann has not had sex with the young pot smoker or with any other guys at the parties, though she has been importuned. Most of the Amish partying girls won't "do it," she says, though one party regular is known for sleeping with every guy who asks her, and another became pregnant and then frantic with worry that the father of the unborn child might decide not to marry her. This would be a huge problem, because within the Amish culture, as Joann says, "Abortions aren't allowed. So if you get pregnant—hey, you've got a baby, you know? And *you* have to care for the baby."

After a few months on the party scene, Joann recognizes that there is a "double standard" for dating among the Amish youth. "Guys are more just like, you know, 'Well, I'll ask her out once; if she doesn't want to go out with me, fine; if she does, fine.' " But for the girls, "dating is serious business," because a young woman has to determine, "Do I want to spend the rest of my life with this guy?" Too much is at stake for an Amish girl just to have a fling. The much greater pressure on the girls, Joann feels, explains why it is understood that they, rather than the boys, will make the decisions about sexual intimacy. The guys actually seem to prefer that, readily agreeing to abide by the girls' decisions.

During the week, and despite her job at Das Essenhaus, Joann feels "trapped," having to listen politely while her parents express their dismay about her weekend activities, even though they seem "more upset about me wearing jeans than going to parties."

But Mom and Dad also and repeatedly ask her, in various ways, "Do you really want to do this?"—meaning the partying scene—and she responds that she is not certain but that all her friends are in it. "Go seek out different friends," her parents advise, friends more attuned to pious Amish ways. That seems to Joann difficult to do, since those straight arrows are almost as clueless as her parents about the thrills as well as the perils of being out in the world.

Lydia T is going to "get it" from her parents when she finally rolls home after this weekend "away," she knows, so she is prolonging her time out as best she can, going to two movies and staying over with her non-Amish friend who has an apartment and has agreed to hold for her the things she bought yesterday at the mall. This weekend has been particularly exhilarating. For years, Lydia has been annoyed by having to turn over her weekly paycheck from the venetian blind factory to her father—as Amish custom dictates—while her non-Amish friends are able to spend what they earn on themselves. She says, "My best friend, she'd be having her own money, and I'm, like, 'That's not fair.' So she goes, 'Well, keep it.' And I'm, like, 'No, I can't, because my dad wouldn't approve of that.' And she goes, 'Well, how will he know? Just tell him you put it in the bank. He wouldn't know.' "

Lydia laughed at the idea and told her friend that "when the statement would come out, Dad'd be, like, 'Where's the extra two hundred dollars here? It's gone. Where is it?' "

But the idea grew more delicious as Lydia conjured it—money to burn, and a poke at her father's swagger—and so this past Friday, unbeknownst to him, Lydia cashed her check instead of depositing it in the family bank account, and she and her girlfriend went on a shopping spree. Two pairs of shoes, undergarments, some jeans to wear when she isn't at home—she has blown the whole check, and it feels wonderful.

Anger and possible retribution await Lydia at home, she knows, and not only because she has spent her money on worldly things. Unlike the other partygoers, Lydia is not technically in *rumspringa*; she has already become a member of the church, baptized at seventeen. For a while after her baptism, she had tried to stay within the bounds of the church's rules for behavior, which are quite strict. While she is a person of faith, does want to live in a community of the faithful, and agrees with the underlying basis of the community's rules, the Ten Commandments, and the precepts of Jesus on how to exist in this world, the rules often chafe. The unwritten list of them, the *ordnung*, covers everything from the number of pins that an Amish woman may use to hold together her dress to the directive to defer to men's judgment in all-important matters to what constitutes improper fraternizing with the opposite sex.

Lydia has begun to feel that the concomitants of her membership in the church are making her miss out on a period of life, and on the sorts of experiences, that nonbaptized teenage Amish are enjoying—that she has "joined church too early." So she has been sneaking out on the weekends on the pretext of sleeping over at a friend's house; since the community has few telephones, that is difficult for her parents to verify.

In the past, when her parents found out about her partying, they lit into Lydia, calling her a "troublemaker"—one of their worst epithets—and forcing her to confess her sins to a minister and promise to "correct" herself, adjust her behavior so that it stayed within the boundaries. Surely this time a contrite apology will not suffice to save her from the wrath of her father and of the community. Actually, Lydia doesn't feel very remorseful and says she is "not willing to apologize for what I'm doing—just having fun—and I don't think it is wrong for me."

On Sunday afternoon eighteen-year-old Gerald Y awakes from a drug-induced daze to find himself in his rented trailer-home, with the TV blaring, the smell of beer all about, and other guys, some he hardly knows but has probably met at the back-acres party, passed out on mattresses and chairs. He looks for his girl-friend, Joyce, but she is not there—she probably left rather than spend the night.

His earring studs are still in his ear, which means he has fallen asleep without taking them out. Now he has to pull himself together and prepare to go very early tomorrow morning—4:00 a.m.—to his job, driving a forklift at the RV factory in Goshen. He likes the job, though it is exhausting; lately, his shift has not been getting out until 3:00 that afternoon. The pay is good, but he hasn't been able to save any of it. He blows it on gas, car payments, trailer rent, beer, and cigarettes, but mostly on drugs.

Glimmers of the past two days and nights filter through to him. When coming down from his cocaine high, Gerald had "thought about dying," contemplating "all the bad [expletive deleted]." It has happened to him before, which is why he usually tries to "fall asleep quickly" and avoid such disturbing thoughts, intertwined as they are with his deep belief in Heaven and Hell. Right now, living the way he is—unbaptized, outside the church, addicted to drugs—he is afraid that if he dies tomorrow he'll go straight to Hell.

Cocaine is "awesome," able to make Gerald feel like he's "tackled the world and won," and it "opens my mind to new people, new ideas," to enlarging the circle of friends with whom he converses easily. Drugs also seem to cool the rages he has felt since he was a small boy, waves of sudden anger that crested when he dropped out of school after the eighth grade. But cocaine is "very expensive," eating up his money. And during the periods when he is drugged out, he has to be very careful to avoid meeting his father on a street, because he "couldn't look him in the eye"—Dad is more knowledgeable about the world than other Amish parents and knows when Gerald is "messed up."

Gerald's parents want him to give up the trailer, move back home—no rent, and "everything free," including the food, they promise. When he first started at his job, his mother would prepare lunches for him and leave them in the refrigerator. And when his punch-in time was "normal, like six in the morning," she would wake and make him breakfast, but he asked her not to do so when he had to go in earlier than that, wanting her to have her sleep.

Gerald's parents have taken care to maintain his room as he left it, although a sister is sleeping in it. Those aspects of returning home entice him, but then, if he does return, his parents will also expect him to join the church and become Amish like them—and just now that is the furthest thing from his mind.

He is a person of faith but doesn't think he'll ever want to become Amish. He cherishes his independence—except that he misses having Joyce to wake up next to. She is absent because she wants him off the stuff; that has become clear this weekend. No more cocaine, not even a toke of marijuana—she has tried pot a few times but is not smoking, or drinking, at all anymore, and she wants Gerald to be "clean," too. Her threat is now also clear: he can continue to go out with her, or he can continue to do drugs. It is his choice.

Marlys B is feeling a lot older than the Amish-born young men and women around her this weekend, though she has just turned nineteen. Small-boned and short, rail-thin, with hollow cheeks, dark eyes, dark hair, and penciled eyebrows, she often wears black, though not the black of the Amish on Sundays: her blacks are turtlenecks, bell-bottom jeans, and platform shoes, the whole outfit set off by her big silver hoop earrings. She also drinks her coffee black, with six packets of sugar substitute.

She feels older because while the other kids at the parties are truly running around, looking for a mate, she's past that stage. The only girl and the baby of a family that moved about quite a bit in her youth to be near her father's construction jobs, at age sixteen Marlys had decided that her parents' home was "claustro-phobic" and that she was "ready for rebelling, big time." The first few months of her *rumspringa*, on the party scene, she had been by herself and enjoying it, but then she met Steve. Amish-born and four years older, Steve is "smart and philosophical," has a car and a good job; they "clicked right away" and within a year were living together. Steve had even helped her obtain a job at the RV factory where he worked.

Residing away from the home in her middle teens, Marlys opines, was good for her relationship with her family, because just then the family hearth would have been too "suffocating." "I wouldn't have stood for anyone—my parents or the ministers— trying to tell me what clothes to wear or how to arrange my hair."

A few months after taking the job at the RV factory Marlys had to leave it, and then she and Steve "had a terrible fight" and broke up. Marlys found a new place to live, and a new job, sewing drapes at a factory that serves the RV industry, and tried to enjoy herself on her own. Two months later she and Steve "hooked up again."

This time around, they continue to reside in separate places but spend many hours with each other. In retrospect, Marlys is "glad we'd had our breakup when we were still single," because there would have been terrible consequences had the split occurred after they were married. She hadn't realized until after that time-apart episode that "he's my best friend, my lover, my everything, and I can talk to him about anything." This "anything" included her "female problem." For the longest time, until Steve prodded her, Marlys had put off going to the doctor, because, among other reasons, her current job doesn't provide health insurance. The doctor diagnosed a benign ovarian cyst and prescribed birth control pills to shrink the cyst and regularize her menstrual cycle.

Marlys now thinks it is time for her and Steve—at ages nineteen and twenty-three—to begin thinking seriously about marriage, which means they'll also have to seriously contemplate joining the church and giving up their English lifestyle. They are people of faith, and of the same faith as their parents, and they have talked before about wanting "a slower life out of the rat race." But are they really ready for it?

At twilight on a Sunday after a weekend of *rumspringa* parties in northern Indiana, twenty-one-year-old Johnny Y, his girlfriend, Becky, and his sister Jody are speeding back east in the F-150, along the Indiana Turnpike, which, soon after it reaches the border, becomes the Ohio Turnpike. They had a good time at the parties near Shipshe, which are better than those closer to home; besides, these trips enable Jody to see her sometime boyfriend from Middlebury. It bothers Johnny that Becky will go on a road trip with him in the half-truck only if Jody comes along as chaperone, but that might be expected from an Amish schoolteacher.

Becky is talking over the seat to Jody in the back while he drives and listens intently to the Indians game. Cleveland radio has a good range, and the truck's receiver picks it up easily. The drive to the Y family farmette, at the eastern edge of Wayne County, will take another several hours, and listening to the game might take up the whole ride. The Tribe is at home, at Jacobs Field, playing the Seattle Mariners. In the gathering darkness, Johnny no longer has a need for the shade that his Indians cap has been providing; he reverses it on his head, putting the beak at his neck, like the rally caps the bench jockeys sport when Cleveland

has to come from behind late in a game. He looks forward to jaw-
ing over tonight's game with his co-workers at the brake factory
tomorrow at lunch.

Growing up in an Amish household with no television or radio, Johnny had known little about major league baseball, although he had played in the infield in softball games at school.
Then, early in his *rumspringa*, a group of the slightly older Amish
guys had taken him with them to a Saturday game at Jacobs Field.

"I never seen so many people in one place at one time," he recalls. "It was amazing. Everybody yelling and shouting, drinking
beer and eating hot dogs, waving towels. It was great. And then I
started whooping and hollering along with them because, well, I
mean, I don't know how to describe it—it was, like, *so* fantastic.
One of those games where the lead goes back and forth, y'know?
You hang there on edge—we're ahead and you're up, then we're
behind and you're down, then you zoom way up when we win.
And it was perfect, too, because Omar was the hero."

Omar Vizquel, legendary shortstop of the Indians, had not only
made the game-winning hit but also turned a double play to snuff
out a threat in a late inning. Johnny, having played the infield
himself a bit, had been amazed at the acrobatics of this play. "A
four-six-three, y'know?" Second baseman to shortstop to first
baseman. Those numbers and the number 13, which Vizquel
wore, became Johnny's lucky numbers. "Even bet on them in the
lottery, a few times," he confides. That first game was back when
Vizquel's teammates had included Jim Thome, the first baseman
and home-run hitter who wore his socks high in honor of his
grandfather's ball-playing career—Thome, who had later broken
all Cleveland fans' hearts, including Johnny's, by deserting the Indians and signing with Philadelphia for "something unreal, like
eighty-five million dollars."

Johnny admits to having become a fan, with his Indians cap
and a laminated card containing the team's schedule in his wallet;
he has not put a bumper sticker on his truck, though, "because
that might get my parents in trouble" with the church. Nor is he
a sports fan in general; he has no feeling for the Cleveland Cava-

liers of the NBA, or other Cleveland teams, but he adores "the Tribe." "I mean, like, I know it's only a team, and *Thou shalt make no graven images* and all that, but still, it's fun being a fan."

Having turned twenty-one, and "five years on the loose," Johnny realizes he is getting a bit old to continue "rumspringing," but he likes partying, likes these road trips, and likes having one too many beers now and then. He's not ready to give it up, join church, and become Amish, as his parents want him to. "Besides," he teases, "how would Jody get to Shipshe if I wasn't driving her?"

At the turn of the twentieth century, there were 5,000 Old Order Amish. Because of various defections and splits, and economic conditions, their numbers increased only gradually until the 1950s, when they began to soar. Twenty-five years ago, there were 100,000 Amish; today there are an estimated 200,000 Amish individuals, of whom about half are under the age of eighteen. The Amish make up less than one-tenth of 1 percent of the population of the United States, but their numbers are increasing very rapidly. The doubling of the Amish population in two decades is due to the high Amish birthrate—the average family has seven children—and to the very high retention rate.

In 2003 there were 333 Amish church districts in 28 states from Montana to Maine, Wisconsin to Florida, and in Ontario Province in Canada, though most are concentrated in Ohio, Pennsylvania, and Indiana. A recent census of church districts reports that the traditional leading centers of Amish population are being closely challenged by fast-growing "daughter" settlements in other states. A new Amish settlement is established somewhere in the United States or in Ontario, on average, every five weeks. A correspondent to an Amish weekly newspaper, *The Budget*, suggested that the rate of increase for the Amish is the same as that of the Jews in ancient Egypt: Joseph arrived in Egypt with a dozen men and six dozen women and children; twelve or so generations later, when Moses prepared to lead the Jews out of Egypt, they were 600,000 souls.

Ten million Americans each year come as tourists to the enclaves of the Amish. According to a survey done for Shipshewana
businesses, 90 percent of the town's tourists come from nearby
states and the non-Amish areas of Indiana, and they come primarily to shop in Amish-themed shops and eat in Amish-themed
restaurants. Viewing the Amish themselves ranks third as a reason
for a visit. A county survey in Lancaster found that tourists to the
Amish there spend about $1.3 billion a year, and perhaps $4 to $5
billion countrywide in Amish homelands.

From my interviews with young Amish shopgirls, waitresses,
and buggy drivers in Indiana, Ohio, and Pennsylvania who deal
with tourists every day, and who try to answer visitors' questions,
a portrait emerges of what the usual tourist knows or wants to
verify. To tourists, the Amish are the people who wear "plain"
clothes, travel by horse and buggy, speak Pennsylvania Dutch,
do not use electricity, do not watch television or other entertainment, and do not want to be photographed. Most tourists
also impute to the Amish a collective character of moral purity,
naïveté, willful ignorance about the world, the ability to survive without creature comforts, and adherence to old-fashioned
virtues.

Tourists also are of the opinion that the Amish life nurtures
qualities that visitors do not have in their own lives but yearn
for—simplicity, innocence, close touch with nature, a slow-paced
existence. The evidence for this, shopkeepers say, is the types
of souvenirs and Amish-themed gimcracks that tourists choose
to buy.

As David Weaver-Zercher concludes in his study, *The Amish in
the American Imagination*, mainstreamers have come to view the
Amish as "homespun saints," a "saving remnant" of devout Christians who demonstrate by their intense Christianity and the rules
for behavior that they derive from the Bible how far the rest of us
have strayed from true faith—and this is a very merchandisable
image.

Most visitors idealize the Amish, to the absurd point at which a
fair number are annoyed to learn that Amish farming is not usu-

ally organic, that the Amish are not monks and nuns, that they gab on a telephone when they get the chance, and that sin is not unknown in Amish communities.

For casual visitors, though, Amishdom remains a nice, romantic, and safe place. It is historic, Pilgrim and Puritan combined, and it speaks American English—a foreign country that Americans can tour without having to go beyond our borders, and from which they can easily return, bearing tidy packages of sentimental and symbolic value. In the postcards available for purchase in Amishdom, cows are always beautifully groomed, though in reality cows, Amish or not, are frequently messy with mud and manure.

What truly distinguishes the Amish from the rest of us is not as visible: their interior lives. Old Order Amish dress and travel as they do, reject the use of electricity from the common grid, worship in their homes rather than in church buildings, end their children's formal schooling after the eighth grade, and engage in many other nonmainstream behaviors because these activities are mandated by and in congruence with their religious beliefs. The Amish are charged with the task of being "in the world but not of the world"; maintaining that separation requires a constant battle with the surrounding culture, and in that endless conflict it is the depth, strength, and completeness of their beliefs that sustain them. *Rumspringa* as a cultural practice exists partly as a result of this need to keep separate, and equally from the basic Anabaptist belief that only informed and repentant adults should be baptized.

In the late Middle Ages, when Anabaptism began, it was a radical movement, born of the desire to separate church and state—then entirely conjoined—and to baptize only adults, which was then contrary to civil law. The first substantial Anabaptist manifesto was issued in 1527, at Schleitheim, in Switzerland. In the Schleitheim Confession, the sect's leaders pledged devotion to seven tenets that articulated their shared faith and that still form the basis of the Amish brand of Protestantism.

The Schleitheim's first tenet addressed the prime difference between Anabaptists and other Christians. Labeling infant baptism "the greatest and first abomination of the Pope," the signers agreed that baptism must be an active choice, made only by adults "who have been taught repentance and the amendment of life [and] who truly believe that their sins are taken away through Christ."

Although *rumspringa* is not mentioned in the Schleitheim or in any subsequent important church document, the practice is intimately involved with the Anabaptist credo because *rumspringa* is the time during which the young person accumulates the knowledge to make the informed, adult, and repentant baptismal decision. Absent such a period, and the wisdom presumably gained in it, the aspirant could be argued to be uninformed.

The second and third tenets of the Schleitheim are also central to Amish practice today, and to the prime reason that Amish kids feel themselves "unleashed" during *rumspringa.* They deal with the discipline necessary to maintaining the "purity" of the church. The Anabaptists' revolutionary conceit was that the brothers and sisters of the sect were to hold one another accountable for their behavior—for obeying the rules, today known as the *ordnung*.

The rules are backed up by a system of punishments, the most important of which was outlined in the Schleitheim: a member who sinned or erred was to be warned twice, and if the bad practice continued, the third time he or she was to be "publicly admonished before the entire congregation" and banned, that is, excluded from communion, so that only those who were pure would receive that sacrament. "As Paul indicates, we cannot be partakers at the same time of the table of the Lord and the table of the devils," the document explains.

The bann is the harshest punishment that the sect can mete out, among other reasons because it forbids members from having certain kinds of contact with the former church member, even if the shunned person is in the immediate family. The toughness of "shunning" has been a bone of contention throughout the history of Anabaptism. One hundred and sixty-six years after the Schleitheim Confession, Jacob Amman would permanently split with his Anabaptist brethren over what he saw as the need to apply the bann strictly, and that split would separate out the group who would come to be called the Amish from the majority, called Mennonites after the earlier leader Menno Simons, who also believed in the bann but whose followers did not want to apply it as frequently.

The fourth tenet of the Schleitheim is also central to Amish life today, stating specifically that "everything which has not been united with our God in Christ is nothing but an abomination." The list of "the evil and the wickedness which the Devil has planted in the world," and which is to be avoided, includes winehouses and houses of worship, as well as loans and mortgages that cannot be signed in good faith, "and other things . . . which the world regards highly, and yet which are carnal or flatly counter to the command of God." The Amish have interpreted this tenet to mean that the faithful do not have to live completely apart from the world, just that they must separate themselves from its wickedness. Another element of this separateness is the imperative to "fall away from us the diabolical weapons of violence," such as the sword. A later section takes the prohibition against the sword beyond a nonviolent ethic to a rejection of almost anything having to do with "worldly matters." For example, the Schleitheim states that Anabaptists are not to sit in judgment in the outside world either as jurors or as judge, nor should they accept election or appointment as state officials, because the "citizenship [of magistrates] is in this world, that of the Christians is in heaven."

The other critical tenet has to do with the absence of a church hierarchy. Leaders of the Anabaptists are not to be priests who, in the Catholic manner, are appointed by a central authority at some distance from the congregation. The faithful are to be their own flock, and to choose their own shepherd. This, too, was a revolutionary concept in its time and reflected the radical revisionist aim of the Anabaptists: to re-create the church of the first generations following the death of Christ, a church that was, in their view, purer and closer to Christ's teachings than the Catholic church in the Middle Ages. The Anabaptists wished to follow a direct form of Christianity that brooked no intermediaries between congregants and the divinity—no saints, no priests, no religious hierarchy.

One hundred and five years after the Schleitheim, in April 1632—still sixty years before the 1693 split—that Confession was augmented by another, signed in Holland by several dozen Anabaptist elders and known thereafter as the Dortrecht.

Far from being a dusty, historical document, the Dortrecht Confession is also integral to today's Amish practice: youth in *rumspringa* know that if they return and join the church, they will be taught the Dortrecht's provisions and will have to agree to abide by them. Among the interesting specifics in the Dortrecht is that adherents are obliged to obey civil laws "in all things that do not militate against the law, will, and commandments of God." Anabaptists were to pray "for the government and its welfare . . . so that we may live under its protection."

Throughout the Dortrecht "confession of faith" are reminders that it is a guide to a "nonresistant Christianity." The Amish tenet of peaceableness is based on one of the important instances in the New Testament where Jesus specifically disagrees with the ethic of the Old Testament, the old "eye for an eye, tooth for a tooth" justice, insisting that his followers leave vengeance to the Lord and when attacked turn the other cheek. What seems to others to be passivity by the Amish is nonresistance, the ultimate pacifism.

A second basal attitude, implied in the Schleitheim and made more overt in the Dortrecht, is that Anabaptists must behave in ways consistent with their knowledge that their presence in this world is transitory, and that the aim of a person must be to live a life in imitation of Christ's—a life of service.

These concepts set out a vision of Christianity as a particular kind of discipleship—of the church as a brotherhood of laypeople whose rules are ethical and concerned with love and nonresistance rather than with slavish adherence to an abstract kind of worship. In a word, Anabaptism is concerned with orthopraxis, how to live rightly, rather than with orthodoxy, how to live within doctrine.

The directives to be humble and to yield to authority are logical derivatives of a nonresistant Christianity that views the most important action as faithful adherence to the way of Jesus in this world. Anabaptists must eschew whatever might unduly yoke believers together with unbelievers; that is why they wear simple clothes and do not follow the dictates of fashion, and that is why they do not use electricity from a common grid also used by the non-Amish, or own motorized transports—such activities would link them too closely with the outside world.

As time went on, and the Amish moved from the Old World to the New—in the mid–seventeenth century, at the invitation of William Penn, they resettled in Pennsylvania—the rules became more detailed, and in some instances ossified. Thus, Amish men today must not wear mustaches because in the seventeenth century mustaches were sported by military men who used swords. The rules came to govern the precise size of hats, the colors permissible for buggies, when a man was to grow a beard, the procedures to be followed when a member was shunned, and so many other aspects of life that the provisions seem to regulate minutely every facet and moment of an Amish person's existence. Underlying all the rules is the belief that these are but extensions of the tenets agreed to at Schleitheim and at Dortrecht, themselves based on close textual reading of the New Testament and, therefore, on the word of Jesus, son of God.

Amish youth in *rumspringa* know that what awaits those who choose to return and join the church is the expectation that they will thereafter live within the tough tenets of the Schleitheim and the Dortrecht. And they have a strong sense of what shape their lives will have if they return—that they are likely to marry between the ages of twenty and twenty-two; that more than half will have their first child during their first year of marriage; and that by age thirty the men will have become factory workers, small shop owners, construction workers, or farmers, the women, housewives and mothers, and as couples they will have become the parents of four or five children.

This vision of what lies at the end of the rainbow may comfort them, but they also know that the safety net of community can be a confining mesh for those unwilling to live within the rules. All the more reason then, while "unleashed," to drink the cup of experience to the dregs and ready themselves for the most important decision they will ever face: to be or not to be Amish.

The choice is all-encompassing. To be Amish means to accept a faith and a way of life that has made the Amish the principal naysayers of American civilization, refusing to use many electricity- and telephone-based modern technologies on which most Americans depend; refusing to be entertained while living within the borders of a nation increasingly defined by being overentertained; refusing to permit children to be formally educated past the eighth grade in a country increasingly participating in a "knowledge-based" economy; refusing to own and operate vehicles other than those fit to be pulled by animal (or human) power in a landscape irrevocably shaped by cars and highways; and refusing to encourage individual achievement—artistry, acquisitiveness, learning, science, politics—despite mainstream culture's idolization of all matters individual.

All adolescents in America today face a version of the basic task of the Amish teens in *rumspringa*: to accumulate enough evidence and impressions to enable them to shape the course of their futures, insofar as they can. Mainstream American youth may not have as detailed a sense of what awaits them when they conclude their adolescence, but they have other equally useful advantages, namely, several points at which they can make such a decision— on graduating from high school, or college, or graduate school— and a wide panoply of careers, locales, lifestyles, and potential life partners from which to choose. Mainstream adolescents also retain the latitude to later change their choices, to revise their decisions about their futures. One of the chief characteristics of American life in the early twenty-first century is its number of second chances—several careers, multiple marriages, lots of moving of residences, and plenty of opportunities for starting over.

Amish youth have few such options, and only one moment in which to make the most important decision—perhaps the only significant decision—of their lives, one that will then define their lives until the end of their days. For once they have agreed to reenter their ancestral culture, it becomes difficult to leave again, and the consequences of doing so are harsh.

The Amish *rumspringa*, its choices and its implications, raises questions for us mainstream parents. Are we bringing up our children properly? Can those children find a way to coexist with the blandishments of American pop culture—the MTV lifestyle, the NASCAR pace, the Wal-Mart shopper mentality—and not become entirely lost in them? How, and on what terms, will and should they interact with the world during their adolescence and, for that matter, during the rest of their lives? Are the boundaries that we set for them tough enough? Or liberal enough? What will induce and enable our sons and daughters, after their time in adolescence, to become adults who share with us parents our core moral and ethical values?

2

"A Glory Old Time"

On a brisk winter Saturday morning, the parking lot at the Leacock Shoe Store, located on a back road connecting Paradise and Intercourse, in Lancaster County, is packed with a dozen Amish buggies and a half dozen vans with their non-Amish drivers. Though the store is in the heart of a tourist area, it is a place into which almost no tourists wander.

Another van arrives and parks. The eight members of the E family step out. The eldest daughter, Katie, fifteen, carries an infant brother. The E's have come by van because the shoe store is too far from their home for travel by buggy, and because they have at least two other stops to make this day, the only day of the week that Katie's father is not at work in the outdoor furniture shop or at church. The van is expensive but necessary, he has told her. As the family goes toward the entrance, the driver settles down to wait; he leaves the motor on to keep warm and dons earphones to listen to a tape.

Katie totes her infant brother in her arms; the three-year-old twins hold on to her by the waist, and her other brother and sister, eleven and nine, respectively, also stay close to her while the parents pick out shoes for them to try on. The store is barnlike, capacious, stocked with boots and camping and hunting equipment as well as with shoes. The atmosphere is crowded but mostly orderly, with nearly a hundred Amish and salespeople moving about, the children trying on shoes, the salespeople repacking and reshelving pairs that do not fit or are otherwise found wanting. Two cash registers at the front desk clang regularly as fathers hand over large rolls of bills to pay for their families' purchases.

Katie is in charge of the E little ones because her mother needs help, and Katie is out of school now and has been unable to find a paying job outside the home. The morning's hubbub demonstrates to Katie that she is truly needed for child-minding, a view shared by her mother, who indicates by a raised eyebrow the horde of other children in the store, loping through the aisles, pulling down pairs to try on, then running to find their parents to ask their opinions. Katie does not mind assuming some responsibility for her younger siblings; she loves being part of a large family, loves being the oldest daughter. She likes how at home the whole family—except for Papa—fills the kitchen, singing songs as they bake, and how they all pile on Papa every afternoon when he comes home from work. What she doesn't like as much is when she must strain to keep the younger children under control, as she is now having to do.

Katie can hardly wait to be sixteen, to be eligible for a paying job, for something that will take her out of the house for a while each day, so she can be a teenager instead of her mother's chief assistant, can play volleyball on a Friday night or even go to one of those parties she has heard about. She spots one of her former school classmates, seated on a bench in an aisle, unencumbered by siblings as she tries on a pair of sneakers that Katie knows her own mother would reject as too brightly colored. Her father has advised Katie that she is going to have to wait until next month for her new pair, since this month the family can afford new shoes only for the younger children. Maybe when they make their next stop, at Kauffman's, the bulk-food supply depot in Bird-in-Hand, her mother will allow her to buy some of the lemon drops she favors as a sweet. The thought of the sweet-sour candies makes Katie smile.

"My family's picture-perfect," asserts Johnny Y, the Cleveland Indians fan from central Ohio, "and we're rednecks."

What does he mean? "We're all together, all-American, old-fashioned, pretty religious, and just like everybody else. And *my* family taught me morals."

"Just like everybody else," he explains, means that he and other Amish are "normal, not odd" in their behavior. As we talk further, I understand that "picture-perfect" and "all together" are short-hand phrases for him that indicate the Y family has an ample number of children, three generations living in the same house or in nearby homes, and no divorced members—in contrast to English families, which have only one or two children, plenty of divorced members, and whose generations are scattered.

"Redneck" and "all-American" also come from his contrast-and-compare vocabulary; they convey that the Amish are white-skinned, native-born, and rural, rather than nonwhite recent immigrants or city dwellers, that the Amish are as "patriotic" as anyone else in America, and that their wish not to live in lockstep with the mainstream does not make them un-American.

"Pretty religious" for the Y family means that they are more devout than most mainstreamers, that they read the Bible, attend church regularly, and are good Christians; this phrase and "old-fashioned," combined with emphatic mention of the teaching of morals, conveys that Johnny's Amish family honors older virtues while implying that English families no longer teach—or practice—moral values.

He hastens to add that while he is not currently wearing Amish garb, the Y's are fully Old Order Amish—"gas lamps, plain clothes, hats, proper beards, the works . . . My dad never did any farming, and neither did his dad. Oh, we got horses to pull the buggies, and we had a cow for a while and a few chickens, and Mom's got a vegetable garden, but not real farming."

The Y home is a ten-acre farmette in a rural community. "Our lane," he says, "you could go for hours without seeing a car on it." He remembers his childhood days and nights as idyllic, featuring activities that changed with the turns of the wheel of the seasons: planting, swimming, harvesting, wrestling in the leaf piles, ice skating and sledding, canning. He recalls "not wearing shoes" except in the winter or when the family went to church, and has pleasant memories of helping his mother with the garden and the cow, and with the younger children as they came along.

By Amish folklore standards, his family is small, four children, though according to statistical studies, four is now about the average for a mid-Ohio Amish family that does not farm. Johnny is the oldest child. He implies that his limited number of siblings is a result of his parents' conscious choice, though he will not say so directly, because family planning is not permitted by the church.

Ever since he turned sixteen, Johnny has been working at the nearby brake factory where his father worked for more than thirty years before his recent retirement. Since Johnny is not yet a member of the church, Social Security and health insurance costs are deducted from his paycheck, as well as federal, state, and local taxes. He "has no problem" with the employer diverting some of his pay into a retirement fund, and partly matching it. Johnny aims to retire from the factory relatively young, as his father has done, in order to have plenty of years for activities other than making money. "Thirty and out," he says, quoting the phrase that has become a tradition in many midwest factories, particularly nonunionized ones that fashion attractive packages to retain employees: you put in thirty years and can retire at fifty-five with a reasonable pension.

Johnny speaks warmly of his factory's well-respected position in the industry; he is proud of the products they make, but— mindful that a central tenet of the Amish is to cultivate humility, *demut*—he sees this sort of pride as no different from that of a farmer in bringing in a good harvest. Aware that his questioner knows the Amish detest *hochmut*, wrongful, arrogant pride, he further explains that what he feels as pride is not the "I'm better than you" attitude that leads to "vanity" and "buying too much stuff."

His relationships with non-Amish co-workers and bosses are "comfortable," as his father's were, and he shares his father's antipathy toward labor unions. "No 'yoking together,' y'know?" he says, referring to an important biblical phrase used by the Amish, II Corinthians 6:14: "Be ye not unequally yoked together with unbelievers." This phrase underlies the Amish mandate to separate themselves from the world's wickedness. Johnny's distrust of unions also seems cut from the same cloth as his characterization of his family as rednecks: unions, he says, are full of "slackers" who join to obtain easier working conditions—groups directed by "Washington" that he finds "too political." The idea of going on strike if union demands are not met is, to him, "un-American."

Now that his siblings are old enough to "take care of themselves," his mother is working as a waitress at a local restaurant that caters to tourists. Actually, the entire family is employed at enterprises that serve the wider world. Jody, his nineteen-year-old sister, is a secretary at a sand-and-gravel pit operation, and his seventeen-year-old brother works at a woodshop specializing in lawn furniture that is generally sold in suburban areas populated by non-Amish. When asked if all the children still reside at home, Johnny bristles. "Yes—is that so unusual?" The Y children also contribute some of their salaries to the family coffers, he asserts with the same prickliness, because "we like the idea of sharing the load."

While each family member earns only a modest salary, their combined incomes, and relatively low expenses because of their Amish way of life, allow the Y's as a family to live reasonably well. Unlike non-Amish families, Johnny's does not have to pay electric bills, tuition bills, and insurance bills, spends much less than the average American family on clothing, almost nothing on entertainment, and raises some of its own food. But the family income does provide enough money for hunting weekends for Johnny and his father—he likes hunting with Dad—for whitewater-rafting weekends for the brothers, and for household appliances and trips to fancier food emporiums for his mother and sister. Since several Y children are in *rumspringa*, the family has cars, a convenience that benefits Mom and Dad, who as church members are not permitted to own cars but may ride in them. Johnny is pleased to "help out" in this way. He "thinks the world" of his parents, and they appear to be tolerant of his road trips and of the various minor excesses attendant on Johnny's time outside the

Amish church. "And we kids're saving money for when we, you know, get our own homes." Will he ever be a farmer? "No way— it's just too hard, too much work."

Farming is associated with Amish core values, and Johnny's lack of interest in it is the sort of attitude that has raised the hackles of numerous letter writers to the Amish magazine *Family Life*, who worry that jobs "working away" from the farm will eventually result in more Amish youth leaving the fold, especially now that less than 20 percent of Ohio Amish adult males farm. Johnny has no interest in farming because his father had none; the son is a fan of his father's and, so far, a willing follower in his footsteps.

Johnny's *rumspringa* began, he recalls, in ways little different from his father's, with "supper crowd" at one farm after Sunday service and "singing" at the next farm, all properly chaperoned. That style of *rumspringa* was left behind during a four-day Easter weekend, the first spring after he turned sixteen. Easter is the most significant religious holiday of the Amish year, and that weekend, while his family was at church and at social gatherings, Johnny attended unsupervised parties, drank enough beer to knock him out, had revealed to him a "whole new world" of grunge rock and sexual titillation, and didn't sleep at home for several days. He recalls being "lucky" that he was able to make it home sober enough not to arouse recriminations, allowing him to get a few hours' sleep, shower, and stagger into work on Tuesday. Thereafter, attendance at weekend parties became a regular thing for him, perhaps the most important objective in life other than making sure that his "sweeper" job at the factory at sixteen would turn into a regular line job when he reached eighteen. It was during this period that he attended that first Cleveland Indians game.

After Johnny and other Amish male teens sat in the bleachers for a second ball game in Cleveland, they went to a city bar, where, despite the fact that most of them were underage, they had no trouble being served; they also easily "scored" pot and cocaine. "Don't know how we got back home without getting killed or busted," he recalls. After that, "I tried all kinds of things. Don't like going to one of them big concerts if I'm not wasted." At a concert, he met a non–Amish young woman, and on another date with her received his sexual initiation. "Me 'n' her went together a couple of months," he says and shrugs. (He did not meet his current girlfriend, Becky, until recently.)

After his initial burst of activity, Johnny "pulled back a bit," perhaps fearful of being so wasted on a Monday that he would jeopardize his job prospects. His father importuned him to go fishing one weekend in Kentucky; Johnny had dreaded the trip but ended up liking the experience. Soon he had settled into a routine where "maybe once a month I'll stay home on a Saturday, take my mom to the Wal-Mart, that sort of thing," before going out for the evening, and on another weekend he would hunt, fish, or target-shoot with his dad. And once in a while, on a Sunday, he "even go[es] to church with the family when I don't have to."

"Yes, my parents put food on the table, clothes on my back, but it was my older sisters took care of me," says Phil T, an Amish-raised RV factory worker in Indiana. He is the second youngest son of a family of eight boys and four girls. His father had spent his working life in such factories, which meant that he was not home for large stretches of the days. When Phil was growing up, he says, "If I had a problem, I went to my older sisters, I didn't talk to Mom and Dad. Now if I got into trouble, my ass got beat by Dad, but that's just the way it worked. And I guess that contributed to my not being really close with my parents."

He recalls his childhood as "generally happy," even though "there were moments when I wished I'd never been born, much less born Amish." His father and mother were so busy with the myriad tasks of handling a household of fourteen that they had little time for each child. Frequently his father would call one son by another's name, unable to keep straight in his mind each of the towheads with bowl haircuts and identical outfits. Having lots of siblings, Phil recalled, meant that he was "never at a loss for a playmate" at home; but he later came to realize that most of the brothers' interaction took the form of "having somebody to beat your ass to keep you occupied. Always picking on each other. Always nagging, always something to do, never boring. If it was boring, it was because you were hiding by yourself somewhere."

By age eight, Phil became conscious of being different from non-Amish kids and chafing under the restrictions of the *ordnung*, the unwritten list of rules. Why did the T family have to travel by buggy when the world was whizzing by in cars? Because they were Amish, he came to understand. He says, "I couldn't see myself sitting behind the horse and going 'gee-yah giddy-up' or anything, whatever" for the rest of his life. For him, there were "places to go and people to see," and he could not countenance wasting time traveling by buggy to those exciting destinations.

Despite expressing some resentment toward his parents, Phil maintains a great respect for them, especially for his father. John T was a legend in the RV factories because of his deeply ingrained work ethic and productivity, a legend enhanced when Phil's older brothers followed John into the factories. John transmitted many work-related lessons to Phil and his other sons; among them were "You don't try to get a dollar out of a person unless you do something for that person . . . If you want something, you work for it . . . If you set your mind on something, you don't let hell or high water stop you until you get it." Perhaps the most coruscating of Phil's father's tenets was that you should never settle for second best, because coming in second meant that you were "first loser."

John regularly pitted Phil and his brothers against one another in physical and mental contests. Phil recalls, "He'd say, 'Well, he can do this better than you can,' or 'He's much faster at this than you are.' " This relentless family competitiveness left Phil with the sense that if what he wanted—a goal, a job, a girl—did not present a challenge, it was not worth competing for. "It's like, once I do something for a while, and become good at it, or convince myself that I'm good at it, it becomes boring. And this leads to never being satisfied."

Phil's desire to leave behind Amish restraints—and his parents—quickened at thirteen, when the *ordnung* permitted him to quit wearing the suspenders that had identified him to other

Amish as a prepubescent. This coincided with the family's move from Indiana to Jamesport, Missouri. John T had tired of the grind of the factories and wanted a less pressured work situation; he also evidently wanted a stricter church district, which he found in Jamesport. Newcomers there, the T family had to observe all the rules of its *ordnung*, even those that they had tiptoed around in Indiana. In Jamesport, after Phil finished eighth grade at fourteen, the jobs he could find were uninteresting. It also galled him that he had to turn over his earnings to his parents, though they told him that, as he reached sixteen and eighteen, he would be permitted to keep more and more of his pay. Many Amish parents who confiscate their children's earnings also promise that in the future—when the children marry, or want to set up their own businesses—they will give them large gifts of land, money, house furnishings, business equipment, and so on. But for Phil, such promises were so far off in the future as to seem meaningless. His brothers hadn't stuck around the house—a couple had remained in Indiana to work, and another had just left the Missouri home, ostensibly to seek higher-paying work—so why should Phil stay?

On turning sixteen, Phil secretly applied for a driver's license. He passed the test and arranged to have the license mailed to an older brother's place in Indiana. He soon left home, wearing his Amish clothes and with a small bag holding nothing but an extra pair of pants. He caught a ride with a van full of young Amish heading north to Indiana for a party, and did not tell his parents that he was going or when he might return. Dropped off near Goshen, ten miles southwest of Shipshewana, he made his way to the brother's home, where he stayed for several months and looked for work. He had no idea what was going to happen next and was a bit frightened by the uncertainty, but he also felt that he had had no choice but to leave home. It was either that or be stifled forever.

"Adolescents are scared and well they might be," writes the psychiatrist George H. Orvin in a recent authoritative text called

Understanding the Adolescent. "What other period of life is more frightening and anxiety-ridden?"

On this subject, the experts and most parents whose children have been through the tunnel of adolescence agree with Orvin's rhetorical question. He and other researchers trace the anxieties to the teenagers' needs to complete important emotional and mental developmental tasks that are the key to their becoming well-functioning, mature adults. Parents of teenagers also agree with researchers on precisely what teenagers must learn: to fashion their own identity, to reason abstractly, and to make a set of rules to which they are willing to adhere in the future. As Orvin also suggests, and as most parents of teenagers will attest, teens figure out who they are, in part, by learning to view their parents as ordinary human beings rather than as omnipotent ones, and in part by figuring out how to relate to their peers and to society as a whole.

As for abstract reasoning, what sharpens the ability for that mental function is the characteristic teenage struggle to form one's opinions of the world. In making their own set of rules, teenagers incorporate some rules taught in childhood, but they also reject others and substitute new ones, until the mix becomes acceptable to them and useful as a guide for adulthood.

With such major tasks before them, it is no wonder that teenagers are drawn to taking risks, both constructive and destructive, to try to establish control over their lives.

Adolescence is a period of transition, and a chief characteristic of any transitional period—grief, postdivorce, and new parenthood are others—is experiencing a high degree of ambiguity about one's status. Students of adolescent behavior believe that only when the adolescent's "status ambiguity" is resolved can adult life begin. Adolescence, therefore, is a second birth.

When Emma M was very young, eight or nine, she estimates, she worried that when she went to Heaven she'd be "bored." She wouldn't be able to swim, eat ice cream, or in other ways have fun, because "all you'd do was sit there all day with your wings."

As she grew up, first in Missouri and then in Wisconsin, Emma had a passel of older sisters who were as much a trial as a delight. The middle daughter of eight girls in a family that eventually included twelve children, Emma recalled always being mischievous. She characterizes her childhood as "happy" but is quick to add that there were times when she was "insecure because I had four older sisters, and sisters have a way of hurting each other, especially when I was nosy." She was frequently nosy, would "do the normal thing . . . spy on them and their friends, and read their diaries." She would then deliberately reveal choice morsels that could only have come from the diaries or from espionage—and suffer the consequences as her older sisters became angry and said "bad things" to her, which would sadden her and make her "lose confidence" in herself because of her willingness to accept their assessment. "I had a problem with insecurity as a child, thinking that nobody likes me, stuff like that. Or that I am so ugly."

But Emma enjoyed the security of knowing that, unlike some English neighbors in Jamesport, her parents would never get divorced, never lose themselves to alcohol, never be out of touch with God; she took comfort from the "peace" and "closeness" of her family life. Schoolwork, too, comforted her, because she was good at it, an apt student. And she did housework chores competently. Back then Emma could imagine no future other than one inside the community, following in the footsteps of her mother and older sisters, living within the borders of the *ordnung*.

Emma did not realize for a while that her household was stricter than some others. But gradually she came to understand that other Amish families nearby, such as those that included her cousins, the children of her mother's sisters, were permitted more leeway in their dress and behavior.

"Very lonely" at times, Emma soon "tired of wearing the bonnet and the long dresses." She could talk to her mother, though not to her distant father, but the notion of growing up to become a wife and homemaker, guardian to a flock of children, began to seem to her impossibly "dreary." She also worried about becoming the sort of parent who had so many children that she would be incapable, as her parents now seemed to her to be, of giving enough individual attention to each child. She "wouldn't mind" having children someday, but what she really wanted was a career, though she didn't know what she would do or how she would manage to hold down an interesting job while residing within the community; few Amish women had good jobs, and those who did, she had observed to her chagrin, were almost always the spinsters. "I didn't really want to be just an old maid if I didn't want to get married and have children right away, but I thought I'd probably have to do one or the other."

Emma's possibilities began to change when her older siblings entered *rumspringa*. Now she heard more from them about the outside world, and what she heard was exciting. Running around with boys, non-Amish boys, cars, parties, forbidden delights. Her oldest sister became pregnant and was married soon after to an Amish man. The next eldest also ran around with boys, and the one after that, and soon the young males of the area, both Amish and English, began to pay attention to Emma, who by thirteen had developed a fashion model's tall frame, figure, and pretty face. Secretly, when her parents were not watching, she would go out with the older teens. Tales of Emma's gallivanting reached her parents. Because she rode in cars with older guys, she was accused by neighbors of being "wild" and a "slut," accusations she insists were inaccurate.

Her father decided to move the family to rural Wisconsin, to take them away from what he considered an overliberal atmosphere of drugs and drinking. Emma's mother did not want to go, since her birth family was from Missouri, but Amish tradition dictated that she yield to her husband's wishes. The move to Wisconsin coincided with Emma's graduation at fourteen from her Amish school, and Emma couldn't shake the suspicion that her father had taken the family to Wisconsin partly to curb her escapades.

In Wisconsin, Emma wanted to go on to high school, but her parents refused to send her. She threatened to move in with a friend's family and attend high school from there. Her parents said that if she took up residence elsewhere, they would send the police to fetch her home, since she was under sixteen. Not yet willing to have a full-scale confrontation, Emma gave in but was "very bitter" and became "very stubborn." She also "went behind my parents' back" to find ways of escaping and annoying them. Having blossomed into a tall, attractive brunette, she had no difficulty finding boys to take her around.

"In this society, Amish or not, if you want to be cool, you be bad," Emma says. "For the Amish kids, they go out and get a radio, watch TV, start smoking cigarettes, drink. They hate drinking, but they drink. They smoke cigarettes even though it makes them sick." As a rebellious fourteen- and fifteen-year-old, Emma did all those things. And she watched and listened as her mother tried to keep in touch with her children who had previously done those things and then left the church. Communication with them on the outside was hard for her mother and for those sisters.

New friends told Emma that she was so pretty that she could become a model or an actress, like those she saw on the TV sets in their homes. Male attention helped the "confidence in myself" she was developing from growing beyond the rules and regulations. When younger, she had "cared too much" about the lies other people told about her, but it no longer mattered to her if they said something untrue, if she knew it was not true.

Emma chafed for a few months more at home and then, still before her sixteenth birthday, found an excuse to leave her stifling environment: she would go for a short period to Shipshewana to help an older sister who was in the last months of a medically difficult pregnancy. She would stay with the family of a second cousin.

Her parents felt unable to object to this scheme, since there was no work for Emma near their home and she was becoming ever more difficult to control. They allowed her to go to Shipshewana. Once there, Emma obtained a job in the kitchen of the Blue Gate restaurant, the town's largest, and did not look back.

. . .

The *ordnung* is an unwritten list of rules that members of the Amish community must follow, rules that the Amish hope will lead members to achieving their social goals—the continuance of their church and its way of life. Today's foremost scholar of Amish culture, Donald Kraybill of Elizabethtown College, calls the *ordnung* "the social blueprint, the oral policy manual so to speak, that spells out the 'understandings' of acceptable and unacceptable Amish conduct." There are more than fourteen hundred Old Order Amish church districts, and each is more or less independent, with its own *ordnung*.

The *ordnung's* rules are what enable the faithful to properly imitate the life of Christ. Over the centuries, the rules have evolved to govern everything from the proper appearance for garments and facial hair; through permitted and forbidden technologies in the home, on the farm, and in the shop; to encouraged and disallowed ways of earning a living. The *ordnung* is flexible and organic, Kraybill suggests, frequently revised in reaction to the challenges presented by the outside world. However, its rules are not guidelines; infractions can bring reprimands and usually set the member into a confrontation with the leaders, which, if continued, can result in suspension from the church or, in the ultimate instance, excommunication.

Formulated by the church elders of a district, the *ordnung* is ratified and personally agreed to, twice yearly, by all the members of the congregation. Though at each semiannual review some changes to the *ordnung* may be made, an unwillingness to alter the *ordnung* too radically or quickly gives the Amish the latitude to make unhurried evaluations of technological innovations, to contemplate what modifications in their way of life will be produced by, say, a portable calculator, a new hay baler, or a youth recreation facility before agreeing to their use, or before disallowing them as encouraging behaviors that are un-Christ-like: pride, overcompetitiveness, worldliness. The Amish consider that the sin of *hochmut*, a word that connotes arrogance and haughtiness as well as pride, is among the worst, the root of many other sins.

The *ordnung* is designed to prevent the members from falling prey to sins such as *hochmut*, and while Amish teenagers may well agree with that objective, they perceive the rules as so strict that upon entering *rumspringa* the teenagers feel relieved not to have to live up to all of them for a while.

Traveling between Amish settlements, one becomes aware how the *ordnung* differs from area to area and, sometimes, from district to district. In Indiana, the norm is lots of teens (as well as other Amish) on bicycles. In Lancaster County, one seldom sees bicycles, which are forbidden by most districts' *ordnung*, but does see a great number of scooters. Less obvious to a visitor but notable to the Amish themselves, is that battery-powered electrified fences are allowed for farmers in LaGrange County but not in Lancaster County. And one finds teenagers in one area complaining that they have to hand-push the family lawn mower, while their cousins in another state are permitted to use motorized mowers, and their second cousins elsewhere must mow their lawns by hand but can trim the edges with a motorized tool.

The diversity is not only the result of decentralized authority; it also reflects the evolving of the *ordnung*: the motorized lawn mower technology was not permitted years ago, but when the battery-powered edge trimmer came along, a newer generation of church leaders decided to permit that tool—but not to retroactively expunge the older rule against the mower. On the whole, differences in the *ordnung* between Old Order Amish districts are minor; the similarity of the districts' basic codes is what makes the disparate Amish settlements, and their members, seem cut from the same cloth in terms of physical appearance and behavioral practice.

For outsiders, among the most difficult of the *ordnung*'s rules to understand are those dealing with activities that to us may seem not to warrant moral regulation, such as sports. Many Amish children attend public schools but are not permitted to wear school or team uniforms. The only uniform they can wear is the Amish habiliment, whose character and boundaries are carefully set. But the Amish are not against sports; Amish kids may play sports in public school in their own clothes, and several sports—even ones that can be highly competitive, such as soccer, basketball, and softball—are enjoyed in Amish school yards. "Softball is okay in the Amish school yard," a minister explains, "but people can get carried away by playing sports like softball on organized teams, and forget their duties to their families and church." As a contemporary letter to *Family Life* puts it, "For people who preach separation from worldliness and practice nonconformity in dress and other areas of life but then are caught up in adult play . . . this is inconsistency and a form of worldliness to be alarmed about. Is this not a form of idolatry? . . . Our leisure time activities should be home centered rather than youth group centered."

The Amish believe that the greatest danger to them from the world outside is the threat of becoming assimilated into the "worldliness" of the secular culture. Any step in the direction of assimilation, however small, must be prevented; if a teenage boy's allegiance—or, for that matter, the allegiance of a young married man—became entangled with a secular softball team, to the point that he would rather go to a game on a summer evening than perform some Amish community duty or familial chore, then who knows what sort of unapproved behavior might come next?

As the softball restrictions suggest, the Amish view themselves and their children as inherently weak and vulnerable, capable of being led astray by almost any activity. Clothing must cover up nearly all flesh, for even the sight of a naked leg might incite uncontrollable desire. Total abstinence from alcohol is required (in many communities) because no one can be trusted—no individual is strong enough—to consume in moderation. Children must leave school at fourteen because the courses taught to them at a public school in the ninth grade might warp their minds beyond retrieval.

All teenagers complain of having too many rules, but Amish teens have substantive objections to some of the rules that constrain them. Christina G, who helps her brother at his farm, fulminates about *ordnung* restrictions on farm equipment that make it nearly impossible for their chicken farm to compete with non-Amish neighboring ones. Wilma D, a clerk in a retail store, lives too far out in the countryside to commute by buggy to work in the nearest town, and because the *ordnung* forbids her family to buy a car, she has to pay seven dollars a day—an hour's wages—to be transported to and from work. Regina E, a sixteen-year-old wait-ress, wails in a more characteristic teenage way that without a set of wheels she "can't go anywhere, can't do anything." Emma M, Marlys B, and other young women in the party scene in northern Indiana are the envy of their younger sisters and brothers because they are in *rumspringa* and can buy cell phones for themselves.

Ordnung restrictions on phones and motorized transport vex today's Amish youth, not only because their non-Amish acquain-tances all seem to have cell phones and wheels but also because all of America now seems connected by phone and by car. The two technologies, telephones and automobiles, have been bothering the Amish for a century. When telephones were first introduced in rural Pennsylvania, early in the twentieth century, the *ordnung* forbade their use. Even then, writes the historian of telephones Diane Zimmerman Umble, there was a recognition by the Amish that the telephone "is not merely a neutral instrument. Its use in-trudes into already-established patterns of communication, poten-tially reorganizing and reordering practices that have long held 'the world' at bay." The elders feared that using telephones would mean substituting electronic communication for face-to-face give-and-take, and that would weaken community ties—a good reason for forbidding their use. A similar fear had given rise a few years earlier to vetoing the introduction of the automobile: it would enable church members to travel too easily, and either exit the community altogether or cause the community to be more scat-tered geographically than was considered ideal. Retaining horse-drawn buggies as the only permitted transport effectively limited members' trips to a ten-mile radius—after traveling that distance, a horse has to be rested, watered, and fed, else it will start to break down physically. Thus, the reliance on horses helps to assure the continuity of the community.

Some Amish thought the ban on phones and autos absurd, and between 1907 and 1910 there was a major fissure in the church over it, which resulted in the splitting off from the Old Order of those "liberals" who wanted to use phones, cars, and other modern technologies. The decisions to forbid ownership of telephones and automobiles drew a very important line in the sand for the Amish. Anyone who could not live without phones and cars could not be in the Old Order; moreover, once the phone and car lovers left, the church was better able to enforce its conservative and purist tenets on those who remained within the fold.

Years after the split, in the 1930s in some areas, even later in others, the Amish began to allow telephone use for business, because they understood that phones had become necessary for commerce with outside buyers, though phones were still forbidden in homes as unwarranted intrusions into members' privacy and separation from the world. Since then, as mainstream society has grown ever more communicative, pressure has mounted for the Amish to be able to be more connected. "When we first wanted to put a phone in here for the business," one current business telephone owner recalls, "all the neighbors urged us to do it so they could use it." Those uses are to keep in better touch with family members who are too far away to visit on a regular basis. Today, a structure that looks like a whitewashed privy with a solar panel on the roof and a lock on the door sits in the front yard of the home, adjacent to the workshop from which the business is conducted. A half dozen "key holders" have access. Each has an individual code for making long-distance calls, so that monthly bills are easily apportioned among the holders. Incoming calls ring a bell inside the house and shop, and someone runs out to answer the phone; if the call is for a neighboring family, they are fetched to respond.

Recently, a public school bus driver reported that for the first time, every single one of the Amish children who rode her bus regularly gave her a phone number, along with his or her address, for emergency contact purposes.

A columnist for *Family Life* addressed the process by which the *ordnung* changes in response to the changing norms of the mainstream and pressure from within the community. The pioneer Amish drew water from a stream for all their needs, he wrote, but the following generations, taking their cue from non-Amish neighbors, judged that practice too backward and insisted on having wells. In another thirty years, wells were deemed too cumbersome; newer generations did not want to haul water up in buckets, they wanted pumps, so the *ordnung* began to permit windmill-driven pumps. "What one generation thought was so easy, the next found tiring." When a more modern generation balked at having to work the pump every time they wanted water, they petitioned for the right to use holding tanks. Their children, not satisfied with having only cold water coming out of spigots (and needing to heat water on the stove to wash clothes and dishes), wanted water heaters, a request that eventually put household water heaters into the category of acceptable technologies. "Satan likes to make us believe that if we only had this or that, we could be so much happier," the columnist concludes. "If only the church would allow this, we'd be satisfied. We wouldn't ask for more. We'd be content. Would it really work that way?"

To be fair to the church, we must recognize that the task of constructing and administering an *ordnung* is a difficult one. The elders must balance accommodating to changing technologies with assuring that alterations in their way of life caused by new technologies do not compromise the essence of being Amish. Successful accomplishment of this task is, in large measure, what has preserved the Amish from the fate of other religious sects, assimilation into the mainstream. After studying many different sects, the sociologist Laurence R. Iannacone found that the stricter the church, the greater the likelihood it will survive and increase; the key to survival, according to Iannacone, is the strict churches' ability to "penalize" or otherwise prohibit members from engaging in activities that would make them drop out. The more severe the rules and the potential sanctions, the greater the likelihood of the church retaining its members.

Lydia T, the young venetian-blind factory worker who blew her paycheck one weekend rather than put it in the family bank account, learns that she was absolutely right to fear she was going to "get it" when she returned home. When her father discovers that the money is not in the family bank account, he is furious.

Under his pressure, she admits to cashing her check; she does not want to apologize but eventually, to please her parents, agrees to see the minister. In the presence of the minister, she "corrects" herself—agrees to stick to only those behaviors permitted by the *ordnung.* But everyone in her family and the community senses that it is just a matter of time before she heads out the door entirely, because she has been a "problem" since her early childhood.

Lydia might disagree; she remembers in her earliest years being a "good child," encouraged to think of herself that way by her mother and father. The pace of Amish life in Wisconsin was "slow, very slow," which made childhood, for her, "a glory old time, just poking and moseying—didn't have to worry about this or that—basically a simple life."

Only later did Lydia come to understand that her family's life in Wisconsin was even more restricted than that lived by Amish in Indiana; the rules of the Amish church district in Wisconsin forbade factory work for the men and did not permit women to do any paid work outside the home except as cleaning women and babysitters. There were no enterprises there that plied the tourist trade, and, consequently, fewer jobs were available for Amish who did not farm. Lydia did realize that her family was a bit unusual in having only two children, Lydia and her sister, six years younger. Her mother, she later figured out, had had a hysterectomy after several problems with failed pregnancies.

Lydia attended a public school; there were no Amish schools in the area. She loved school, especially the art classes, and her English and Amish friends. "And," she says, "I loved going to church, looked forward to Sundays."

Discipline in the T family reflected that of the church district; Lydia was spanked many times, and when she and her sister forgot to wear their hair coverings at home, their father would yank their long tresses to remind them to put on the coverings—after all, you never knew when an Amish neighbor might come calling; if one saw you improperly covered, she might whisper about it to others, which would likely bring rebukes and sanctions against the family.

When Lydia was thirteen her family moved to Middlebury, Indiana, where an Amish school was available, and her parents made her attend that. Though Lydia acted properly toward her all-Amish classmates—shy, quiet, and respectful—they did not warm to her. Partly as a result, the new friends she made were English, and when she was around them, "I was all over the place, knocking the walls down, having a good time. My mom used to say, 'Well, why don't you have more Amish friends?' And I'm, like, 'I don't know, I just don't get along with them as well.' " Shortly thereafter, Lydia decided that she had "two different personalities," one that was on display inside the Amish world, another when she interacted with the outside world.

During this period, Lydia recalls, her mother was "lonely and bummed out," having left behind in Wisconsin all the people she knew; then, tired of being alone in the house all day, her mother took a factory job. It lasted six months, after which Mrs. T returned to babysitting jobs. For four years after Lydia finished school at fourteen, while living at home, she worked for just one family, cooking and cleaning their house, caring for their children. Her paycheck was dutifully given to her father, who would hand her twenty dollars when she wanted something. Frequently, her father would tell Lydia that she could not have any money that week because the family had none to spare. But he would leaf through a tool catalog and buy himself a tool that cost several hundred dollars. She would ask why he needed that tool, and he would tell her he might use it someday, maybe ten years hence.

As the T girls sat on the porch in the early evening, watching the traffic on the highway, one would say, "Look at that car," and the second would invariably answer, "Wow, that's cool." A female cousin, almost the same age as Lydia, would join in, and all three vowed that someday they would have a car, a sports car, and it would be red—a Mustang, a Corvette, or maybe a convertible.

It was when she turned fifteen that Lydia's parents "knew they were going to have problems with" her, because her "outgoing" side came increasingly to the fore. And they, perhaps fearing that her participating in *rumspringa* activities at sixteen would result in her getting entirely carried away from the faith, "pushed" her to join the church.

The Amish believe that a "still, small voice," the Holy Spirit, will tell a young person when the time has come to be baptized. Lydia was religious, a believer in Christ and in Christ's way, and had no desire to exist separately from the Amish church, but at sixteen she did not hear that voice. Nonetheless, aware that every family member on her father's and mother's sides had joined the church, she was not eager to become the first to stay outside it. Her parents counseled that even if people are sometimes unsure about their commitment, they become spiritually fulfilled by going through the motions until the Spirit moves them, as it eventually will. Lydia dutifully began the nine sessions leading to baptism. She faltered several times, wished to drop out, arguing to her parents that "this is not right," but her mother calmed her fears and, Lydia says, "made me feel comfortable with it again, and I'd go back the next Sunday, happy." Her father chimed in, telling her that being baptized was "breaking down the wall between you and God instead of building it up—bringing more brothers and sisters into the family" of the church; once she had joined, he insisted, the church would keep her "under its wing" and "protect" her.

On the day of her baptism, when Lydia balked once more, her

mother took another tack, arguing that not going through with the ceremony would embarrass the family.

Lydia was baptized and became a church member. She hoped and prayed that God would help her follow the Amish way. At times she would think, "I can't make this," but at other times she was able to cope.

Her circumstances changed when the mother of the family for whom she had been housecleaning and babysitting decided to give up her outside job and return to being a full-time home-maker, thereby throwing Lydia out of work. For the first time, Ly-dia had reason to venture out of the community altogether to find a job. She did, and went to work making display boards for a venetian blind company that sold its products through JC Penney and other chain stores. The pay was much better than she had been making, two hundred dollars per week, though, still being under twenty-one, she was required to hand over her salary to the family. Her new work arrangement meant that she had to travel to the factory and back in cars, which resulted in her developing more English friends.

This was when she began to go out in secret on the weekends, which eventually led to the time that she blew her paycheck on clothes, movies, and enjoying herself.

Shortly after that event, Lydia's father sits her down at the kitchen table, hands her a pad and pencil, and demands that she "make a list of what all you want on your buggy."

"Oh, cool, this is kind of cool, brand-new buggy," she thinks. She is not certain that she really wants a buggy, but she sits down and writes, in order to "make my parents happy again." Her list includes everything she can think of, especially extravagant items such as "windshield wipers, horn, brake lights, turn signals, bright lights, dome lights, clock." She hands her father the list, and now it is his turn to be surprised. He complains that such a buggy will cost him "an arm and a leg." She counters with an additional de-mand for fenders on the wheels.

Next week, he goes to a buggy manufacturing emporium and orders the vehicle. It is to cost four thousand dollars, quite a large sum for this particular Amish family. A month later the buggy arrives, looking wonderful, smelling of fresh paint and new leather, and outfitted with all the latest gadgetry permitted by the district's *ordnung*.

Lydia takes one look at the buggy and knows that from then on she is going to have to settle down and be fully Amish. She hopes that God will help her do so, and that the months until she turns twenty-one—and can keep her paycheck for herself—will pass quickly.

In the preindustrial era, there was no such stage in life as adolescence. People went from being prepubescent children to being working adults with no interim hiatus. During most of the industrial era, until around the year 1900, the amount of time that it took for the transition from childhood to adulthood, a period educators began to refer to as adolescence, was short and coincident only with the teen years. Its psychological and developmental tasks were presumed complete by eighteen or nineteen, by which age most young men and women were already employed, married, and otherwise functioning as full adults in society. A brief, condensed period of transition made social sense when the life expectancy was fifty years, as it was in the year 1900.

Today, adolescence is long; the years that a young American mainstreamer spends in transition from childhood to adulthood now include the early twenties, the onset of maturity having been deferred until an education-based emancipation date—graduation from college or, in an increasing number of instances, completion of an advanced degree. Marriages are also routinely postponed until the participants are in their late twenties, and having children is being put off until several years after that. Full adulthood, in the opinion of some psychologists, may not begin until the first child is born.

A contributing factor to the prolongation of adolescence, and certainly a concomitant, is the huge panoply of sensations, options, and fantasies provided by our society. "What is offered to our teenagers by the outside world is vaster and more complex than it was twenty-five years ago, when I was young," says Norman Y, a forty-three-year-old Amish minister who is also a businessman in Shipshewana, a father of three children, the oldest nineteen, and one of the people in the community principally involved with shepherding youth. "Evil has so many more faces than it used to have," he adds, among them one that stunned him when he was recently shown it: pornographic images imported to a camera phone—something unimaginable even a few years ago and an evil, he points out, that can be dialed up by a teenager without parents being aware of it.

In a mainstream culture characterized by information glut, the adolescent's task is separating wheat from chaff. He or she must discern true role models from packaged ones, soul mate from sex partner, diversion from devastation, helpful community from hindering community, morality from mere rationalizing. We adults recognize that these tasks have increased in difficulty as the world has become more complex. Less well recognized is that mainstream children, long before reaching puberty, are regularly exposed to many of the culture's temptations, an exposure that helps them develop the social equivalent of antibodies, and that enables our children to complete their various tasks as adolescents. Amish prepubescent youth do not have access to such advance protection. Their childhoods have been structured deliberately to block out the sensations of mainstream culture. Without television or the Internet, without access to unapproved ideas, they know very little of the worldly surround in which, as American adolescents, they will have to operate.

"You can always spot the Amish teenagers at the Wal-Mart," says Rob Schlegel, an Ohio social worker who grew up in the Wooster area; he is not Amish but speaks Pennsylvania Dutch and has worked with the Amish for many years. The Amish teens in *rumspringa* go to Wal-Mart to buy clothing for their outings in the wider society. "Even though they may not be wearing Amish clothes, their behavior gives them away. They have their hands in their pockets, they walk quietly, with their heads down but their eyes trying to take in the sights; they don't talk loudly—hardly speak to each other. The boys walk with the boys, the girls with the girls, and a few steps behind the boys. They try to convince outsiders that they belong—'We're fooling everybody by the way we dress, but we really are different.' "

3

"Straightforward Conversations"

The carpenter Enos S and his family of five are seated around the table at a farmette well off the main roads in Elkhart County; the house is quiet, the air echoing with the faint, early-morning sounds of chickens in the yard and horses in the barn. Mother and daughters, ages nine and fifteen, have brought the food to the table, where the males await, and now all are ready to begin breakfast. They are four people in Amish garb and haircuts, and the eldest son, Ben, eighteen, in English clothes and with a crew cut.

The parents are deeply worried about the soul of this son in rumspringa. Basically Ben is a good boy, sometimes going to the parties, sometimes satisfied with Sunday singings, a son who continues to live at home and is respectful of all things Amish—but yesterday evening he brought home a car that he had purchased. Twenty years ago, when Enos was in rumspringa, he did not have a car, never saw the need for one; but Ben has paid for this car with his own money, and Enos is afraid that if he tells his son the car cannot be countenanced, Ben will leave home in order to keep it—and his parents will lose all influence over him.

Enos knows what will happen then, because one of his brothers, in his rumspringa period, grew so used to cars and English clothes, and to the supposed freedom of the outside world, that he never came back to the church. Enos does not want that future for his Ben. He recalls what the preacher says in Ecclesiastes 11:9–10,

> Rejoice, O young man, in thy youth; and let thy heart cheer thee in the days of thy youth, and walk in the ways of thine heart and the sight of thine eyes: but know thou, that for all these things God will bring thee into judgment. Therefore remove sorrow from thy heart, and put away evil from thy flesh: for childhood and youth are vanity.

How can Enos instill in Ben the understanding that playing on the edge is not good for him? How can he convey that family life is more sustaining than any of the momentary pleasures provided by the outside world?

A partial solution occurs to Enos, and he presents it this morning at breakfast. He tells Ben that he can continue to live at home, and even park the car near the house—though his parents consider it a bad thing— if he will agree to breakfast with the family every day, and to participate in the five minutes of prayers around the table prior to the meal.

Ben assents. They all bow their heads at the table and begin the morning prayer session.

In a holding cell in the central Ohio police station, Eli K cannot get out of his mind that he is in a "whole heap of trouble." With two of his *rumspringa* buddies, the red-haired, lanky eighteen-year-old had started drinking vodka and beer early Saturday night, and they were "all a little drunk" when they climbed into the beat-up sedan he'd bought for $750. He and his pals were talking loudly, he didn't properly gauge part of a curve on the two-lane, brushed a car opposite that was going south, and "everybody ended up off the road." The guys in his car received only scrapes and bruises, but the couple in the other car—English, tourists—were more seriously injured, the man with a broken leg and the woman with cuts and worse from the impact, seat belts, and air bags. His car was a mess, and the tourists' car looked as though it was "totaled."

The Ohio State Police arrived on the scene and, in the glare of their whirling lights, made Eli take a DUI test. He flunked it, and so after they were all transported to the hospital, where their wounds were treated, the police released his pals but took Eli to the station and held him there. The cops told him he was going to be charged with DUI (driving under the influence), speeding, and "reckless endangerment." He guessed the last charge meant causing injury to the tourists.

"Scared of going to jail" and "scared of having hurt people," Eli also fears that his entire life is ruined because he carries no insurance—not on the car, not on himself, and nothing that will pay the medical bills for his pals or for the English people who have been injured, or for their car. The cost to clean up the mess could be in the tens of thousands of dollars—which he doesn't have.

There is no one he can turn to for help now, except someone he is also scared of, his father, Elmer. Eli doesn't get along with the old man, at least "not like my older brothers did . . . Maybe he was just tired of daddying by the time they had me." Eli, the youngest son and second youngest child of six, was a "slow learner" in school, though he always "got there eventually." He much preferred toying with carpentry in the home woodshop; he likes to "make stuff, do the corners, get everything to fit right." But when he graduated eighth grade, there were already too many carpenters in the area and none willing to hire him. At that moment, Elmer badly needed an apprentice in the small-engine repair workshop, so Eli had reluctantly gone to work in the dingy, greasy place. His two older brothers, when they had been fourteen and fifteen, had done the same. But each, upon turning sixteen, had found work elsewhere.

Eli has been unable to follow their route and escape the repair shop because he is the youngest son and there are no younger K boys coming along to replace him. But he has also learned a great deal about small-engine repair in four years and discovered, to his delight, that he is good at it—better than his brothers were—

though his aptitude has not shielded him from Elmer's blunt criticism and occasional rages at his mistakes. Painstakingly, Eli saved enough money to buy the car three months ago, and he had been thinking of using it to go apply for a job at a factory twenty miles from home, where he could make more than the minimum-wage salary his father has been paying him. Eli has also yearned to do something new because there has seemed no possibility that Elmer would retire and turn over the repair business to him.

From the hospital Eli tried to phone the family, but the number at their neighbor's down the road rang forever, and he was uncertain that the message he left would be picked up even the next morning, a Sunday.

Sitting in the cell, Eli hopes that when one of his pals reaches home, he will alert the K family, but he knows it will take hours for the family to travel by buggy to this larger town to fetch him.

When Elmer K arrives at dawn, Eli is so relieved to see him— and to note his father's look of concern rather than of rage—that he cries. "I'm sorry, real sorry . . . The whole thing is my fault," he says and tells Elmer that he is "ready for punishment. I'll take whatever comes, but I don't know how I'll ever pay for everything."

While waiting for the police paperwork to be completed so that Eli can be released, father and son converse, in Pennsylvania Dutch, which they believe the police do not understand.

Elmer reports that he has spoken to the deacon and has been assured that the church will take care of Eli's bills from the general fund obtained by tithing; but since the bills might amount to a considerable heap of money, Eli will have to agree eventually to pay it back.

"Sure," Eli says, without hesitation, though he is unclear how he will be able to repay many thousands of dollars from a two-hundred-dollar-a-week salary.

Elmer must have considered the same problem, for he next tells Eli that on the buggy ride into town he has thought about the ownership of the shop and is now prepared to sell the repair business to Eli, since it is time to retire anyway. Eli understands that the shop must be sold rather than simply turned over to him because it represents the family's accumulated wealth and therefore belongs to all the children. The price mentioned is relatively low, though, and Elmer believes that the steadiness of the repair business will allow Eli to pay for the shop, and for whatever assistance the church will have to provide, in less than ten years.

Eli is quietly amazed by the arrangement but even more by his father's demeanor. "He seems, I don't know, almost happy about it—not that I'm in jail, or that bad stuff's happened, but that there is something he can do for me; like I'm the prodigal son, y'know?"

Implicit in the deal, Eli understands, is that he will now fully yield to his parents' wishes, end his *rumspringa*, join church, and settle down. Well, Eli's girlfriend, Regina, won't mind that, and, truth be told, neither does he. "It felt like it was meant to be," he says in recalling the story to a visitor some years later; he pinches his thumb and forefinger together as illustration, and says, "I come this close to losing it all. But God really has a plan for everyone, y'know?"

Gerald Y is worried. The young man who tries hard to fall asleep quickly when he is coming down from his drug-induced highs, so he will not be bothered by visions of being condemned to Hell, feels he's stuck in a rut. For more than a year, all he has been doing is work and blow: putting in his daily eight-plus hours at his job at the RV factory, cashing his paycheck to buy cocaine, getting the stuff into his system, partying, then crashing on Sunday and pulling himself together so he can go to work the next day. He cherishes his independence, but, sitting in his trailer, exhausted after a day of driving the forklift, his thoughts wander back to his mother and father in their Amish home. He says, "My parents supported me as best they could, but I wouldn't listen. I had to do everything on my own. And I was the one that messed my life up. They didn't have nothing to do with it. They tried to make my life good, and for that I love them. But everything I screwed up in my life is my own."

His father is incredibly agile and strong. "He weighs two hundred some pounds and can run the forty-yard dash far faster than I can . . . and he can lift me and my brother at the same time—combined, that's almost three hundred pounds." And yet his father has never been in a fistfight. His parents married at eighteen and seventeen. "That's young," Gerald now realizes. He now also admires the way his parents "stick together, make decisions together." Moreover, Gerald says of his father,

> even if somebody he knows does something wrong, and he knows it, he won't judge that person for it, and that's the coolest thing about my dad. He'll still be as friendly as ever; but just don't try to lie into that aspect of his life because he's straightforward. He'll tell you what he thinks—I admire that, too, but I always try to stay out of those straightforward conversations because I hate hurting the person's feelings.

Gerald also hates lying, which he's had to do many times when his father and mother upbraided him and his younger brother for taking drugs and doing other "stupid" things.

For a long time the Y boys shrugged off such harangues, refused to hearken to the parents' pleas on this subject. Now reality is intruding. Gerald's brother has recently been nabbed for possession and is facing a court date. Both brothers have decided to go cold turkey, stop doing drugs completely. There are no Amish community programs to help them, but they have some of their father's strength and resilience, and believe they can do it.

A few weeks later, the Y brothers are past the roughest of the withdrawal symptoms and the cravings, and are holding on to their sobriety. Gerald's girlfriend, Joyce, is ecstatic. Neither brother is thinking about returning to the community and "joining church," but Gerald, at least, has come to a realization about their upbringing in comparison to that of their English friends:

The way we grew up, you had to live with what your parents gave you. It seems like the way the English kids in school lived was for something else. It was, like, "If we don't have what my friends have, I need it." So, okay, you go to school and you see one guy talking about one thing for, like, a week; then the next week he'll come in and his friends have it. Wow! We Amish could talk about it for years and never get it. Okay, fine. I'm glad they have it and I'm glad they're happy. All I needed when I was younger was a basketball hoop, a book, and a basketball.

Back then Gerald had read all the books in his house, all kinds of books, those belonging to his mother, father, and siblings. Now, he says, "I kind of watch all kinds of movies. Reading is work, you know? It tires you. Anything that tires you is work, to me. TV is just, like, laziness. You sit there and do nothing. But I love it."

The key moment in his life, he now recognizes, was when he dropped out of school. He was fifteen, his basketball days were about over, and the final touch came when a pony fell on his leg, which gave him leg and back problems. In eighth grade, he

got to partying a little bit, so I was, like, "[expletive deleted], I'll just go make money. That way I can go buy my party supplies." And now I wish I hadn't done that because I'd be a senior this year. Kind of weird: four years ago, dropped out of school—but, you know, I can't complain. It's my choice. I got to face what I did. I'd get so insane mad. Irate. At everybody. I always had this mean look on my face, like I was a [expletive], and I wanted everybody to leave me alone.

Now he feels calmer than he did at fifteen, and he has more friends. And a girlfriend who is pleased that he has quit taking drugs. What is next in his life? He is unsure, but he has realized that he has to "grow up" and stay off drugs, or he'll be "lost."

. . .

When Tobias K was sixteen, though he had enjoyed growing up on the sixty-acre family farm in Lancaster County, helping his father with the herd of twenty-eight dairy cows and the fields of alfalfa and corn, he had no intention of ever becoming a farmer. As the eldest son of a family of six—including an older sister, three younger ones, and a much younger brother—he understood that the farm could be his when he reached adulthood, if he wanted it. His not wanting it then had caused difficulties for the family.

More sons in the family might have eased the problem, but an older brother died before Tobias was born: that child, then two years old, was standing on a fence watching the pigs and slipped; his head wedged between the rails, and he choked to death. "It was hard on Mom," Tobias recalls, "but she got over it." Other Amish families in the area had suffered similar losses.

The fate of the family farm, Tobias knew, was of increasing concern to the elder K's as Tobias entered the *rumspringa* years. A small farm like theirs, while able to sustain a family, was much more labor-intensive than non-Amish farms, since the K's did not use tractors, other complicated mechanical equipment, or electrically powered milking facilities. The prohibitions on such labor-saving devices were dissuading many sons of neighboring farmers from taking over the running of their small Amish farms. Tobias chose masonry, particularly because he found it "easier than farming." Most of the other young Amish men of his acquaintance also chose to do construction work—it paid more and was less exhausting than farming.

The K family farm sits adjacent to a rural road, a quarter mile from the nearest neighbor; in the previous twenty years, only a few homes have been built along that road, but just over a hill, in the next church district, developers recently erected several hundred homes on what used to be four hundred acres of farmland. The K's didn't want that to happen to a farm that had been in their family for generations.

Tobias liked building with bricks and mortar. There was satisfaction in seeing a project through from start to completion, in being able to drive by it, point to it from the road, and say, "I made that." The money that masonry put in his pocket allowed him to go "fooling around" with the Pilgrims, an Amish "gang" that he joined because his elder sister already belonged. The Pilgrims were not as wild as the Antiques or as mild as the Quakers: when Tobias first joined, along with a dozen other Amish kids his age, on Saturday nights the Pilgrims did little more than have coed volleyball and, on Sunday, singings and hoedowns. But soon a few of the males bought cars, and, when Tobias turned eighteen, he did, too. "Satisfied with a horse and buggy" until then, he came to love his car because it gave him the freedom to indulge his liking for rock music; he used it to travel to Philadelphia and Wilmington for concerts.

At first, Tobias says, the fact of the car "was pretty hard for my mom. She wasn't going to accept it. I had to hide it a little bit. I didn't drive up front right away." Eventually, though, he stopped parking the car behind the barn and left it nearer the house, in full view of the Amish neighbors—who also had sons working off the farm. "Later on, we Pilgrims had more cars, and we did wilder things," Tobias recalls. "Everybody wanted them hot cars, to show 'em off." The Pilgrims would frequently drink and become "rowdy," and occasionally there would be "a little damage" when they "lost their respect" for others' property.

The K's watched patiently, over the course of nearly a decade, as most of the men and women in Tobias's age cohort in the Pilgrims joined the church and married—while the rest stayed out, as he did. The ones who stayed out, Tobias observes, did so because "the car and driving's the toughest thing to give up. Horse and buggy's too slow after driving. Another thing they don't want to give up is playing baseball." And television sets.

Some of his pals joined the Beachy Amish, a sect that permits cars and electricity, though not televisions. Two drifted away from church completely, never joining any other denomination. Tobias's closest friend from the Pilgrims had to "go non-Amish" because of his job: he puts in rumble strips on highways that are more than a hundred miles from home, a task that sometimes requires him to stay overnight in motels. "That don't fit in with the Amish family schedule," Tobias says. "It's different when you can go out and work a construction job and be home at night."

The majority of the young Pilgrims who joined the church did so because they had met potential spouses whom they wished to marry. "Finding a girl sort of settles them down," Tobias says. As for himself, "I guess I had a little bit of crazy blood in me yet that I wanted to get rid of."

In the same decade, the K's married off all four daughters, one of them to an Amish farmer who had his own family farm. The other sons-in-law were in businesses that they had no wish to abandon in order to take up farming.

The K house has emptied out; only the two sons are still at home—Tobias, the eldest, and the baby of the family, now old enough to take a first job pouring concrete for foundations. Tobias's father has nearly doubled the number of cows in the herd, making the farm more economically viable. But he is also now in his early fifties, and somewhat tired after more than thirty years of farming.

One evening, the elder K's sit twenty-five-year-old Tobias down and tell him that it is "time to make a change." They plead with him to come home and take over the farm. In the absence of a wife for Tobias, his mother will keep the house for the three males. Father K will help out on the farm as necessary and will find some outside work to bring in cash for the household—but the farm, a going concern easily worth several million dollars, will be Tobias's.

For Tobias, farming means the chance to "be my own boss," to run a business from which he can make more than an hourly wage, and to own a property that he can improve. On the negative side, he knows that most of the successful Amish farmers have apprenticed to their fathers or fathers-in-law for a half dozen years or more before being considered fully trained and ready to take over a farm. He will not have the benefit of that full apprenticeship, though his father will be there to help him avoid the pitfalls.

He agrees to the deal and becomes, overnight, an Amish farmer.

There is one thing left for him to do. He has been putting off this decision, but when by age twenty-six he has not fixed on a mate, he decides to join the church anyway. In preparation, he gives up his car, the CDs with the rock music, the weekends of hot-rodding, drinking, and carousing. He misses those things, but since he had been raised knowing how to live and farm in the Amish way, he believes that he won't think the quiet life of an Amish adult farmer too boring.

The day of his baptism quickly arrives. "Shaking like a leaf on a tree on a windy day," he stands in the center of the congregation, answering the ritual questions about his willingness to submit his life to the church. Conquering his nervousness, he accepts his membership and all that it entails. At the celebration afterward, he is only gently teased about having had the longest *rumspringa* of anyone in the community.

Adolescence is a difficult season for all parents, but the parents of Ben S, Eli K, Gerald Y, and Tobias K have a task during their children's *rumspringa* periods that exceeds those of mainstream parents. As an Amish minister put it in an article for *Family Life*, "It is the duty of parents to bring up their children in the nurture and admonition of the Lord so that when they reach the age of decision, they will also choose to serve God."

Plenty of community lore exists on how precisely to achieve the objective of having the children all join the church when they are of age, and some of it has found its way into the letters and opinion pieces in *Family Life*. Many correspondents suggest that if children are forced too soon to choose between English and Amish lifestyles, they may well permanently turn away from being Amish; therefore, parents should bide their time, let the children have their fill of the fast lane, until they are more amenable to yielding to their parents' wishes, to giving up the English world and becoming Amish adults. Other articles in the magazine suggest that teenagers will be most likely to yield to their parents' wishes if they have had their wills broken early in childhood and been trained to obey. "Some children can be taught to give up by the time they are twelve to fifteen months old, while others develop more slowly," a grandmother writes. "If we are observant, we can easily see that children who are taught obedience at a young age are far more pleasant to be around and are much happier. Children who are not taught to obey are handicapped, often for life." "The greatest lesson we learned while raising our children was the importance of teaching submission," writes another grandmother, who cautions that the mother must not wait until the father comes home to spank a child to instill "discipline." A minister writes that "young children do not always need a detailed explanation of why you require certain things, or why you forbid such activities as boys and girls tussling together. 'Sometime when you are older. Right now I want you to obey because Mother said so,' is sufficient."

Submissiveness, accepting discipline, and willingness to yield to higher authority are seen as Christ-like by the Amish—part of living in imitation of Christ. Thus, mothers are encouraged to discipline their children firmly, by physical means if necessary, because unless they do, the children will not respect the authority of the schoolteacher—likely to be young and female—who is the primary person outside the home teaching them the Amish way of life. Mothers are also cautioned not to let children play by themselves too long because they "have the carnal nature, which Satan will appeal to in any way he can." A writer who signs herself "a spoiled child" traces her "headstrong nature" as an adult to the fact that "my will had never really been broken" and laments that "life would have been much easier for me" had her parents done their duty and taught her obedience. Children permitted to do whatever they want to when young will not as teenagers willingly quit the fast lane after a few laps around the track, many letters suggest.

A pamphlet aimed at Amish youth who will soon graduate eighth grade, "Timely Talks with Teenagers," warns against "the pursuit of pleasure or amusement" in the outside world, so that the youth can "direct their minds heavenward" and get ready to live a Christ-like life of service to fellow man. To be avoided on the outside are "all foolishness," amusements that make one "less thoughtful and sober," and gatherings that are "popular among giddy-minded and ungodly people." "Worldly pleasure is ruinous because it always has the sting of sin in it," the pamphlet insists.

> You are growing in body, in mind, and in knowledge. Are you also growing in morals? . . . What the world wants is manly men and womanly women . . . who have the courage to stand for the right and against everything that is wrong. This is the time of your lives when you want to see that you are right spiritually . . . If you are not growing as a young soldier of the cross, you are growing in wickedness, and becoming hardened in sin. Don't make the mistake of your life by starting wrong!

Why do some Amish youth "start wrong," drift away after *rumspringa*, while others have no problem returning, joining the church, and becoming responsible Amish adults?

"I used to think I knew," Mrs. Ruth M says, her brow furrowing. A slim, studious-looking grandmother with steel-rimmed spectacles, she lives in Shipshewana, as she has done all her life. "I thought it was the sort of family you grew up in."

The M's personify that sort of family. Ruth and her husband, DeWayne, live a mile east of town, in a *daadi* house— grandparents' house—not far from the main house in which they lived during most of their married life, and just a few hundred yards from the farm on which Ruth and her eleven siblings were raised. DeWayne, after many years of being a building contractor, now operates a woodworking shop next to the larger house on the property, a house currently occupied by one of their three daughters, a son-in-law, and three young grandchildren.

Today, Ruth is in that modest dun-colored home, serving as a nurse for her daughter, who has just returned from the hospital after an outpatient tonsillectomy. Treatment at home includes ice packs for the neck, cool drinks, and rest in a recliner. Later in the afternoon Ruth will also do what she has been "doing a lot of, lately," babysit for the grandchildren when they come home from school. And there is another generation to care for: in the middle of the day, a buggy pulls up and unexpectedly drops off Ruth's mother, who is in her eighties, not as mentally sharp as she used to be, and needs looking after—especially so that her visit will not unduly tire the recuperating patient.

Another of Ruth's focal points today is an upcoming meeting of an advisory board for the middle school. She is on the board because she spent more than a dozen years working in administrative capacities in the Shipshewana public school system, at first in an elementary school and later in a middle school. She also brings to the board an Amish perspective—important for a school whose student body is 40 percent Amish.

Ruth wants a visitor to understand that a high percentage of Amish youth do not participate in the wild parties scene, that a few weeks ago the church districts held three "singings" on a Sunday in three separate locations, with two hundred Amish youth at each one, crowds that almost overwhelmed the homes where the evening activities were taking place. However, she also reports that a week after these singings there were "a thousand Amish kids" at one of those back-of-the-farm parties with deejays and drinking.

While at first she thought family was the critical factor in who came back to the faith and who did not, when Ruth saw evidence that controverted that idea—some kids from conservative families, families whose child-rearing practices she admired, not returning to the fold, while others from liberal families were—she could no longer argue that family was the only element that mattered. "Then I thought it must be the church district," she says, the more strict districts being better at retaining kids than the less strict. That notion, too, she had to give up, because she discovered more than a few exceptions to the rule. Nor does she think birth order the answer—I point out that some scholarly research has identified it as a factor—since she knows families where the older children partied and the younger ones did not, and other families where the reverse was the case. The real answer is "complicated, a mix of factors."

"It's the 'cool' kids who drive everything," she opines. "In school, if they're inclined to do well academically, others follow, and everybody does better. Same thing with the band and the choir: once you get the cool kids excited about an activity, it takes off." That's the positive side of peer pressure. On the negative side, "peer pressure by the 'cool' group" can push an individual toward activities he or she may not want to participate in but feels forced to in order to run with the "in" group and not be ridiculed. During the teenage years, as Ruth has observed to her dismay, peer pressure displaces parental influence, and "that's how the kids learn about drugs and can get lured into doing bad things."

The solution to drug and alcohol abuse, she believes, lies in part in substance awareness education, on all levels and in all venues, including "the parochial schools," the Amish schools, where it is not now taught. But the solution also, and even more fundamentally, lies in teaching children—at home—how to deal with peer pressure. When she was a teenager, "I learned that if I could lay the blame for saying no to something on my parents, I could still be cool with my peers." These and other skills for resisting peer pressure can be taught, she avows, but the teaching task cannot be wholly abdicated to the school; it must be done as part of a parental program that involves setting good examples and exerting proper discipline.

The essence of parenting teens, according to Ruth, involves establishing rules for kids and sticking to them. To her this means "making good on your threats and punishments"—such as "grounding" kids if they need that sort of corrective, a practice she had to put into effect with her own teens from time to time. "Most people think you can't make rules for kids, or you'll be laughed at when they disobey them. But you can, and you have to." Moreover, if rules are to be "taken seriously" by the teenagers, "you have to explain your reasons for every ruling." What you cannot assert, at least not often, is "Do it because I say so." If you utter that too many times, rebellion is likely to follow.

Kathryn L, an open-faced, sturdy woman in her forties, feels that everything is happening at once. Her two eldest children are in *rumspringa* in northern Indiana, and she and her husband, Vernon, are each going through their own difficulties. A few years earlier, their last child was born and was discovered to have a heart defect. Though the L's are quite traditional, they did not hesitate on agreeing to a costly operation and extensive postoperative care for him. Today, looking back on that, Kathryn believes that worry about the health of her youngest was an element in her becoming clinically depressed. "It started coming out a few years ago," she recalls. More important as a contributing factor to that depression, in her view, are her household's continuing "financial difficulties." Vernon, an "easygoing man who doesn't like to disagree with anybody and always wants to do what's right," is, because of those very traits, having problems in his cabinetmaking business. "Too accommodating," Kathryn says, and shrugs. "Customers take advantage—force down the price, ask him to endlessly redo the work," resulting in no profit on his fine cabinets. When he hires workers, he finds they do not perform well enough or fast enough, and he has to take up the slack. "His situation makes for problems with the kids reacting to him, and him with the kids." The house had to be remortgaged to pay off bills. Kathryn became "moody" and "depressed."

When she talked about her depression to church officials and to family members, the advice given was to "try harder to be Amish," to work more diligently, be more devout and more accepting of one's lot and of God's design for one's life. Kathryn did all of that, but her black moods, tears, and bouts of rage did not abate. Eventually she was convinced to seek outside help. "I started talking to this counselor, taking some medication, and I'm okay now. I only take it in the winter, because in the summer I'm outdoors, working in the garden, getting a lot of sun, and I don't need it."

Her son Jerry's difficulties, Kathryn believes, are separate from hers and did not start in *rumspringa* but date back to his troubles in grade school. Though bright, artistic, and athletic, able to draw well and to play ball, he was "a hyper child, hard to handle," and had tics and spasms. His arms would shoot out when he did not want them to, or he would involuntarily make strange sounds and facial grimaces—spurring schoolmates, especially boys, to make fun of him. "It got really bad when he was twelve," she recalls. Jerry was so spastic that he almost had to be removed from school. Kathryn and Vernon took Jerry to *brauchers*, Amish healers who manipulate people's bodies as chiropractors do, but the *brauchers* could not fix what was wrong. "We wondered if we were to blame," she recalls. Maybe they had been too focused on their youngest, before and after the heart-repair surgery, and had not paid enough attention to Jerry.

A friend suggested that Kathryn look at some information about Tourette's syndrome. The descriptions of the behaviors associated with Tourette's, Kathryn saw right away, matched Jerry's, and when she took him to a medical specialist, the doctor agreed and quickly verified the diagnosis. He also gave Jerry medication that calmed the tics. The teasing at school continued. Jerry asked his mother to come and explain to the kids about Tourette's, which she did; some of the teasing stopped.

Since then, Jerry has graduated and found a job as a dishwasher and busboy at a large tourist restaurant, five miles from the L family home. When he turned sixteen he "wanted to go out like the other kids did." In their area, remote from the nearest town, the pattern is for a group of boys to travel together in *rumspringa* activities; because his choices of companions were limited, Kathryn says, Jerry reluctantly agreed to "hang out" with two of his former tormentors. Kathryn is concerned about this arrangement but has not interfered, because, after all, the other boys are Amish and they went to the same school as he did.

As this was happening, Kathryn's oldest daughter, Susanne, fifteen, found a first job at the flea market in Shipshewana, a huge enterprise that runs several days a week for most of the year—and was asked out by Joe, a young Amish-raised co-worker whose parents are in the same church district as the L's. A few years older than Susanne, Joe wears English clothes and has a car.

Kathryn recounts for a visitor, with great aplomb, what Susanne told Joe: "I'll date you but I won't dress English, I won't sleep with you, and I won't drink." Joe agreed to the conditions. Kathryn might have chosen a more traditional boyfriend for Susanne, but, as she did with Jerry, she feels that she must allow Susanne to make her own choices.

Dennis L of Shipshewana, an Amish grandfather, has held many jobs during his lifetime, among them farmer, blacksmith, carpenter, general contractor, and furniture finisher. A big man with a magnificent beard, he is missing a digit on each hand, testimony to having spent a life working around machinery and tools. His three daughters were all married in the space of eighteen months, and he and his wife, Mary, now assist in the care of their grandchildren. Dennis is the second son of a brood of ten born to a farmer on a farm not far from the county seat of LaGrange, which is about fifteen miles from Shipshewana; his parents now have some seventy great-grandchildren, most of them still in the area.

"I started working when I was fifteen, and gave all my wages to my parents, without them asking," he says. "I didn't start keeping the money until I was nineteen, about to get married." Hewing to the straight and narrow path came naturally to him: "I knew what was acceptable behavior and what was not." It wasn't that he had memorized the *ordnung*. His parents did not have to enumerate precisely what was permitted or forbidden; they and his older siblings and relatives and neighbors had communicated it to him, mostly by example. "That's what happens when a family is functioning properly," he avows.

Dennis admits that he strayed a bit during his own *rumspringa*—

"I had some things to apologize for"—but not much, because he had effectively internalized the proper code of behavior. "We don't obey the *ordnung* because we fear the consequences of not obeying the rules but because we think they are correct," he says. On a society-wide level, he goes on to suggest, this same inculcated sense of right and wrong is what makes us behave courteously toward other oncoming vehicles at a four-way-stop-sign intersection—and, in his view, this internalized sense of what is right and wrong must underlie the justice and governmental structure of any good society, as he believes it certainly does with the Amish.

While to outsiders the *ordnung* may symbolize the odious restrictions and absurd contradictions in Amish society—a barbed-wire fence that keeps in more than it keeps out—in the view of thoughtful Amish adults such as Ruth, Kathryn, and Dennis, the *ordnung* functions as a white picket fence surrounding a lovely garden and a community of the faithful who find it neither unreasonably burdensome nor oppressive. They know that part of their parental task is to help their children accept the need for this fence and to stay willingly within it and their faith.

That is also the explanation of the *ordnung* set down some years ago in an authoritative note to the scholarly journal *Mennonite Quarterly Review*. The writer, who originally signed himself an "Amish minister," was later identified as the historian Joseph F. Beiler, a cofounder of one of the only libraries established by the sect, the Pequea Bruderschaft Library in Gordonville, Pennsylvania, and also of a monthly magazine edited and published by the Amish, *The Diary of the Old Order Churches*.

Beiler wrote that the usual English translation of the word *ordnung*, "discipline," was inadequate. In his view, *ordnung* had three "meanings."

1. To arrange or draw up a rule of degree to induce equality.
2. It creates a vision of contentment.

3. God's example of the universe—nobody doubts the time of sunrise or sunset, nobody argues the timing of the moon, etc.

The dos and don'ts of the *ordnung*, he implied, were the human equivalent of God's "rules" for operation of the universe, reason enough for any Amish to follow them. This was also, in Beiler's view, why properly observing and obeying the rules of the *ordnung* would "generate peace, love, contentment, equality, and unity."

Beiler's historical research convinced him that there was an integral relationship between the *ordnung* and the survival of the Anabaptist creed—that adherence to the *ordnung* was what permitted the most conservative Amish and Mennonite churches to endure, while the absence of a strict *ordnung* contributed to the fading of other Christian denominations.

Yet in the early years of the Amish sect, during the period when its members were being hounded in Europe and continuing on through the first decades of transfer to the New World, the *ordnung* was "not a major problem," Beiler wrote. The first list, a written list, was made in the wake of the Revolutionary War, which, Beiler observes, almost destroyed the Amish sect with its promises of freedom and individuality; fixing the rules that governed behavior helped to keep the community intact. According to Beiler, adherence or nonadherence to the *ordnung* became a full-blown subject of discussion and controversy during the American Civil War, when changes in fashionable clothing and inventions of new farming technologies made it imperative for the Amish to address such issues directly, in the hope, as Beiler puts it, of preserving intact "their old-time religion." Today the *ordnung* remains, Beiler asserts, a matter of "holding the line" against changes in the way of life that if left unchecked would demolish the church.

Beiler charges that a "rebelling" member will generally deprecate the *ordnung* by saying that it is man-made law with "no scriptural base," and that the *ordnung* "causes discord" among members. But it is the sinner who is to blame, not the church's rule against the offense, Beiler asserts; and while the *ordnung* may be made by men, it is divinely inspired and in imitation of rules given in Scripture. Adherence to the *ordnung* "is a symbol that tells if you care for the church or if you don't care; if you love the church or if you don't. You are either in the church or you are outside; there is no happy medium." People inside the church's white picket fence, he asserts, have "more freedom, more liberty and more privilege than those . . . bound to the outside."

An example of the *ordnung* being enabling is given by David Wagler, a columnist for the Amish weekly *The Budget*, in an article titled "Why the Amish Can Live Without Television." Citing the Fifth Commandment and its instruction to honor one's parents, Wagler writes that the concomitant of being honored by children is the obligation to guard them, to bring them up "in an environment that exposes them as little as possible to the temptations of this world." If Amish parents allow a TV set into the home, "we are abdicating our position as head of the family . . . and turning over the key to our homes and our hearts to the world." Furthermore,

> when the world is invited into our homes, it accepts the invitation and proceeds to take over . . . This monster will demand complete submission to its own set of values . . . We admit it would be convenient to have television sets in our homes to get the news, the markets, and the weather report. But we don't think we can afford it. The price is too high . . . We don't think it is fair to ourselves or to our children to be constantly exposed to the example and teachings of those who do not have the knowledge of the true God. We will not invite the false gods that personify the goals of this world to enter our homes.

A main purpose of the *ordnung*, then, is to regulate the family lives of the Amish. It is important to recognize how markedly Amish family lives differ from those of mainstream American families, especially in regard to raising teenagers.

Some basic differences are mandated by size and situation:

Amish families are far larger than mainstream ones, with an average of seven children each; they are usually intact families, with both birth father and birth mother in the same house, rearing the brood to adulthood; they often have several generations living under one roof; most extended Amish families contain ministers or bishops, which most mainstream families do not; and in many Amish families, the fathers are the only breadwinners, while the mothers work solely in the home.

Further differences are illuminated by scholarly research into the attributes associated with "competent" mainstream families. In a study widely cited by academics as thorough and revealing, the psychiatrist Jerry M. Lewis of Kent State University and his associates observed dozens of mainstream families in different situations over the course of decades and found that "optimally competent" ones—who were also the most successful in rearing "mentally healthy" adolescents—share the following half dozen characteristics:

1. A well-defined leadership shared by the parents, with the mother taking the lead in some areas, the father in others. The roles of each parent are consistent and clear to each other and to the children.
2. Authority exists; authoritarian behavior does not.
3. Individuality among the children is permitted and encouraged.
4. All family members are allowed to express their opinions, and all human feelings are expressed and reacted to within the family circle.
5. There is an understanding that each member of the family speaks only for himself or herself, and does not presume to speak for the others.
6. Family members respect one another.

The "parental coalition" that best supplies the family with "strong, effective leadership" features "flexibility, shared power, and considerable psychological intimacy." And its pattern for successfully dealing with a teenager is "not authoritarian" but one in which the parents "listen to their adolescent child's ideas and feelings and seek solutions through negotiation."

Most Amish families meet very nicely Lewis's first criterion for competent families, well-defined leadership, and his last, respect for one another, to a degree seldom found in mainstream families. But they don't do well on the "communication of feelings" criteria. While Johnny Y's parents evidently have a high tolerance for adolescent needs, many of our other Amish families do not. Lydia T's parents seek an accommodation with their rambunctious daughter through an ingenious deal for a buggy. Kathryn and Vernon L seesaw between allowing Jerry and Susanne to do as they wish and disagreeing with their children's choices. The parents of Emma M and Phil T appear not to communicate with their children in an emotionally open way, or to tolerate their high jinks, or to be willing to negotiate.

Another psychiatrist, George H. Orvin, who surveyed a slew of similar studies of patients and added observations based on his own practice, found many parents in marginally competent families expressing the firm belief that

> if they worked hard enough, their children would become well-adjusted adults. Seldom were these parents negligent in their parental responsibilities. Rarely were these children deprived of physical necessities. When neglect did occur, it was more frequently in the sphere of emotional deprivation. Many of these families were uncomfortable in the open expression of affection—in expressing not only love but also anger, jealousy, fear, or sadness.

In Orvin's view, what prevents such families from producing mentally healthy children is parents carrying over the "attitudes, beliefs, sentiments, and behaviors from their childhood into their relationships with their children." He explains, "Parents who have grown up in families in which feelings were not indulged" find difficulty in "expressing feelings within the family they come to lead."

Such difficulties in parental homes are familiar to Amos and Anne Beiler, proprietors of the well-known Aunt Anne's pretzel chain, headquartered in Gap, Pennsylvania. Both were raised Old Order Amish in Pennsylvania, and each left the church without being baptized. According to Amos, they brought into their marriage very little sense of their own emotions or how to convey them but began to realize this as a painful lack only when one of their children died in a terrible accident and they had difficulty dealing with the emotional consequences of the loss. "Neither of us had any experience expressing our feelings on any emotional matter, let alone one this big," Amos recalls. "The Amish don't encourage that kind of expression, not even love for your spouse in front of the children. We had to learn all that." From therapy the Beilers gained knowledge about feelings and expressing them, and then Amos, with Anne's encouragement, and with some of the proceeds from their pretzel enterprise, founded a clinic to counsel Amish and Mennonite people in emotional distress.

On Lewis's list, Amish families would perform well on three items and not well on three others; in Lewis's terms, this score might put Amish families into the category of less than optimally competent. Yet in mainstream society's terms, Amish families are clearly functional: they do not disintegrate into divorce; they are law-abiding, pay taxes, and rear children who become productive citizens, offspring who decide in overwhelming numbers to follow closely the tracks taken by their parents.

The discrepancy between the psychiatrists' characterizations of "normal" families and the facts of Amish life reinforces how greatly Amish norms differ from mainstream norms. From the Amish standpoint, American society's norms are skewed in the wrong direction by an overemphasis on the notion that family mental health and parental success depend upon fostering certain kinds of individuality and growth in the children—as in Orvin's summary contention, "A healthy environment for children must

promote growth toward individuality and connected autonomy . . .
If that environment stifles growth, individuality, and connected
autonomy for the parents, it will do the same for the children."

Nevertheless, Orvin—who champions the nurturing of individuality—sees as essential to well-functioning families a "disciplined environment" of the sort that Ruth M, Kathryn L, and
Dennis L speak of as central to Amish child rearing. Orvin writes
of the "necessity of setting limits" for children through establishing
"clearly stated" rules that "should have value," should "have a purpose," and should be "genuine." "Parents ought not to impose
rules that they do not respect." Rules should convey to adolescents
what is right and what is wrong, should set limits that the parents
can enforce, and "should help adolescents 'not cross the line.' "

Joann H, the shy girl who started slowly in *rumspringa* but with
her older brother's help had soon gotten in up to her chin, is conflicted about what to do now, having turned seventeen.

She is out in the wider world on the weekends and having new
experiences, but patterns of behavior from her past keep recur-
ring. She recalls that even before she began *rumspringa*, she had
been having near-continual "spats" with her parents and Amish
girlfriends. "I had a really, really bad temper. Any little thing could
set me off, and it was just, like, 'Okay, I'll get *you* back.' And I guess
the bitterness just welled up in me when I turned sixteen."

The focus of that bitterness was her mother, who had married
at eighteen and was—then as now, in Joann's view—a "real Little
Miss Goody Two-shoes," naïve, a woman who has never set foot
in the outside world and therefore does not have a realistic perspective on it. Joann herself has some experience of the world
now, most of it garnered at Das Dutchman Essenhaus, the big
tourist restaurant at which she waits tables, and from the Baptist
church that she now attends.

Her father, she knows, is more worldly. In her early youth he
was a duck farmer, but then, in a search for cash, he had started a
wood shavings business, "a dirty job" that entails going around to

workshops, baling the shavings, and selling them for horse bedding. The eldest daughter of a brood of eight, Joann attended Amish school, where she was an "easy learner" but which she was "glad to leave" at graduation. She had yearned to go into the world but could find only babysitting work until she became old enough to take the restaurant job.

Now that she has turned seventeen, her parents say, it is time for her to give up her wild ways. Joann responds, "I'm, like, 'You guys don't understand.'" Her parents seem not to care how much fun she is having, or to countenance her unwillingness to stop having fun. So Joann, a dutiful daughter, tries to meet their expectations halfway, agreeing one weekend to attend a party but not to drink; she manages that feat, but the experience is not enjoyable.

From out of the blue, the church offers her the opportunity to teach at an Amish school. She wonders, "Do I really want to? Because basically, if a new teacher comes to the school, well, 'This isn't the way we did it last year,' and it causes a lot of confusion," so she decides to wait for a few years; if she still wants to teach then, she is certain, she can.

Also in reaction to this not-so-subtle offer, she takes a huge step in the other direction. An older woman with whom she works at the restaurant, and with whom she has been discussing matters of faith and independence, suggests that Joann move into her apartment as a boarder. Joann's parents are upset, but she wants to be independent, as her older brother has become. So she does it: moves out.

No longer under her father's roof, she keeps for herself more of the money that she makes, and with some of it has her hair cut and buys sneakers. She takes up jogging. Every day after work she puts on shorts and a T-shirt and runs a few miles. "Sure can't do that in an Amish dress," Joann tells herself.

She likes the way running clears her mind. So does something else that is new: with her landlady's coaxing, Joann starts to attend Baptist church services regularly—and discovers that they are very different from those of the Amish church in which she grew up. Everyone at the Baptist tabernacle, she observes, is "reading the

Bible and talking about the Bible instead of 'which guy is the cutest?' which us Amish girls had always talked about." She truly enjoys talking with others about the Bible, an activity that is even more intense during Wednesday-night classes and Sunday school. And she learns to "trust Jesus more."

In Joann's Amish church, individual Bible reading is not exactly forbidden but is difficult to accomplish, since the Bible is in High German and substantially different from the Dutch she speaks; there are German-to-English translations to be found, but few people bother using them—most members of the congregation are content to leave interpretation of the Bible to the ministers.

Joann feels an emotional tug when her mother reports that her littlest sister is crying and unable to eat her meals because Joann is not home. She resists that guilt trip but transmutes it into another worry: "What if I don't go to Heaven because I left the Amish church?" People at the Baptist tabernacle assure her, " 'It's okay, you know; if you have Christ in your life, it's okay.' But there is always that fear."

Steadied by her attendance at services and studies at the Baptist church, Joann weans herself from partying and drinking. Her brother turns eighteen, which means he is legally able to buy a vehicle, and he does, a truck. "And all of a sudden—wham! wham!—he's involved in two accidents and lucky both times" in that he is not badly hurt. "It's like God watching over him still, you know? 'Still got a chance.' He better take it!" Her brother was not drinking at the time of either accident, but Joann recognizes that he has become quite a drinker, and also a smoker of a carton of cigarettes each week.

Smoking and drinking to excess are wrong, Joann knows, and the error in what her brother has been doing becomes so obvious that she can no longer avoid the same understanding of her own actions; she begins to feel "guilty" about smoking, drinking, petting, rock music, partying till all hours. The guilt, she believes, "comes with the territory," but she does not discuss it with anyone, and none of the other Amish party girls ever mentions it—though Joann is certain "they're also feeling the same thing."

She has some fights with her Amish and non-Amish girlfriends over stealing boys, backbiting, gossip. "Having little spats with friends" seems to her to be a popular pastime among her peers.

The fights hurt Joann. She also suffers when some of her close colleagues at the restaurant leave for other jobs. Life on the wild side, she is now realizing, is "not what I expected it to be. You think, 'Well, I could go do this and that now.' Well, you can't. Because you're still going to have to live with the consequences." It is an echo of what her parents have always told her.

Her parents' anguish finds renewed voice when Joann's next youngest sister turns sixteen and hastens to join her and their brother in partying. This, finally, is too much for the parents. One child on the wild side is bad enough, but three at the same time! Their upset is exacerbated when neighbors ask questions that are really accusations about the parents' lack of supervision of their children. The subject comes up at the Amish Sunday church sessions, not directly but by obvious inference, with the entire congregation requested to pray for the guidance of the young folks who are currently in danger of falling permanently into Satan's hands and never returning to the church. When the H trio of party-scene teenagers touch down, however temporarily, at the family home, the parents corner them and harangue them to give up their wild ways.

The confrontation style is not two parents against three kids, Joann notes as she waits her turn; rather, it is father and son, or father and daughter. Her mother stays out of the argument, often out of the room altogether. Joann's older brother, in his truculent way, simply listens to Dad's diatribe and offers nothing in response; this makes Dad become even more exercised, and the atmosphere gets "a little tense," but there is no resolution—her brother isn't about to give in, and neither is Dad. Her next youngest sister, under the same sort of pressure, takes a different tack—argues with their father, which also incenses him.

Joann tries a third approach when her father has her alone in the room. She reasons, "If you talk back, they're going to get mad, and if you don't say anything, they're going to get mad. But if you just kind of agree with them, 'Yeah, I know, I shouldn't be doing this,' then they'll accept that." And they do, for a while. But for how long? What can she do about it? Run farther away? Run home? Be baptized in the Baptist church and seek comfort in that group? Join the Amish church? Joann doesn't know what to do, and that is bothering her, big time.

Put in more abstract terms, what bothers Joann—what bothers many Amish teens and, for that matter, almost all of us during our adolescences—are matters of identity, belongingness, and meaning in one's life. I find it striking that Donald Kraybill and others who have studied the Amish over long periods have pinpointed identity, belongingness, and meaning in life as basic satisfactions of an adult Amish existence.

Earlier in this book I asserted that the Amish are the great naysayers to American cultural experience, but we must also acknowledge that they are the furnishers (to their members) of certain kinds of positive social satisfactions that mainstream Americans complain of not having—such as belongingness and meaning in life. These satisfactions are, in the phrase of a sociologist who studied the Amish a generation ago, the fruits of that society's "cultural reward" system. Victor Stoltzfus identified the cultural reward of family as "the single most important item in the Amish reward structure . . . the carrier of other important rewards." Among these are the comfort of not having to feel alone in the world, the pleasure of having multiple siblings with whom to share childhood, and the stimulation and variety of interactions that derive from the mingling of several generations. Learning about life from a grandparent or an older sibling, or from the chore of caring for a younger sibling, is a further benefit of being in a large family, often under one roof or in adjoining homes on the same property. Another benefit derives from the Amish tradition of "visiting" other families in association with one's own and participation in other community events, including funerals, which are always held at family homes. Two related rewards have been more recently identified by Kraybill: contentment with one's lot and the satisfaction of being satisfied.

One hundred and fifty years ago, Henry David Thoreau famously observed in *Walden* that "the mass of men lead lives of quiet desperation." The Amish seem to exude not desperation but rather its opposite, contentment. Amish parents have reason to hope that their having provided their children with structured childhoods and comforting family experiences will act as a bulwark against the world for when the teenagers go out into it—that their home life will have given them the strength to resist the temptations, wants, and comparisons with other people's lots that are at the heart of desperation.

Thoreau's remark is often misinterpreted because our culture has moved beyond his definition of desperateness. He believed that most people lived lives of desperation because they were not engaged on a high enough mental level with the world around them; in his day, Americans expended most of their energy and time keeping themselves fed, clothed, and housed, and did little conceptual thinking beyond that necessary to accomplishing these tasks. Today's Amish children, just as American mainstream children, are furnished with adequate quantities of food, clothing, and housing; but while mainstream children must often discover their own rationales for living, working, and relating to the world around them, Amish children are taught—by their churches, families, and schools—specific patterns through which to conceptualize their work, their engagement with the world, and their relationship to the people around them. A poem in *Family Life* called "The Joys of Folding Wash" tells of the homemaker, while she creases and stacks each item, thinking—as the church would have her do—of the wearer's presence in the family and the blessings that wearer brings to the familial group. Such a conceptual context makes a humdrum task more endurable; it is the engine of the satisfaction of being satisfied. Ruth M keeps a songbook on the window ledge above the sink in which she washes her vegetables and dinner dishes; it is a religious-themed songbook that, she says, makes a chore such as washing dishes into something enjoyable and celebratory.

If secular mainstream society has fewer of these sorts of satisfactions, that lack may be the unwanted product of the quickly mounting accumulation of desires that our culture asks us to slake: we are exhorted not only to live well but to become rich and famous, to be elected to high office, to have our talent recognized, to live in grand comfort, and so on—in short, to embody the American success dream. Those who unquestioningly accept that achievement goal are the most susceptible to the lure of needing bigger cars, the latest technological gadgets, more money in their pockets, superior political power, greater individual accomplishment, and louder applause from ever larger audiences. The escalation of desires also teaches mainstreamers to be perpetually unsatisfied with what we do have, or else to feel out of step with the American dream.

Young Amish men and women are Americans who are taught a different American dream. As shaped by their parents, church, and community, their dream highlights the satisfactions of providing adequately for the family rather than only for the self; contributing to the social welfare of the community by imitating Christ— by assuming responsibility for their neighbors' well-being, doing brotherly and sisterly good deeds, bringing up children to serve the Lord and preserve the church; living a life stripped of unnecessary frills so that it can be devoted to religious goals and to the deep soul pleasures that faith can offer.

4

Education: "Prepare for Usefulness"

At age thirteen, after moving with her family from Wisconsin to Middlebury, Indiana, Lydia T has a strange moment: for the first time in her life she is attending an Amish school—just for a year, until she is old enough to graduate. Her entire previous schooling has been in the public school system. The Amish schoolhouse in Middlebury is the smallest school she has ever seen, just one open room with children from five to fourteen in it. No separate lunchroom, no gym, no library, no television set on which to watch educational videos: not a lot of fun. Her classmates in Middlebury are, she estimates, years ahead of her in English and mathematics. They are also not very friendly, perhaps because she is new. The teacher can't give her enough attention to compensate for her being so far behind, especially in math, a subject that, she says, is "absolutely not soaking in." She has been hating every minute of this year. Fortunately, the school is going to allow her to graduate next spring, no matter how well or badly she does.

Today, however, an instructional subject comes up about which, for once, she knows more than her peers: sex education. Their casual comments have convinced Lydia that they know virtually nothing about sex. She had basic sex ed in public school, somewhat to her mother's chagrin—her mother forbids talk in the house about women being pregnant, even if they are

visibly so. Now Lydia's age-mates in the Amish school have found a chap-
ter on sex ed in the public high school "health" text that they are using
and are importuning the teacher, "Let's read that."

Lydia starts to chime in, to assert that it's really important—basic in-
formation that everyone, especially every girl, ought to know in order not
to inadvertently become pregnant—but the teacher interrupts. "Oh, no,
we're not reading that. That's nothing for you guys to know about."

Lydia is more amazed than amused as her classmates just say, "Well,
all right," and, without further protest, agree to skip the lesson.

Elaine W is a bright and athletic Amish-raised girl of seventeen
who, unlike most Amish her age, is attending high school—she's a
senior at Westview High, near Shipshewana. Her being in high
school is the product of a lengthy series of fights within her family. She was in grade school when she became aware of the battle
going on between her parents and her oldest brother over his education. He threatened to leave home if they did not permit him
to attend high school, and, so as not to lose him, they gave in. But
every morning as he prepared to catch the bus, Mrs. W would try
to dissuade him from going to the school, telling him as he went
out the door, "It's wrong, it's wrong." The mother's distress wors-
ened as two other children followed the eldest to high school and
the eldest, when he turned sixteen, refused thereafter to wear
Amish clothes while in school.

When Elaine was in the fifth grade, she went with her father to
the high school to see her brother play in a tournament basketball
game. She remembers, "It was so cool" to watch him and "see all
those people" in the bleachers, cheering. Her father, a dairy
farmer who had begun a furniture-making and retailing business,
had yielded to his son's entreaty to attend this game, at which the
seniors and their parents were to be honored. Mrs. W had stayed
home. For attending the game her father "got in trouble with the
church," but for Elaine the event was salutary, because it piqued
her interest in sports—and in going to high school.

The basketball-playing brother went on to college and became an accountant; by the time he had finished his advanced degree, it had become obvious that he would never return to the Amish fold. But the two next eldest W children did return. They graduated high school, then married and settled down in the community with no apparent deleterious effects from having been exposed to worldly education past the eighth grade. Elaine completed junior high while another two siblings were working their way through high school: one brother then breezed through college and into medical school, and a sister entered nursing school. "As time went on," Elaine recalls, "it was easier for each family member to go on in school, and for me it wasn't very difficult at all. My mom said something about it, but I guess that was kind of expected."

Elaine has become a vigorous athlete. She is not hampered during games by her long brown hair, which she pins out of the way in the Amish style. A mainstay of the basketball team, she also does well in classes and has set her sights on obtaining a college degree in sports therapy as a stepping-stone to later studying medicine.

Elaine considers herself fairly straitlaced. Although she is in her *rumspringa* years, she has never attended a back-acres Amish party; she is unwilling to participate in excess drinking and licentious behavior. Her elder brothers and sisters were the same way, and she finds it "hard to believe" that Amish parents "would rather have their kids go out and drink and do that stuff than have them go to school and get an education and try to make, you know, a life for themselves." Still, she was deeply disappointed when her parents would not come to see her play basketball. On her sixteenth birthday, Elaine stopped wearing Amish clothes so that she would not look Amish in her yearbook photo.

Thinking about her Amish friends from elementary school, Elaine is convinced that one "could have been class valedictorian" had she attended high school and that others could have done equally well. "I do think that a lot of the Amish would probably be some of the smartest people in high school; I think they would be some of the better athletes; I think they are just cheating themselves of something really great by not going on."

. . .

Emma M, the tall, willowy girl whose friends told her she could be a model, was refused permission to attend high school, but now, sixteen and working in Shipshewana, she says she is "not embarrassed about not having my diploma, because I learned nearly as much in my eight years as my non-Amish friends did through their twelve."

Back in Missouri, in her prepubescent years, she had been a "scholar" at a one-room schoolhouse. "All the schoolwork, we did in school. There was no talking in class, you just studied and did your work." There was no homework, so the children could devote their out-of-school time to household chores. One class unit per week, in Spanish, was taught by a convert to the Amish faith who had previously taught public school. "He said he could teach the Amish kids as much in a half hour as he could teach the non-Amish in three days." Emma attributes that to her classmates' fluency in two languages. Another assurance that her education was better than that of a public school came from a non-Amish girlfriend who was "amazed" that Emma's seventh-grade English assignments were the same as the friend's twelfth-grade ones. But "some subjects we never had," principal among them science:

> The Amish feel the world began as the Bible says it, God created earth and man and the sun and it just grew from there. And they're definitely against everyone thinking they came from apes or something, because it goes against the Bible. Which is kind of why we didn't have science. If they could have had their own science books, written by them, we probably would have had. But science had too much of evolution in it, the books that they saw, so we never did have science.

A middle child in a family of seven, Velda B attended public grade school in northern Indiana. Her family operated a chicken farm, and Velda enjoyed family tasks such as collecting hundreds of eggs from the henhouse. "It was great," she recalls. "It was when us kids connected the most." Sometimes they would have egg fights.

In school she was full of questions, and she was rewarded for these and for being bright. In junior high, though, Velda's attitude toward school changed. An English friend offered to let her borrow shorts and a shirt for a gym class; she put on the outfit but says, "I just couldn't wear it—it just felt so strange because for so long I was used to wearing the dress. And the hair covering. And I felt very naked without it. . . . At that point . . . the basic things that formed my identity were the things that I was taught to be and told to believe."

Such experiences made her acutely aware of how different she was from her non-Amish classmates and damped her interest in formal schooling. Velda began to keep her questions to herself, though at home she could not help but query her parents on why the family had no car or telephone. "It's not something that the Amish people allow, it's not part of our way of life," she says they would tell her, "and that was the end of the conversation."

She tried to come to terms with those restrictions, and to take sustenance from the Amish culture and community, while at the same time she came under pressure from her Amish peers, perhaps because she was physically mature when most of the others had not yet begun to blossom. On a hot spring day she went to junior high wearing short socks called "booties," which she thought "cool and sophisticated," and which were often worn during the summer. But soon after this display she received a letter from her Amish girlfriends saying that, because she had dressed inappropriately, they would no longer "hang out" with her. Velda was stunned.

Near the end of junior high, she "lost interest" in school altogether—mostly because it had become obvious to her that she would not be going on to high school. "My parents didn't support that idea, or couldn't support that idea."

After eighth grade Velda stayed home and helped with the household chores but dreamed of something unfamiliar to Amish girls: having a career. She had no particular career or job in mind, she just wanted a life out of the ordinary Amish channels. She developed a passion for music, listened to on a secreted radio in her room or from CDs played at the homes of non-Amish friends. Soon she edged over into more forbidden behaviors.

Physically well developed and darkly attractive at fifteen, Velda looked older and tried to act it. She would pretend to be at a girlfriend's, sleeping over for the weekend, but they would join the older teens on outings and, Velda says, "do all the things we were so much denied to do . . . We'd get into a lot of trouble. We'd go out and drink and—that was a period of time when to us it was just like being, it was like being unleashed." Being "drunk every weekend," she later thought, "kind of dulled some of the pain that I wasn't even aware of, and relieved the confusion for a little bit, but it didn't help solve the problem," which had its seat, she later came to believe, in her desires for a career and more knowledge about life. She wondered, "Am I wrong to feel this way?" because she knew that her desires and questions were causing a lot of pain at home.

Velda took up with "a much older guy, a Mennonite." On their first date, he escorted her to a steak restaurant, and she was embarrassed when she did not even know how to use the knife to cut her meat properly. He taught her that, and how to drive, and encouraged her to wear clothes that accentuated her good figure and jewelry that highlighted her dark eyes.

She found a job in a factory that manufactured campers; at fifteen and sixteen she was not permitted by law to do the "heaviest" work, but she prepared parts for the men to use. The work was "very fast paced," stressful and exhausting. But Velda was "trying to prove something . . . trying to prove that I was worth something."

In being in the community yet out of it, conducting an affair and having a job, Velda felt she was slipping in and out of "an emotionally enclosed environment," just like a jack-in-the-box. "You know: he'd pop out, they'd push him back down. He'd pop out, they'd push him back down. And that's sometimes how I feel.

Like if I would step out, there's so much conflict that it would, you know, make me go back down."

DeWayne C, a strapping lad of nineteen, now wears his hair buzz-cut short and is bothered by his lack of a high school education.

As a young boy, he was happy when his parents permitted him to attend public grade schools instead of Amish school in northern Indiana. In junior high, he made friends with non-Amish basketball teammates and wanted to go on to high school with them. "I begged Mom and Dad," he says, "but they said the reason you can't is if you go, then you'll more likely leave the Amish church, have a profession—like, you know, 'You're doing something else, then you won't come back at all.' "

That seemed unreasonable to him. His older brothers had gone out and partied, and they had returned to the Amish fold. So at fifteen, DeWayne helped his father in his workshop and enjoyed racing in the family buggy that had been given to him. But being kept out of school seemed so wrong that he began to question it and other church edicts he had previously accepted. Why would his having as much education as his basketball teammates harm him, his family, or the church? What logic could explain the church permitting his father to keep a telephone in a shack outside his workplace but not inside the shop or the house? Why was an Amish person allowed to accept rides in cars and trucks yet forbidden to own or drive a car? Why would cutting his hair in a non-Amish style prevent him from entering Heaven? "The way I was brought up, I thought that if I had short hair, and shorts on [instead of long pants], I was pretty much going to Hell."

A friend from school whose family had left the faith would occasionally give him a ride in the family car; the attraction for DeWayne of having his own buggy began to fade.

At sixteen DeWayne went out partying, timidly at first because he did not like the liquor being shoved at him by slightly older Amish teens. But he did have his hair cut short and in other ways soon came to enjoy his new freedoms. On turning eighteen, he obtained a job in one of the several large RV factories in Middlebury, bought a Harley, joined a motorcycle club, and rented an apartment. None of these gave his parents pause. On one of DeWayne's weekly visits home to enjoy his mother's cooking, his parents asked him to let his hair grow so that when he took part in a brother's wedding he would not look non-Amish. Unwilling to offend, he agreed.

Now, however, bothered by his lack of a high school education, DeWayne takes courses that will lead him to a GED degree. Once he completes that, he wants to try a few college courses, just to see whether he likes them. Being on his own, he can pursue education even if his parents don't approve.

Eli K, the red-haired young man "rescued" from the mess of a terrible automobile accident by an arrangement in which the church paid his fines and he took over his father's small-engine repair business, is now twenty-three and sports a red beard grown to denote his status as a married male member of the Amish church. He married his childhood sweetheart, Regina, settled down, and is the father of two boys, and of another child on the way. Today the K's live on a five-acre farmette, where Regina spends most of her time with their two sons while Eli is busy in the repair shop. "We are truly blessed," he says.

He reminisces about his early years at an Amish grade school. "That's where me and Regina really met," Eli recalls. "I known who I was going to marry since I was eleven." School was a "mostly happy" experience for him, though he recognized that he was far from the brightest student in the one-room schoolhouse.

In such schoolhouses, as a way of assisting the lone schoolteacher, older students are expected to teach the younger children their lessons. Regina was twenty months his junior, a taciturn girl with sturdy legs and wire-rim spectacles, growing up on a farmette about a mile beyond the school in the other direction from the K house. As Eli tells it, their bond was formed when, instead of him teaching English to her and the other eight-year-olds, "she ended up teaching me," in part because her English was very good, which everyone attributed to her family's operating a bakery stand, where she had to interact daily with English-speaking customers.

Regina also became Eli's "only real friend." He was uncomfortable with the incessant competitiveness of the other boys in the school—including two of his brothers—and unwilling to match their ardor for "fighting about every little thing." Regina became his refuge from the teasing of his siblings and, eventually, from the world.

Eli managed to graduate, but barely. Today, he thinks the curriculum was not practical enough. Besides, he didn't need formal education as a basis for becoming a repair expert, and his classmates didn't need it either, since, he says, "You don't have to have a high school degree to work in the factory or be a farmer.

"What I like is knowing what to do," he adds, speaking of his work and the repair business. This attitude also characterizes how Eli thinks about other aspects of his life. He likes having figured out that since Amish housewives do the wash on Mondays, on Tuesdays he will be summoned to repair various washing machines. Alternate Wednesdays, Eli, Regina, and the toddlers have supper with his parents or hers; Sundays their cow is not milked or her bedding changed, so on Monday mornings there is a mess in her stall; church is held at their home thrice every two years, which gives Eli ample time beforehand to call in his brothers and brothers-in-law to help paint the place and spruce it up.

His most profitable line is converting washing machines from electric-powered to gas-powered, since "every woman getting married has to have one in her new home." A nearby wholesaler of appliances usually recommends him for the conversion job and, of course, expects and receives a small commission for doing so.

Recently, to expand the business—and perhaps because he feels the need to repay his debts more quickly—Eli started a sideline of renting out small gas canisters. People bring in their empties and he replaces them with filled ones, which he obtains weekly from a distributor. "If people're coming in anyway for the gas," he explains, "they sometimes bring along a lamp to fix."

In addition to renting out canisters, Eli plans to offer a plumbing service. Newer generations of Amish men, no longer being brought up on working farms, have not learned from childhood the repair of plumbing and other household machinery, so there is now a need for plumbing services in a community where in the past there was not much call for them. And eventually, Eli says, he will offer gas-powered appliances for sale, used ones at first.

When will his plans be translated into action? "No hurry," he replies. "Do it when I'm ready."

How will Eli be able to afford to buy washing machines for resale, much less add the space necessary to display and sell them from his shop? He has no answers for such questions. He thinks that maybe elementary economics and management subjects would have been covered had he gone on through high school, but he's not sure about that. Perhaps he'll take a correspondence course to make up for his lack of knowledge. Regina could help him with it, because he "sure wouldn't want to fail any of the tests."

The Amish use of formal education reminds me of schooling in the colonies and in the nascent United States of America. In the eighteenth and early nineteenth centuries, all schooling was church-based and deliberately limited in intellectual scope— aimed at giving children just enough education to become productive members of society. It did not seek to create geniuses, artistic stars, or even particularly learned men or women. Students were taught enough math to run a household and a small business, enough ABCs to write a letter to a relative or an advertisement for the weekly paper, and little more. Accumulation of knowledge for its own sake and the development of the ability to think critically about a wide variety of subjects were seen as neither important nor useful. This limited kind of schooling was very appropriate for a growing nation, and it was not replaced by education with loftier ends until the 1870s. Before that era, for example, a very low percentage of the American population attended high school, and less than 1 percent went on to college.

Some Amish, like the historian and school board member Sam Stoltzfus of Gordonville, in Lancaster County, believe that what has gone wrong in American society can be traced back to that moment in the 1870s when American education diverged from its earlier configuration. In his view, when communities ceased to be farm-centered, the need for more education to handle city-based and industry-based jobs arose, as did the push toward individual achievement. As he sees it, "From then on, you saw everybody trying to get more and more education, more than anybody needs—leads to being overeducated, everybody special-izing, very few farming, and that leads to rising divorce and crime rates and your other social ills."

Until the 1940s, the majority of Amish youth attended public schools. Since many of these were in districts populated almost entirely by Amish, local school boards saw to it that Amish chil-dren were not exposed to unwanted academic subjects such as science or to social experiences like dance parties. And federal laws encouraged and permitted farming families, Amish and non-Amish alike, to take their children out of school at fourteen to as-sist on the farms. But when rural school districts began rapidly to consolidate—there were four thousand one-room schoolhouses in Pennsylvania on the eve of World War II and many fewer after it—the Amish slipped from being majorities in the schools to mi-norities, and the need for them to establish their own schools be-came more pressing.

Amish schoolhouses were one-room affairs with no electricity and few creature comforts, facilities little different from those that had served all Americans a hundred years earlier. They were sup-ported by levies on the church district's families, generally of a few hundred dollars per year per family, and most of the money was spent on books and supplies; teacher salaries were minimal. Today the facilities are much the same but the pay is better, Sam Stoltzfus says, though it is still less than fifty dollars a day in Lan-caster County. "Can't pay a mortgage on that salary," he observes;

and one result of the low pay is that only twenty-five teachers in all of Lancaster County's Amish schools have five years' experience on the job.

After World War II, the movement to establish a network of separate Amish schools collided with the pushes in mainstream education toward consolidation of districts, compulsory school attendance for children under sixteen, and permitting only state-certified teachers to teach in public schools.

Through the 1940s and 1950s, Amish parents were taken to court, fined, even sent to jail for refusing to permit their children to attend schools past the age of fourteen or for sending them to Amish-run schools whose teachers were not state-certified and whose educational and safety standards were deemed inadequate. The culminating case in a long series was *Wisconsin v. Yoder et al.* Its issues and outcome underlie Amish schooling today.

The case began in October 1968, when Jonas Yoder, Wallace Miller, and Adin Yutzy, farmers in New Glarus, Wisconsin—the first two Amish, the third an Old Order Mennonite—were arrested and charged with keeping several of their children, then aged fourteen and fifteen, out of public school in defiance of the state's compulsory attendance law. The complaint had been signed by the New Glarus school superintendent immediately after he learned that the Amish community had set up a private school and was planning to prevent its teens from attending the regional high school. In Green County Court, the three fathers were readily convicted and fined five dollars each. The next highest court affirmed those convictions.

The Amish fathers refused to pay and appealed to Wisconsin's Supreme Court. Aiding their appeal were William Ball, an attorney with a long interest in First Amendment matters involving church and state; the recently formed National Committee for Religious Freedom for the Amish, led by the Reverend William C. Lindhold, a Lutheran pastor; and Dr. John A. Hostetler of Temple University, then the country's leading academic authority on the Amish.

In Wisconsin's highest court, the Amish asserted that the state statute requiring them to send children to school until the age of sixteen violated their right to exercise their religious beliefs, among which was the belief that children should not receive formal schooling past the age of fourteen. Their advocates told the court that the Amish did not wish to have their children exposed to science and civics, or to a high school's social life, its entertainment, or its general encouragement of competition. The Amish parents also feared the deleterious effects of what Hostetler characterized to the court as a public school's effort to " 'teach values' with respect to life and moral conduct—without, however, offering the law of God as normative."

The state argued that the Amish were refusing to understand the ramifications of denying children a high school education, which Wisconsin believed was required for them to become productive members of society; without such an education, children might well be unable to support themselves as adults and could become wards of the state. Wisconsin interpreted "religious freedom" as meaning the freedom to worship, not the freedom to act in a manner that contravenes state law.

In a six-to-one vote, the state's highest court agreed with the Amish. Wisconsin then appealed to the United States Supreme Court, which heard oral arguments in December 1971. A *Washington Post* reporter noted that the justices were "clearly fascinated" by Ball and Hostetler's word picture of a people for whom "wisdom is learned in the household and at the plow, and secondary schools are seen largely as purveyors of temptation and worldliness." Associate Justices William Rehnquist and Lewis Powell declined to vote in the case, so it was left to be decided by the remaining seven justices, led by Chief Justice Warren Burger.

The court heard some of the biblical bases for the Amish rejection of schooling conducted by institutions that did not embrace their beliefs and values. Citations included I Corinthians 1:19–20: "I will destroy the wisdom of the wise, and the cleverness of the clever I will thwart . . . Has not God made foolish the wisdom of the world?"; II Corinthians 6:17: "Wherefore: Come ye out from among them and be ye separate, saith the Lord, and touch no unclean thing"; as well as Luke 10:21: "I thank Thee, O Father, Lord of Heaven and earth, that Thou has hid these things from the wise and prudent and revealed them unto babes."

The defense asserted that the Amish believed only in education that was "proper"—in that word's connotations of being moral as well as adequate—that is, proper to the tasks that awaited their youth within the community. They declared,

> Only those will disagree who, like the State of Wisconsin . . . insist that all education must be aimed at life goals dictated by the state, or who demand that the values derived from science and technology, or related to consumption and competition, must be imposed on every child.

The decision of the seven justices, issued in 1972, was unusual: 6.5 to 0.5. The half votes came from Associate Justice William O. Douglas, who sided with the majority while dissenting in part. In effect, by this decision the U.S. Supreme Court extended the free exercise of religious beliefs to the matter of school attendance, deeming a refusal to send a child to high school because of religious objections a right fully protected under the First and Fourteenth Amendments. Chief Justice Warren Burger reasoned that formal high school education

> places Amish children in an environment hostile to Amish beliefs . . . and with pressure to conform to the styles, manners, and ways of the peer group, [and] it takes them away from their community, physically and emotionally, during the crucial and formative adolescent period of life . . .
>
> Once a child has learned basic reading, writing, and elementary mathematics, these traits, skills, and attitudes admittedly fall within the category of those best learned through example and "doing" rather than in a classroom. And, at this time in life, the Amish child must also grow in his faith and his relationship to the Amish community if he is to be prepared to accept the heavy obligations imposed by adult baptism. In short, high

school attendance with teachers who are not of the Amish faith—and may even be hostile to it—interposes a serious barrier to the integration of the Amish child into the Amish religious community.

Burger cautioned that not everything in which the Amish believed could be subsumed under constitutional protections. He cited Thoreau's rejecting of mid-nineteenth-century social values and isolating of himself at Walden Pond, which stemmed from a philosophical rather than a religious basis; Burger suggested that a similar rejection of mainstream social values by the Amish, though they might claim it was mandated by their religion, might not be protected under the First and Fourteenth Amendments.

The decision in *Wisconsin v. Yoder* opened the way for the establishing of Amish schools everywhere, and for the wholesale removal of Amish teenagers from public high schools. Today there are more than 800 Amish schools, serving approximately 25,000 Amish children. This result, writes Donald Kraybill, "has helped the Amish to propagate their own values, insulate their young from alien views, as well as monitor the social relations of Amish youth with the outside world. The schools, in short, have contributed in a significant way to the preservation of the culture of separation."

Thomas J. Meyers of Goshen College, a sociologist who has also taught in Amish schools, examined in a statistical analysis the relative strength of various factors affecting the ability of the Amish to retain their children in the church as adults. The factors he examined were the father's occupation, the location of the church district, the severity of the district's *ordnung*, the child's position in the birth order, and whether the child had ever attended a public school. Meyers concluded that "Amish schools are critical in retaining the Amish way of life," and that a young person's attendance at an Amish school was on a par with the strictness of the district's *ordnung* in correlating to a high retention rate. Moreover, those church districts in which a larger proportion of children attended Amish schools through to graduation had a higher retention rate than those in which the children attended public schools, or attended a mix of public and Amish schools.

"Drill rather than variety, accuracy rather than speed, proper sequence rather than freedom of choice" were the instructions from an Amish school board to the new teacher Daisy Spangler. A grandmother with a doctorate in education and a lifetime of teaching in public schools, from kindergarten to college, she had wanted to see what teaching in a school with firm moral foundations would be like. She found the key in a 1981 handbook, which stated that "The Goal of the Old Order Amish Parochial Schools is to prepare for Usefulness, by Preparing for Eternity."

Spangler's school board translated that mission statement into instructions to her to emphasize "shared knowledge and dignity of tradition rather than progress," because "we want our children to have only the knowledge they need to remain faithful religious Amish children." Spangler realized that the curriculum was similar to that of the public schools in elementary English, math, spelling, with a bit of geography and history thrown in, but that no other academic subjects were even touched on by the Amish school. Though Spangler was irked a bit by the shallowness of the curriculum, she swept aside her misgivings because, as a devout Christian, she was overjoyed at being able to work in a school that actively taught fair play, humanity in history, honesty, respect, sincerity, humility, and other moral virtues that public schools excluded or glossed over. The Bible and religious thought were continual presences in her Amish classroom, she marveled, not just mentioned once a day in a perfunctory prayer. She was, however, both intrigued and dismayed that every school subject was used to reinforce religious tenets. Among the questions in a history lesson book:

1. Who discovered America? When? How long ago was that? Did Columbus believe in God?

2. Describe what and how Indians that Columbus found were living, farming, and speaking.
3. Who is president of the U.S. now? Who was our first president? Was he a Christian?
4. Was our union established on a Religious basis? How do you know?

For Daisy Spangler, who had struggled in public school classrooms to maintain decorum and a proper atmosphere for learning, the Amish classroom was a teacher's dream: the children were always polite and quiet, attentive to the teacher, and willing to take instruction. And the parents' stance was even more helpful:

> If a child misbehaved and his parents learned of it, the very next day they brought the child to school and wanted to know, "Do you think your punishment was severe enough? We also punished this child at home. We want him to apologize to you—now." Then the child, usually in tears, would apologize and I had no more problem with him.

She noted other advantages for the pupils in the Amish schools, such as the one-room schoolhouse atmosphere, in which children heard the lessons in subjects over and over again, years before they had to study them. She applauded the teaching of younger children by older ones, and that the students could stay with one teacher for several years rather than having to switch instructors when they went on to the next grade.

Also relevant here are research studies that have compared Amish children's scores on standardized tests with those made by non-Amish students in nearby communities. Some of these studies confirm statistically Spangler's observation that, in terms of math, reading, and use of English, Amish schools teach their children at least as well as non-Amish public schools do. However, in geography, world history, vocabulary, science, literature, and critical thinking, Amish students do significantly less well than their public school peers. Most such comparative studies were done in the 1960s, as part of assessing the legitimacy and adequacy of Amish schools; since the 1972 *Wisconsin v. Yoder* decision, few similar studies have been completed. One was done in Iowa in 1987. The state's basic skills test was given to 197 children in Amish schools; the only curriculum areas not tested were those that were not taught in the Amish schools, science and social studies. The Amish scholars scored above the state average in all the tests except in English, where they were at a slightly lower level but still above the national average. Another 117 students, tested the following year, confirmed the Amish achievements.

There is more to learning, of course, than curriculum lessons, and in this department there are also some interesting findings. In the late 1980s, the researcher Melvin R. Smucker administered four sets of personality tests to about two hundred Amish children in a half dozen Amish schoolhouses in Lancaster County and to about one hundred non-Amish children in nearby public schools. He found that the average Amish child in the fourth grade was questioning the sect's values and was "somewhat critical and resentful of the demands placed upon him by his family, and . . . not yet able to fully embrace the Amish way of life." However, by the time the Amish pupil reached the eighth grade,

> he has made a significant turnabout in how he views his family and culture . . . This would suggest that the Amish child, upon reaching puberty, is a more stable and less critical individual than he is at age nine or ten. Having weathered the storm of early childhood, he has now come to terms with the demands of the Amish adult world and has internalized the basic values of Amish culture. The opposite was found to be true of the non-Amish.

"That leg is not quite right," Susie Riehl remembers her Amish sixth-grade teacher saying, after the teacher viewed Susie's efforts to draw a horse. "No, not quite right. Try it again." After such gentle prodding and correction, Susie would attempt to improve her "freehand drawing" technique in the one-room schoolhouse in Berks County, Pennsylvania. "We used postage stamps for the models of the animals," she recalls, the moment still vivid thirty years later.

Today an accomplished artist whose works are regularly sold, a mother of six, and a member of the Old Order Amish, Susie credits her early encouragement in the Amish school as providing the foundation for a lifelong interest in art. "My teacher believed that everyone can draw, and she made us believe that, too."

Although the Amish religion does not value art as art, the church recognizes that each individual contributes to the community in ways based on her or his particular strengths, so Susie Riehl "decided that whatever talent I had came from God, and it was not to be ignored." After graduating the Amish school, she sought other resources from which to learn. She says the books on art available from the public library "were too advanced for me. They spoke of 'perspective' and 'medium,' and I didn't know what either of those things meant and the books didn't define them. So I asked the librarian to find me some beginner-type books."

From those, she began to understand the basic artistic terms of which she previously had been unaware. She chose watercolors as a medium "because they're less messy than oils, and less expensive." She and her husband, John Riehl, a carpenter, had more practical uses for every cent they earned than to spend it on oils and canvases. Watercolors and heavy paper would do. The couple adopted a boy and a girl, and after that Susie bore four children. The family took up residence on a farm in White Horse, and Susie painted when she could, using her kitchen table as her studio.

Watercolors are a demanding medium, less forgiving than oils because they cannot be painted over. Susie explains, "Once it's down, it's on there, and you have to go with it." So she spent a lot of time, in between household chores, thinking about what she wanted to depict; this permitted her, on the infrequent occasions when she was able to sit in her kitchen and work at her art, to know precisely what she wanted in terms of "backgrounds, foregrounds, placement of things within the whole, the way of the light," and in terms of subjects.

In a sense, Susie had decided to teach the non-Amish what it is like to look out at the world through Amish eyes. She depicts what she can see in her farm and yard, what she sees in neighbors' farms and yards and homes. Her watercolors feature carefully wrought, highly detailed quilts in profusion—hanging on clotheslines, resting on chests and beds, near sewing machines—their patterns conveying the many strands of an Amish life. Other frequent subjects are Amish dolls and wooden furniture, flowers and fields, buggies unhitched or in motion, an Amish school letting out. The images exude naturalness, warmth, bright colors, and repose. Tourists to Lancaster County buy many of the images, which exist as watercolors, small prints, and notecards, as well as on magnets.

Susie has always refused to draw recognizable individuals, for doing so would contravene the Second Commandment's prohibition on making graven images. She has not found that this limits her imagination. "Recently I told an artist friend of mine that she has got to stop copying what she did before, and what other people have done before—that all she has to do for inspiration is look around."

Margaret M, an eighteen-year-old teaching the lower grades in an Amish school in southern Lancaster County, loves her students. She says, "They're great, they're these phenomenal little children," especially the "beautiful, brilliant little girls," who are "going to grow up to be ladies." They all have such promise. "The whole world" is "opening up for them." They love bright colors and paint them gaily.

As a child, Margaret had also loved such colors and had wanted to wear bright dresses. She remembers having been bitterly disappointed when her mother told her she could not do so, and with some difficulty accepting that because she was an Amish girl and would be an Amish woman, her habiliment would be drab.

Toward the end of her year of teaching, in a flash of understanding one day, Margaret realizes that the bright colors her pupils love will soon be banished from their lives as they were from hers. "They're never going to have a chance. No opportunity for growth and freedom. They're never even going to have a voice." What they have to look forward to, she apprehends in a heartbreaking moment, is suppression of their urges for art, expression, and individuality. Shortly afterward, Margaret resigns her teaching job, and eventually she leaves the Amish faith.

Daisy Spangler, a teacher more sympathetic to the aims and methods of Amish education, nonetheless wrote to her school board after four years of teaching in an Amish school, "I couldn't help but feel that the development of your children's highly intelligent minds gets shut off at their fifteenth birthday anniversary."

Melvin Smucker's study found that "intelligence *per se* is not frowned upon by Amish parents . . . until their child has reached the age where he should be preparing himself to drop out of school in order to take part in adult responsibilities . . . The mere thought that their child might aspire to 'higher' education would be a threat to any Amish parents." That is because having too much knowledge is associated, in the Amish society, with heresy; there is a sense that excess book learning inevitably leads to questioning of the received truth, and from there to rebellion. The Amish reject the notion, so cardinal to Western thought, that fact-based knowledge is power.

Moreover, the Amish community maintains that its children who graduate Amish schools have an adequate education—that they are literate enough to do what they have to do within the community—perform their acts of faith and make their livings from farming or from small, relatively uncomplicated businesses. Andrea Fishman, a pedagogical expert, wasn't so sure that their literacy was adequate to such tasks when she began a year of observation in an Amish school, but her experience at the school, she later wrote, helped her to conclude that literacy truly is a cultural practice, not a decontextualized, universal set of skills and abilities automatically transferable across contexts. It is not the technology or isolated skills of reading and writing that count, but the understanding and application of those technologies and skills within the particular cultural frameworks that truly matter.

Such a focus on context, Fishman realized, explained the Amish schools' emphasis on moral education and their rejection of a curriculum aimed solely at acquisition of facts and cultural literacy.

The curriculum of her Amish and Mennonite school was, by Fishman's lights, quite narrow, featuring mainly texts that supported the moral lessons the Amish community wished the children to learn, foremost among them that the group is always more important than the individual. She explains, "New ideas, unique presentation, and fresh style conspire to make an individual noticeable, to separate him from other community language users. Not only is such visibility undesirable but it opposes the basic community value of group identification."

Fishman was taken aback by the responses of students asked by their Amish teacher to complete a sentence about love. "Love is by behaving well." "Love is obeying parents." "Love is obeying the rules." "Love is to obey." "Love is to behave." "I think love is obeying our parents." To Fishman, these responses echoed the primary lesson taught by the school: learning how to belong to the group rather than how to exist as an individual and pursue personal achievement. When Fishman herself was permitted to give the children an exercise, she asked them to write what someone else ought to know about their school, but she provided "neither model nor implicitly recognizable form" for the exercise. The scholars had difficulty responding in coherent ways.

Also inadequately taught, from Fishman's perspective, was "the most complex reading ability," which involves contrasting and comparing one text with another and treating these as an "organized whole" from which one could "draw conclusions." She decided that the Amish community must think such a complex

ability—to reason to conclusions through analysis—"is a dangerous skill," because individual parsing of texts, and individual
synthesis of the results of thought, is "potentially divisive and destructive." Instead of individual analysis, the Amish school taught
lessons designed to foster "group synthesis" of conclusions.

At the end of her year of observation, Fishman concluded that
the Amish schools deliver what the community wants taught, but
that what the Amish community wants to convey through schoolwork is totally at odds with what mainstream communities want
their schools to do. The goals of all public schooling were set out
succinctly in a Pennsylvania state commission report cited by
Fishman. Schooling was to accomplish three basic tasks: (1) to
help all children develop their individual potential; (2) to help
them achieve individual and psychological well-being; and (3) to
help them find their individual niches in society. These three
goals, Fishman notes, involve choice by the children for themselves and as such are completely at odds with the schooling ob-
jectives of Amish schools. From the Amish schools' perspective,
"Old Order children have no choices to make."

As a parent who watched and helped his children grow through
adolescence, and as a sometime teacher of teenagers and kids in
their early twenties, I am troubled by Amish schooling practices,
particularly by the sect's insistence that children cease formal
education after the eighth grade. My concern is that the years
between thirteen and eighteen are the most crucial mental
development years for a child—and Amish children spend most of
them out of school.

The psychiatrist Ralph Gemelli, summarizing the work of researchers on the mental maturation of children in a recent book,
Normal Childhood and Adolescent Development, writes that the years
between thirteen and eighteen are when people develop their
abilities to do abstract critical thinking, in which comparisons are
made and judgments based on these comparisons are reached.
This is the period, Gemelli writes, when the human mind begins

to register and master the differences between received beliefs and logical consistency, and between received beliefs and observed behaviors. Developing one's critical thinking is what makes it possible to take the mental leap from rudimentary to advanced studies and also forms the basis for understanding complex subjects such as science and literature. Earlier-stage developmental achievements, such as being able to recognize words and know their first-level meanings, are not adequate to the task of reading or evaluating a novel aimed at adults, or a history, or a philosophical or religious tract; nor is mastery of grade-school chemistry and arithmetic adequate preparation for proper comprehension of organic chemistry. To truly understand complex subjects, advanced thought processes must be developed.

These years have also been studied intensively by generations of researchers interested in emotional development, including, notably, the late Erik Erikson of Harvard. The emotional maturation that takes place between ages thirteen and eighteen, he writes, leads to the ability to fashion and to maintain adult relationships with members of the opposite sex, parents, authority figures, and friends. During this period, and especially in the late teens, a person must learn to assert what Erikson labels his or her "personhood," the sense of being an individual, distinct from the various groups to which the teen belongs. A person who does not develop this sense of individual identity, Erikson asserts, may never reach full emotional maturity.

According to Erikson, the danger is that, without achieving "personhood," one may find it impossible to plan properly for the future because of "a decided disbelief in the possibility that time may bring change, and yet also a violent fear that it might." In other words, without full emotional maturity, an adolescent is overly vulnerable to whatever strong influences are acting upon him or her—whether emanating from unprincipled peers or from well-meaning but overly authoritarian parents or church officials. During late adolescence, teenagers adopt thought patterns that will stay with them for the rest of their lives, patterns they construct out of the answers they receive to questions that they put to themselves and to everyone around them: Who am I? What do I believe? What do I have to offer the world?

Because they are no longer in formal school after the age of fourteen, or in some instances fifteen, Amish teens have to rely on their culture for responses to these questions, and those responses are rigid and oriented toward group rather than individual goals. Moreover, because the teenagers have left school so early, they have not had the benefit of analytical training to develop critical thinking of the sort that might assist them in groping their way to their own unique responses to these questions, or that could help them to evaluate the community's responses and put those responses into wider perspective.

The Amish dismiss the need for the development of analytical and critical thinking. They believe that the correct answers to their youth's questions about who they are, what they believe, and what they have to offer the world are provided by their culture. As for Amish schoolchildren having no choices to make, the Amish are adamant that the only real choice in life is between living man's way, which they believe is the way of the outside world—a path polluted by having too much education—and living God's way, which they are convinced is also their way, because their lives are devoted to the imitation of Christ.

Faith and Doctrine: "Stand Fast and Believe the Word as Written"

It is a hot summer night in northern Indiana, and eleven-year-old Faron Y has permission to sleep outside in a tent, with his brother, near the lawn and porch furniture that their father makes in his woodworking shop. Their father, an Amish minister, and the rest of the family remain indoors.

Faron is a slender reed with corn-silk-colored hair. He sees himself as "intelligent but not smart," because he is "always ahead of the other kids in Amish school," and can "figure things out" before they have a clue, but he doesn't get good marks in subjects that don't interest him. He also has the gift of gab and thinks this is why his schoolmates, and his family members, have labeled him as likely to become a preacher. Faron admires his father and his "awesome sense of right and wrong," and he is a religious believer, one of the faithful—but the prospect of becoming a preacher "worries" him, because he does not feel "adequate to be someone to help other people."

The night sky is filled with stars, and he looks up at them and says, "O God, give me a sign if I'm going to be a preacher." No more than a second later, three falling stars pass over him, one after another.

He is petrified by this sign from God.

. . .

In the Amish religion, a minister or a bishop is chosen by lot at a regular Sunday meeting soon after the death of the previous holder of the leadership position. Adult members of the congregation write down on slips of paper the names of men they consider worthy of being their new minister; the men whose names are listed more than once then become candidates for the second stage. There are usually only a few names put forward at this point. These candidates hand in their copies of the *Ausbund*, the hymnal, which are shuffled, and in the process a slip is inserted into one of the copies. Each candidate picks a copy of the *Ausbund*, and the one who has the copy into which the slip has been inserted becomes the new minister.

Norman Y, a forty-three-year-old minister in Shipshewana, recalls that at the moment the lot fell on him a dozen years ago, he was "absolutely stunned." He thought, "No way I can do this." He had never aspired to being a minister and did not want or feel that he could handle the large responsibilities. He had enough to do with a wife, three children, and a business he was trying to enlarge. His work as a maker and restorer of buggies and coaches was renowned—on display, for instance, in the Henry Ford Museum in Greenfield Village, Michigan. But Norm understood that the matter of his ministry was out of his hands: the Lord had chosen him, through the casting of lots, and he must yield to His will. Besides, it was unheard of to refuse elevation. The position of minister was his, for life, and he would have to grow into it. His grandfather the bishop offered assistance, as did ministers from adjacent districts, all of whom knew how overwhelmed and unworthy he felt just then.

"Later I realized I'd been preparing for this for a long time," Norm asserts. He had joined the church at age twenty-one, out of deep conviction that it was "the right path, and the right path for me. Nobody should be Amish unless they believe that." He had become convinced that the doctrine of the Amish church is necessary to "protect us from evil," and serves as a "unifier," instilling the feeling of brotherhood among fellow believers, for instance by showing them that they are all "equal, no matter how rich or poor," and by its insistence on them "wearing the same suit and driving the same buggy."

During the year before his selection, Norm had been rereading his Bible in order to be better able to respond to the questions being put to him by his growing children. Upon being ordained as a minister, he says, he "began studying the Book of Genesis more deeply," because Genesis is the text usually drawn upon for services at weddings, funerals, and communions, where he would first be expected to perform his ceremonial functions. "I had to preach about the Creation, and I wanted to know all I could about it."

The more he studied, the stronger became his conviction that Genesis tells the literal truth about the birth of the world and of mankind. Norm felt impelled to examine the opposite notion, that the earth was created over billions of years, and that mankind had come into being "as the evolutionists think," evolving from lower animals and apes. He went to Chicago to visit the Field Museum of Natural History and was outraged to find on its walls no mention of the Creation as told in the Bible, but he took sustenance from discovering that its exhibits presented, in his view, no solid evidence to support the evolutionist "myth" of creation. "They keep changing the dates, a billion years here, a billion there. Darwin wrote that they'd find intermediary fossils—but they haven't found any. And the zillion years it supposedly takes to make underground deposits of coal? There's a new process where you can do it in minutes or hours, putting pressure on oil. To my mind, scientists have proved absolutely nothing about evolution."

Norm feels it is essential for all true Christians to accept as factual the account of the Creation in Genesis. "How can you believe in the literality of the virgin birth of Christ if you don't believe in the literality of the Creation? It is all of a piece. And we Amish know by experience that things do not happen by random or by chance in this world. There *is* a design. We have to stand fast and believe the Word as written."

Today, Norm reflects that being a minister has brought out the best in him and has helped him contribute to the community's welfare. "Wouldn't have it any other way, now."

As Norm watched his children grow, and his oldest approach *rumspringa*, he feared for them in contact with the outside world and was moved also to keep an eye on the teenagers of his extended family, the church district. A prime motivator was his vision of how the climate in most Amish teenagers' homes has changed from when he was in his teens: "No more parents having chores for the kids to do on the farm," because the majority of parents now work away from the home, which results in children with "too much idle time." A father working away means that his children "don't have the benefit anymore of Dad helping them to put into context the little experiences they have every day," a context that—as Norm learned in his own teenage years, when he worked alongside his father—assists vulnerable youth to behave in an upright way.

The absence of continual fatherly advice and kids with too much time on their hands, Norm came to believe, lead to kids getting involved in the wrong activities—the wild parties, drugs, alcohol, premarital sex, and too much mingling with the non-Amish. Parents and church officials "need to have better contact with the youth" and to "create a moral climate" in which teenagers can understand the moral implications of bad behaviors. "From the time when we make all their decisions to the time when they make their own, we must not let go completely."

Norm had identified the need. But he had not yet figured out how to meet it.

Ruth G, a middle-aged mother with a teenage daughter, recalls a recent moment in her Fredericksburg, Ohio, church district, just after a new bishop was selected by lot. Ruth and her neighbors were elated at the choice of a forty-seven-year-old man, previously a minister, who stood before the brothers and sisters and their children with tears in his eyes.

"We would have followed anybody who was God's choice, of course," Ruth says, but this was a man whom the members already knew as a wonderful minister. "You can see that he and his wife live for God," she asserts; during this man's time as a minister, he had served at every social and religious function, visited the sick—including her, when she had been ill—in the hospital, and he "had love in his eyes for the members." The former bishop, in her opinion, "saw things in black and white," while the new one "sees the grays." For instance, when the members had spoken critically of the district's schoolteachers for requiring too much rigidity in the schooling of Amish children, he opined that "we want a likeness among children; they don't all have to be the same." The congregants had followed the previous bishop because that was their duty; they are following the new one because he is leading them.

Kathryn L, mother of Jerry and Susanne, going through tough times during their *rumspringa*, sees in her own and in their lives signs that reinforce her faithful conviction that nothing happens without a design, and that the design is benevolent and is God's. Frequently the design is not revealed until the events are past, but it is there, evidence that, as she puts it, "God is in control of our lives." As is that of most Amish, Kathryn's faith is of the sort defined in the Letter to the Hebrews 11:1: "Faith is confident assurance concerning what we hope for and conviction about things we do not see."

Eli K, small-engine repairman, father of toddlers, survivor of a car crash, speaks of the similar lesson of "God working in the mystery ways, y'know," and of "seeing every day the beauty of what the Lord made." The older he gets, the more true that seems to him.

Emma M, the would-be model, living outside the church many hundreds of miles from her family's home, is delighted with her independence and her lifestyle, but nevertheless worries whether

God is "happy" with her, "because I am not doing everything for Him like I think I should." She believes that being a Christian means "the individual must be willing to give up whatever God asks for; so maybe the reason I am not feeling bad about my life outside the church is because God hasn't asked me to give it up. But maybe He will—I think He asks different stuff from different people."

Faron Y, the boy frightened by the falling stars when he was eleven, began to run away from home at fourteen and by his sixteenth birthday had spent six months in a state reform school. He later recalled having been very constrained in his behavior when growing up. His minister father would instruct him not to act in certain ways in order to prevent other Amish youth saying to their parents, " 'John's boy does it, and John is a preacher, so why can't we?' Which pissed me off, because Dad was busy thinking about how to preserve his reputation . . . I mean, he had a right to it, I had no right ruining that reputation. I hurt his 'perfect father' image."

By age nineteen, Faron had left his family behind and was a sometime RV factory worker, a drug addict, and a seller of drugs. Though lacking a high school diploma, he had taken some college courses and done well in them when he was interested in the subjects, flunked them when he was not. Still rail thin and highly verbal, he developed charisma and an obscene rant that attracted many Amish in *rumspringa* to come to his side—and to buy his drugs.

Faron still counts his preacher father as one of his heroes; the other, he says, is Tupac Shakur, the angry black rap artist who projected the image of a rebel and made no apologies for his convictions for rape and the shooting of two off-duty police officers. Shakur was murdered, in his twenties, by rivals in the hip-hop music business.

Faron recalls a story that his father repeatedly told, illustrative of what Faron admires in him. The father as a young boy stole five dollars from the wallet of his father and decades later "still felt bad about it." Faron cites this tale as evidence that he will never become a preacher, disqualified from contention because, among other reasons, "I stole a thousand dollars' worth of CDs from Wal-Mart, and have no regrets about it."

The largest divide in this country is between those who have faith and those who do not. The Amish brand of Christianity is highly expressive of faith, and demanding of it, too. What is required of an adherent, in the name of faith, encompasses all aspects of everyday existence and is to be manifest in every action, from praying frequently through wearing austere clothing reminiscent of the habits worn by nuns and monks to having the correct attitude toward fellow Amish and neighbors—in sum, to devoting one's life to *nachfolge*, a word that means literally "to follow some creed or person," and that to the Amish means imitating Christ's example of service to one's fellow man. The essence of *nachfolge*, in turn, is *gelassenheit*, a resignation to God's will that entails self-denial, yielding to others, willing submission to authority, and contentedness with one's lot. It is *gelassenheit* that engenders the Amish gentle handshake, the soft voice, and the slow stride. *Gelassenheit* underlies the Amish embrace of "JOY" as the proper way to live: Jesus first, Yourself last, and Others in between.

The Amish differ from most other American Christians in the degree to which they practice what they preach. Following instructions in the Bible, they give their lives to following Christ in every detail; they deny themselves many "worldly" pleasures and live a deliberately simple life; they revere God in regular services and ceremonies; they read only the Bible, not commentaries on it; they birth large families and raise at home even those offspring who are severely disabled; they tithe to the church; they care for their community's indigent and elderly; they use animal- or human-powered vehicles for transport and work; and they build barns for and otherwise assist neighbors who have suffered disasters, even when those neighbors are not Amish.

Other biblical precepts that they follow include tough measures to maintain the purity of cobelievers by voting sanctions to punish infractions; for instance, excommunicating a member who obtains a divorce in controversion of the "till death do us part" portion of the marriage ceremony and of the specific prohibition of divorce in Matthew 19:9.

In many ways, Amish religious practices resemble those of the Puritans, the early settlers of the northeastern American colonies and the dominant religious force in North America for two hundred years. Puritans and Amish share an emphasis on biblically based community laws, a relatively austere way of life and sameness of dress, and a fondness for sermons about the fire and brimstone awaiting those who do not strictly adhere to the narrow religious path.

Polls show that mainstream American churchgoers now mostly hear sermons that include no references to eternal damnation or to the terrible things that may befall nonbelievers; instead, they hear homilies about the nuances of ethical behavior and the rewards to be expected in Heaven. But Amish sermons still regularly warn of damnation for those who stray from the path, and in many other ways the Amish continue to practice a Puritan kind of religion long after the Puritans have vanished.

The Amish religion exceeds old-time Puritanism in its insistence on the fellowship of baptized believers, which the Amish call the *gemee*; the Amish credo holds that an individual is more likely to get to Heaven in the company of fellow believers. There is a darker side to this credo, one that the Amish share with old-time Puritanism: the tendency for the group's adherents to spy on one other, to meddle in one another's affairs, and to castigate friends, neighbors, and family members for lapses.

Another aspect of Puritanism, an emphasis on individual capitalism rather than communalism, is embraced by the Amish today, yet the Amish are considerably more communal than the Puritans ever were, perhaps because there are more matters today for which the community needs to be responsible—self-insurance, care for the aged, loans to enable young Amish to buy homes and start businesses that will help keep them in the faith. While being basically capitalist, Amish communities sometimes try to limit the growth of members' enterprises to prevent undue disparities between the wealthiest and the poorest members, a chasm that might result in the wealthy leaving the group. Amish businesses are ideally to remain small, and to employ only Amish.

If the Amish religion is reminiscent of the past, Amish cultural practices are very much of the present—so much so that the Amish have become the canary in the mine shaft of American cultural conservatism. They reject abortion, birth control, divorce, homosexuality, and government social welfare programs, and they have long since embraced "moral values" as the core curriculum in their schools and the teaching of "creationism" rather than scientific evolution. They have also long been in the forefront of those asserting that the proper place for a woman is in the home, caring for the children, and that women must yield to men in all important matters. In all of these attitudes, they do more than pay lip service—they practice what they preach.

The Amish religion is not focused mainly on preparing for the afterlife; rather, it focuses on living properly in the here and now. One young interviewee studying for her baptism was warned by the bishop conducting the classes that her entrance to Heaven would not be guaranteed by baptism or by living in the Amish style—such a judgment could be made only by the Lord, after her death—and the bishop enjoined her to live correctly in order to have what the apostle Peter refers to as the "lively hope" of gaining Heaven. In the view of David Wagler, senior columnist for the Amish paper *The Budget*, the combination of having that lively hope and not having the assurance of entry into Heaven is essential to the Amish way of life: were the Amish to believe they were entirely "saved" by baptism, Wagler argues, there would be no need for them to struggle so hard to be "non-conforming" to the world.

Nonconforming, in Amish parlance, means not aping in one's behaviors or appearance the practices of the outside world but instead embodying a highly rigorous Christian life. It is the nonconforming aspects of Amish religious practice that attract the curiosity of a nation composed mainly of Christians whose own religious practices, in comparison, seem less rigorous or complete. The devout Amish feel comforted, even uplifted, by the rigorousness and demands of the nonconforming path—it seems evidence of how difficult it is to walk faithfully in God's appointed ways. The Amish speak of *absonderung*, a sacrificing of some of the pleasures of this world, the better to maintain separateness from the world's sinful, irreligious, and immoral practices.

One added reason for nonconforming and for the practice of *absonderung* is that abstinence from pleasures helps to instill in the Amish a proper sense of suffering—a suffering that echoes Christ's and the agonies of all martyrs to the truth faith, the people whom the present-day Amish claim as forebears.

These progenitors' stories are told in two books that are kept in nearly every Amish home and school, and that seep into the consciousness of Amish children before they venture into the wider world: a history, *Martyrs' Mirror*, and the hymnal, the *Ausbund*.

Martyrs' Mirror, a book of more than twelve hundred pages, was originally compiled between 1562 and 1685, though the version most used today is the one put together by Thieleman J. Van Braght of Holland in 1660. It consists of accounts of martyrdoms—actual deaths and what are known as "witnessings," which is an earlier translation of the Greek root word for *martyr*—of various Christian faithful from the time of Jesus onward. Some stories are told in straightforward narratives; others are transcriptions of letters and documents written by the martyrs, one inscribed with a stick on red earth, another scratched by a pin onto a spoon. The book evolved during the era when Anabaptists were being imprisoned, tortured, and executed for their faith, and its original intent was to instruct Anabaptists on what actions to take and what to say in response to interrogators' questions when their expected turns on the rack arrived.

The first German translation from the Dutch edition, printed in the American colonies in 1748 by Mennonites, Brethren, and the Seventh-Day Baptists, served a similar purpose: to prepare young Anabaptists to follow their faith in the event of war and persecution—the French and Indian War (1754–1763) was rapidly approaching.

A recent publisher of a commentary on *Martyrs' Mirror* laments that it has become a "neglected book that far too often merely collects dust in Grandfather's rolltop desk." That may be true for some Mennonites, but in Old Order Amish homes and schools, *Martyrs' Mirror* is read, and its iconology is a constant reference in Sunday preachings. Its proper use is made plain by the Amish Brotherhood of Holmes County, in an introduction to their highly abridged edition, *Light from the Stakes*:

> Our prayer and sincere desire is that these accounts will serve to refresh many a well-meaning heart, and to strengthen and confirm the true faith, when seeing that in those early and turbulent times many fellow brethren had such love for Christ and His heavenly doctrine, that they did not hesitate to die for it.

There is little overlap between the list of martyrs in *Martyrs' Mirror* and the Catholic church's list of those who, like St. Sebastian, were murdered because of their beliefs. Where a story appears in both, such as that of the ninth-century Spanish sisters Nunilo and Alodia, the emphasis in *Martyrs' Mirror* is primarily on the lesson taught by their lives. Also, *Martyrs' Mirror* devotes only forty pages to the lives of Jesus, his apostles, the early disciples, and one disciple of the apostle John, torn apart in the Colosseum in A.D. 111.

The bulk of *Martyrs' Mirror* deals with the early years of Anabaptism. There are many testaments of people on the eve of execution, in the form of letters sent to relatives, some smuggled out of prisons. They speak of those who go "smilingly to the fire" or to their drowning, beheading, or hanging. These include Michael Sattler, a prime author of the Schleitheim Confession, whom his executioners labeled an "infamous, desperate villain and monk." Sattler's testament, consisting of his answers to accusers as he was about to be hanged, is very detailed, and these are printed together with citations from Scripture that underlie each of his positions. These answers so infuriated his judges, the section suggests, that they decided, instead of hanging him, or possibly in addition to hanging him, to cut out his tongue, tear his body apart with red-hot tongs, and burn him to ashes as a heretic.

The stories' lessons resonate with today's Amish. The theme of being able to bear pain and rise beyond suffering, for instance, emerges from the letters of Raphael Van Den Gelde, who describes being tortured by ropes pulling various sections of his body from his torso. When his pain became "so severe that I thought it was impossible to bear . . . the Lord in a large degree took away my pain every time." He writes that his suffering was ordained by God as a "chastening" that he must "endure . . . with a willing heart," and he reminds his family that those who would not endure suffering are not the Lord's true children but "bastards."

The importance of marital fidelity and affection, and their integration with the Anabaptist belief system, is a theme underscored by a collection of eleven letters written in prison by a husband and wife. Jerome and Lijsken Segers had been married less than a year, and she was pregnant with a child whom the authorities would permit her to deliver before executing her. In one letter Jerome replies to Lijsken's plaint that she blames herself for not having been patient enough with him by contending that Christ "will not remember our sins" because the couple has lived and worshiped properly. In another letter, Jerome tells her of his pride in not revealing the names of Anabaptist midwives. Lijsken writes admonitions "to both of us" to be steadfast in the faith; the lesson to be drawn, a study guide states, is that "as a Christian woman and wife, [Lijsken] takes her proper role and is modest as she gives spiritual advice."

The most egregious omissions of the *Martyrs' Mirror*, scholars point out, are entries from after the year 1700. Since Van Braght's book was a compilation, newer material could have been seamlessly added, but from the eighteenth century onward, no one died at the stake for Anabaptist beliefs. The deletion from the

book of certain facts about individuals that are not directly concerned with their martyrdom and the lack of material about other
martyrdoms—for example, those that stemmed from slavery—
writes the German linguistic expert Werner Enninger, "suggest
that the book can be taken as an attempt at constructing the past
in such a way that it can serve as a framework of interpretation in
which current occurrences can be perceived as irrelevant."

Using the past as a framework for interpretation of the present
is a hallmark of Amish style. The past is used, writes Diane Zimmerman Umble, "to confirm and strengthen social narratives [like
that of persecution] and cultural identity . . . The stories told as
parts of rituals enable a community to appropriate its collective
memory for the interpretation of contemporary challenges."

Martyrs' Mirror is studied in Amish schools. The *Ausbund*, the
hymnal of the Amish and of other Anabaptist sects, is used at
every Amish church service. The *Ausbund* echoes the subject matter and lessons of *Martyrs' Mirror*. In 1535 some fifty-two Anabaptist men, women, and children, imprisoned in a dungeon under a
castle in Passau, a southern German city, kept up their spirits by
singing hymns. Some had been composed by Michael Sattler during his own jailing; others they composed themselves, basing their
texts on biblical passages and their melodies on religious and folk
tunes. Fifty-three hymns survived and became the central collection in the *Ausbund*.

The power and influence of the *Ausbund* comes in part from
the legend that the imprisoned Anabaptists were released because the jailers were swayed by the singing of these songs. Some
emotionally powerful songs in the collection repeat stories in
Martyrs' Mirror. The next-to-last song tells of a man who, having
acted as executioner of some Anabaptists, is converted by his vic-
tims' fervor and becomes himself a martyr to the cause.

The infolding, self-referential nature of the material in *Martyrs'
Mirror* and in the sections of the *Ausbund* where one person's martyrdom and faith enables that of another who is a reader of or lis-
tener to the first's tale is a religious affirmation strategy central to
the Amish way. It is a strategy that ensures today's Amish will con-

sider themselves martyrs, if not as subject to extreme treatment as were their ancestors who died for the cause, then as people who believe they are being mistreated by the world and are suffering for their beliefs. Today's torment may take the form of disrespect or ridicule for their way of life—which to them means for their faith. "God tells us that being different and peculiar will bring about some persecution but that is what Christians should expect," an Amish elder wrote to a university professor. "Persecution will always be part of our lives on earth." This Amish belief in the continuity of martyrdom fuels current litanies of persecution, disproportionately overemphasizing the degree to which the Amish are targeted for hate crimes, harassed by the government, or exploited by those selling "Amish" products and experiences.

Rob Schlegel, an Ohio social worker who has worked for decades among the Amish, contends that the Amish history of martyrdom, and the modern Amish eagerness to keep that history alive in the form of cautionary tales, "plays a large role in many Amish individuals' state of mind. They have a sense of martyrdom." That sense is less acute with those Amish who do not suffer from psychological illnesses, but it is still there in the majority.

To my mind, a sense of martyrdom is what helps the Amish muster the courage to endure the outside world, but it also contributes to their inability to be at ease with that world—if you see the mainstream as waiting at every turn to ridicule you or to make you suffer for your beliefs, you are unlikely to develop deep or meaningful relationships with mainstream people.

Martyrdom stories also encourage the Amish to view other Christians' lives as less worthy if they do not include suffering, self-mortification, and the denial of worldly pleasures. While by mainstream standards, today's Amish lives are austere, by the standard of history, and of their own predecessors, today's Amish lives are relatively comfortable and free from persecution. Even so, the Amish continue to frame the world in terms of the battle of good and evil, an attitude that contributes to their feelings of being isolated and of having to fight the Devil's hand in activities that to most mainstreamers seem fairly devoid of moral depravity.

. . .

Lydia T, owner of the brand-new buggy with bells and whistles, which her father bought to entice her to stay within the Amish fold, is unhappy as she approaches her twenty-first birthday. She says, "Nothing seems to be working out all right." She senses that she is continuing to miss the very years when she should be growing, experimenting with different lifestyles, possible futures. The dishonesty of concealing her wish to be free behind her modest Amish dress and demeanor, and of having to sneak out on the weekends for enjoyment, bothers her.

She prays for guidance, thinking, "Well, if God wants me to leave the church, He'll make it possible." She even discusses these prayers with her parents. "Why would He want you to leave?" they protest. "After all, you were brought up Amish," implying that being Amish is the only sure path to God. She retorts that there are plenty of ex-Amish in the world, most of them quite religious and observant; in her view, God is certainly not absent from those people's lives.

Lydia has looked forward to turning twenty-one, but her birthday is a dud. She comes home from work at the venetian blind factory, exhausted and in need of a shower, to find a hundred Amish youth in her yard, playing volleyball and singing songs— a nice enough celebration but one that was, she says, "totally embarrassing. It was like, 'Yeah, I turned twenty-one, and, hey, man, I'm legal now! I want to go party! I want to do it legally now instead of behind everybody's back.' " As a church member, she cannot do that.

Lydia's buggy, too, is more a burden than a prize. She hardly uses it and is determined to pay her father back every cent of the four thousand dollars he laid out for it. After she has turned twenty-one, Lydia is entitled to keep the entire proceeds of her salary, and that repayment is soon accomplished. Shortly, an "opportunity" arises, in the form of a furnished apartment that she can afford if a friend shares it—and the friend wants to. All she will need to do, Lydia reports, is "move my clothes and hook up my own phone line." The existence of this possibility makes Lydia feel that God is watching over her and is making it easy for her to leave the community.

Two weddings loom, in Wisconsin, in which she is to be part of the wedding party, which her parents will also attend. It would be rude not to take part, or to do so as an ex-Amish. But after she has fulfilled her duties on these occasions, Lydia informs her parents that she is moving out.

"Oh, you got your own place," her father says.

"No, Dad," she tells him. "I'm moving out and I'm leaving my Amish clothes."

That night her father paces the halls until dawn, and next morning, when Lydia wakes up, she sees him with a Bible in his hand and three or four verses written down on a piece of paper that he hands to her. "Here, read this," he says.

She sticks the verses in her pocket and goes off to work. When she returns home that evening, her parents hustle her to an Amish counselor. The local minister comes to dissuade her, then the bishop. Neighbors, friends, and relatives write her letters, begging her not to go, some of them suggesting that if they mistreated her in the past they are sorry and are true friends and will try to be better friends in the future. Some correspondents inform her that if she makes the wrong decision, she will not go to Heaven.

Lydia's response: if her damnation were presumed to be foreordained because she is leaving the church, then "God wouldn't have made it so easy" to leave.

At the last minute, her father offers to buy her a plot of land and build a house on it for her if she will stay within the church. Another bribe! Lydia refuses it and takes up residence in an apartment in White Pigeon, Michigan, with her close friend, the mother of two small children. The kids live with the young women when they are not with their father. During Lydia's first month out, she knows she has to "watch myself, to not let them [the Amish elders and her family] get to me and make me feel guilty," because if she feels guilty, she'll be tempted to go back, and she doesn't want to do that.

To reinforce her resolve to stay out, Lydia makes a few key decisions: to sell the buggy now that she has finished paying her father what it cost, to wear contact lenses instead of bookish glasses, and to cut her hair. First she has her hair cut to shoulder length; the next time she returns to the beauty parlor, she has it cut even shorter. She knows that having short hair will act as a brake on any later decision to go back to the church, for she would have to wait until it grew in again before being permitted to return.

Lydia has imagined it will be hard to sell the buggy, but that, too, is unexpectedly easy: an Amish co-worker's brother buys it for four thousand dollars. Lydia uses part of the check for a down payment on a red Trans Am. She says, "I love driving—I could drive for days." The cousin with whom she shared the fantasy of owning a red sports car or convertible calls on the phone and asks if she is now living her dream. "Which one?" she responds with a giddy laugh. Although Lydia is the first in her set of cousins to leave the church, she is followed by several others, male and female.

She revels in being able to indulge in behaviors like going to the movies that she had been prevented from enjoying when she was a member of the church. It is wonderful, she declares, "not having somebody breathing down my neck and saying, 'Hey, man, that's not right, don't do it.' It's a free world, and I can do what I want . . . and I can talk about it with whoever I want to." Being able to share her most intimate thoughts, including religious doubts, is another element of freedom, one that Lydia appreciates all the more because for so long she felt unable to convey her feelings even to her Amish girlfriends, for fear that someone would tattle on her to the ministers.

Lydia knows that her rejection of the Amish church is difficult for her parents; she has seen what happened to other families when their children left the faith—the parents' shame, the intimations from neighbors that the parents have not brought the children up properly. Her own parents took part in such denigration of other parents whose children had defected—and now it is their turn to be on the receiving end; Lydia aches to think of that happening to them.

And she aches when she finds, jammed into her new mailbox, letters from old friends, former neighbors, and relatives. Some missives plead with her to come back, but as many are hectoring, accusing her of reneging on the sacred promise she made when baptized and prophesying that because she has done so she will never go to Heaven. Lydia tries to put the letters aside without reading them, but the notion of being excluded from Heaven "bugs" her. Will that really happen?

At various Baptist and Mennonite churches, Lydia is assured that if she believes in God and feels that God is within her, she has nothing to worry about; the path to God is through one's self, not through any particular church—Amish, Mennonite, Baptist, Episcopal, Methodist, whatever. She begins to attend Wednesday-evening Bible study classes as well as services on Sundays at Mennonite churches in northern Indiana and in Michigan.

DeWayne C, who fell in love with his Harley and joined a motorcycle club, starts going out with a non-Amish girl, a member of a Baptist church in White Pigeon, Michigan, just across the state line, where he has an apartment. He likes the girlfriend's church and, having always wanted to be baptized, decides to do so and to join this church. When he informs his parents that he is thinking about being baptized outside the Amish faith—that is, converting—they are aghast, because this will make him ineligible to join the Amish church later, as his brothers did after their *rumspringa* years. They ask if DeWayne would like to speak to Amish church elders about this step; not wanting to offend, he says he would.

Nonetheless, he is surprised when one evening, after his regular postwork session at a gym, DeWayne finds two older Amish men waiting in front of his apartment, brought there by a van and driver. The visitors are his grandfather, an Amish minister, and the bishop of the family's Amish district. They want to know why he desires to be baptized in a church outside the faith, and DeWayne invites them in to talk "about everything." He answers some questions and asks some of his own, regarding why they think that leaving the Amish faith is wrong for him.

The threesome talk for hours, during which the older men are, to DeWayne's relief, quite courteous and respectful of his independence and feelings. DeWayne knows that other youngsters in similar circumstances have had visitors who have been far more intimidating. His guests ask about the "rules" in his new church, trying to make him admit that the Amish church's rules are better suited to the regulation of a properly religious life, but DeWayne counters that the Baptist church's rules are the Ten Commandments and not the "man-made" rules of the Amish church. He asks them if they think he will go to Hell because he is not following Amish rules.

"No, no, no, no," they say, but he "challenges" them, saying he has often heard such warnings from members of the community. How can his entry or nonentry into Heaven or Hell, he asks, be determined by whether or not he rides a motorcycle? "It's just a form of transportation, like a horse and buggy," he insists. "It's not like breaking a commandment or nothing."

He also tells them he is bothered by the contradiction of the Amish church permitting him in *rumspringa* to have a motorcycle though it was forbidden before he became sixteen and will again be forbidden if he joins the church. How can they both condemn and condone a behavior? To DeWayne, the Baptist stance on sin is less ambiguous and more understandable: a sin is a sin, no matter what the circumstances. For a Baptist, there are no indulgences, no time-out periods during which something usually forbidden is permitted.

The officials try to explain the church's position, and it takes a while. By midnight, nothing has been resolved, and the men go home. A few nights later, a second delegation arrives: an uncle from Michigan and another from Nappanee, both of them bishops.

DeWayne's uncles confess that, at eighteen and twenty, "they thought about leaving the Amish church, too," but then they

found Amish women, married, and "settled down." DeWayne recounts his uncles' main argument: " 'Excuse me, but you might
know what you want, might be happy with your decision, but
look down the future . . . at, you know—you might have kids. Are
they going to fall away from the religion? . . . How are they going
to be when they get older, because they won't have that background?' " His response: "I'm, like, 'Well, I've got the background;
I think I can pretty much—I mean, I know what's right and
wrong, my kids are going to know what's right and wrong.' "

This meeting, too, ends in a standoff.

In deference to his parents, grandfather, and uncles, DeWayne
postpones his decision to become baptized in the White Pigeon
church. About six weeks later, he and the girlfriend stop seeing
each other, but DeWayne does not lose his interest in being baptized into her church and begins preparations to do so. He invites
his family to his baptism, but his parents do not come, nor do any
other relatives except an aunt and uncle who have long since left
the church and his youngest brother. DeWayne is upset by the in-
transigence of his family, by their refusal to understand his wish to
be independent and different yet still a Christian. He cannot comprehend why they will not see that the apple is not falling far
from the tree.

A year later, when his brother turns sixteen and enters *rumspringa*, DeWayne takes out a loan to buy him a brand-new
Camaro.

Matt E and Lorina L, eighteen and seventeen respectively, are
deep in *rumspringa*, and in love. He is an RV factory worker, she, a
cashier at a hardware store. Currently they are enjoying life outside the Amish community, going places in his car, attending parties on the weekends, but they are becoming "bored" with parties
and drinking, and are trying to figure out what to do with the rest
of their lives.

"I'm in a tough spot right now," Lorina explains, "because I
think I should join church and become baptized, but yet I don't

want to join the Amish church because I don't know what I want
to be. I want to be English, but I don't want to be English. So it's,
like, you know, it seems like God's talking to me one part, but Satan's talking to me, too. It's like 'Do this.' 'Don't do this.' I think
about religious stuff a lot."

Matt suggests that they are going to parties and such now, "because if you join church later, this is the only chance you'll have,
so . . . right now we just go out and enjoy life and do what we
want to do, and then . . ."

"Hopefully someday we can be forgiven for everything we did,"
Lorina completes his thought.

"Yeah—go from there." Matt nods. "I mean, in the future we
might regret everything we did; but right now, it's—you know—
we're in our stage of life where we want to go out and have fun
just like everybody else, and I guess we just go out and do that.
But yeah, I'm sure someday we'll kind of regret it and feel guilty."

Stephen L. Yoder, a Beachy Amish bishop, believes that "mushy,
gushy puppy love, so common in Western courtship, is of Satan
[and] designed to drag one into sin." Yoder was raised as an Old
Order Amish but left the sect and has since risen to the position
of bishop in the Beachy Amish. The Beachy share many core religious beliefs and cultural practices with the Old Order Amish but
differ in permitting the use of automobiles, telephones, and electricity; encouraging individual Bible study; and holding services
in English in regular church buildings under the guidance of professional ministers who do not have life tenure.

Tough and conservative, Yoder believes that no Christian
should drink, swear, or use tobacco; his main concern, though, is
for the purity of Christian worship and the promulgation of an
environment that enables congregants to live in ways reflecting
that purity; the particulars are expressed in his book *My Beloved
Brethren*—a collection of sermons that, he warns in an introduction, should be read by insiders and not by outsiders.

Yoder considers the Old Order Amish to be good Christians

but overly narrow in their worldview and inconsistent in their rules—especially in the practice of *rumspringa*, which the Beachy church does not allow. The Old Order's problems, he writes, originate with the ministers. While most Old Order ministers whom he knows are quite "spiritual," he has also known some who are "carnal" and "corrupt." "Too many," he writes, "are too dedicated to the Amish church customs and traditions to stand out and make a change . . . and they think tradition means more than Scripture."

This fault, in turn, Yoder traces to the Old Order's combination of lifetime appointment of religious leaders and the tradition of these leaders making their decisions in private and only then asking congregants to ratify them. In his view, these practices ensure that the leaders' power over the congregation will never lessen and that the *ordnung* will not evolve, even when its strictures become counterproductive. A minister's authority "places him so far above the laity that the laity is cheated out of their privilege of due consideration on many issues," Yoder writes. While that is "a plus in keeping order," it is "totally Roman Catholic in nature"—an epithet designed to sting a sect that has often charged that Catholics owe their allegiance as much to a man, the Pope, as to God. The result of this neo-Catholicism: "Without any public expression and discussion there is little tendency [in the Old Order Amish church] toward spiritual development among the laity."

The Old Order Amish are "in no way free and joyful Christians," Yoder laments. He praises the ministers' "deep concern about the spiritual welfare of their people" but takes issue with them for not being "evangelically minded enough to be the least bit concerned about the spiritual welfare of [the non-Amish] around them." Being a complete Christian, Yoder insists, means being concerned about all of humanity, and therefore bringing the Word of God, and good deeds done in God's name, to the unbaptized. His own sons and daughters have become missionaries abroad. The Old Order Amish do not proselytize and have no missionaries.

How dare the Old Order forbid individual Bible study and

prayer groups among the laity as "too worldly" when they permit "drinking, smoking, [and] unbecoming courtship practices!" In Yoder's view, "opposition to Bible study and [to] following the fashions and styles of the world" are cut from the same wrong cloth, and for the Old Order to be "worldly in doctrine is much more serious," because that leads to having a people who practice proper religious form but are ignorant of the true spirit of Christianity.

Yoder comes near to written apoplexy in discussing the Old Order's approach to *rumspringa*, which, he charges, produces "wild drinking parties, smoking, dope, fornication, and shameful courtship practices." His prescription for proper courtship: Bible study classes, supervised singings, youth groups traveling together to serenade people in old-age homes, and holiday events at which youth interact with slightly older married couples. He chastises the "hypocrisy" of the Old Order's willingness to forgive a youth's past sins if the youth agrees to join the church and follow its rules. In Yoder's view, these youth are "reformed but not transformed." "TOO MANY SETTLE DOWN BUT DO NOT SETTLE UP! . . . If they only settle down to a different style of life they may look alright but are still lost. . . . *To commit their life to Christ is very much more important than to sell the car, join the church, or marry the girl.*"

"Good people go to Heaven and bad people go to Hell," Velda B, the confused young woman who feels like a jack-in-the-box hemmed in by Amish culture, recalls being told at a very young age. "Rebellious," as she put it, she worried that "I'm too bad, so I can't go to Heaven."

In church, before she was old enough to attend school, Velda was taught to be "silent . . . not to whisper in your friend's ear, not to be rowdy," or you would be "disciplined," spanked or given a stern lecture. Church was "three hours long, and we have to sit on hard benches." Beyond the discomfort, the services bored her, because she could not comprehend what was being read from the

Bible, or the songs, or the sermons, all of which were in High German. The kids would memorize the songs and sing along with the adults, but since they knew only Dutch, they could not figure out the precise meaning of what they were singing. Velda endured church by envisioning the fun the girls would have afterward, a Sunday afternoon of romping in a bunch.

At fifteen Velda dived headlong into partying, drinking, and other *rumspringa* excesses, but she later felt those activities were a cover for the "emptiness I felt inside," which she attributed to her fervent desire to go to Heaven. "I wanted to be sure of my salvation, I wanted to know that that is where I'm going."

Velda "didn't particularly like" the Amish faith's insistence that even the baptized were not assured of entering Heaven—that each individual would be judged on the basis of her or his deeds and life. She wanted certainty, and the Amish church provided none.

It was at the time of this inner conflict that Velda had taken up with the older Mennonite fellow who taught her things such as how to cut her steak and how to dress in a more sophisticated and alluring way.

After two years, at age nineteen, she breaks up with him, and her parents are much relieved. But for Velda the problems have only increased, because while she feels that declaring her independence from him is good for her, she also fears that she is now "back to the old options." Those are only two: being a member of the wild parties bunch or of the prepare-to-join-the-church bunch.

She meets an Amish man and begins to lean toward jumping off the party merry-go-round. Though "joining church" has not been on her "agenda," Velda realizes now that all her "support" is within the Amish community. She decides to resume wearing Amish clothes and to begin prebaptismal classes.

Just before she starts those classes, Velda goes with her family on a vacation to Florida, and while there she sometimes dons English clothes. In such clothes, with her hair recently done up by a beauty parlor and wearing a pair of earrings, she poses for a studio photograph. When she looks at the print, she thinks it is "amazing that I could look this beautiful—glamorous and exotic and bold and beautiful." She stores the photo away, an icon of a life on the outside that she is about to renounce.

Some Amish youth treat the nine sessions of prebaptismal classes in a perfunctory way, but for Velda they are of a piece with trying to satisfy her yearning for religious contentment. Joining the church means "giving up all the bad things that I was involved in. It means living a different life—a life that's more worthy to God." No more styling her hair or wearing fingernail polish or earrings; but those are not difficult to relinquish. Letting go of her music is harder, as is giving up on "the sense of being able to really make my own choices." Velda listens with mounting chagrin to the leader of her class detail the particulars of "what you're not supposed to do," a list that includes women not being permitted to go without panty hose on Sunday, even if the day is very warm and their legs are otherwise entirely covered.

That bishop rehearses with the students the questions to which they will be required to give formal responses at the baptismal ceremony. The questions and answers are in High German, and Velda could just memorize them, but she hunts up an English translation that allows her to understand the full intent of the exchanges between minister and applicant. They involve pledges of acceptance of Christ, of submission to the church, and acknowledgment that transgressing church rules is "almost like committing a sin." This is harsh, but Velda is ready to accept it and hopes that doing so, and becoming a full member of the church, will assuage her inner pain and yearnings, the ones she still cannot fully explain to herself.

Emma M, the willowy would-be model, now sixteen years old, and Faron Y, the intelligent son of a minister who has become a factory worker and drug addict, meet in the party scene near Shipshewana. They become a couple. She adores him so much that it becomes "scary" for her, because she has never before experienced a love that "made you willing to give up what you had been dreaming about." She becomes as enamored of his tormented soul as he does of her bright and calming presence. She extends her stay in Indiana to be with him. Emma does not take drugs and tries to see the good side of everything—including Faron. For her sake, and with her encouragement, he quits drugs and tries hard to go straight.

They talk about everything, including religion. When Emma asserts that "I'm going to believe there is a God" and will act accordingly, Faron challenges her. "What if you're wrong?"

"I'll continue to believe, just to be on the safe side."

"What if the Bible is a sham?" Faron presses on. "What if some smart man wrote it and made a load of money off it? What if God isn't real? What if the earth began like the scientists say it did?"

"Well, if we started coming from apes, when did we quit coming from apes?" Emma counters.

So Faron tells her how the universe and mankind have developed—some of his answers, Emma suspects, are "things he makes up" when he does not know all the particulars.

His questioning and cynicism unnerve her. She takes comfort from later conversations in which he says things such as

> Well, you got to admit that there's a higher power, you know. [Expletive] sun and [expletive] seasons and everything. I don't know: there's got to be something or somebody controlling all that, so I believe that there's a God. I mean, I think if you really, you know, want to do His bidding or whatever, and be like an upright Christian, I mean, I believe it will help you at times, but He'll still [expletive] with you. I just—I don't know—right now I kind of look at it as "[Expletive], God is a big guy that likes to play evil tricks."

Faron understands that most Amish, like his mother and father, have "a personal relationship with God," but he is hard put to know how he will ever achieve one for himself:

I would love to feel like my dad does and, like, get along with my family and be a righteous, Christian, God-fearing person and go to church every Sunday and everything and be happy like that. I would love that, but I can't. I have never been able to. Hopefully, someday I will be, but for right now I couldn't, and what is the use of going to church and praying and reading your Bible if you have absolutely no desire? Well, not no desire, because I do have a desire to— I don't know. If it doesn't make you happy, why do it? It doesn't really make me happy at the moment. I don't know what does.

Emma is pleased that Faron admits there is a God, but the doubts he has raised continue to shake her. "When you believe in something all your life and then someone shows you that you could be wrong," she says, that is "really scary."

The sociologist Denise Reiling studied Amish youth over a ten-year period for her doctoral thesis and learned that, for many of them, experiences in *rumspringa* "generated a high level of anxiety and depression." Reiling traced these feelings to the young people's dread of dying outside the church, which possibility they thought, as they had been taught since childhood, would prevent them from entering Heaven. This feeling was very difficult for them to shake, and in Reiling's view it is what drove many of them back to the church. She also found that among those who after *rumspringa* eventually chose to join the church, regret for previous bad behavior while outside ran very deep: "Anxiety over transgressions committed during [that] period . . . did not diminish for most upon taking adult baptism because they believed their God could still hold them accountable for these [past] acts."

Joann H, the young woman who had gotten into wild partying "up to her chin" and eventually moved out of the community to live with a Baptist co-worker, turns eighteen and realizes that she has been "on the wild side" for two entire years.

Partying, Joann now realizes, is "just plain stupid. I mean, 'Hello?' All you do is drink. And then the next morning you might not even remember what all happened." She also understands the extent to which her own wild behavior has been "hurting" her parents. "Now some people, they can totally shut off their conscience and just go right on partying. But I'm more of a— I want people to like me, I want my parents to respect me."

Joann doesn't quite know what to do about partying but worries more about her older brother and her next younger sister than about herself. It might be only a matter of time before the brother has a third truck accident and dies in a crash without being in a state of grace; and Joann is chagrined to hear her next younger sister, now sixteen, voicing the same arguments for rebellion that she once uttered and is now finding spurious.

Desperate to jump off her wild ride, Joann decides that "what I need is God." Having always been a believer in Jesus, she has been attending Sunday services and Bible study classes at the Baptist church. Now it becomes obvious to her that the Baptist faith is not giving her what she wants. She comes to the conclusion that life outside the Amish church is, if not totally wrong, then certainly not leading her to the peaceful, faith-imbued state of mind for which she yearns. She hangs fire until a crisis arises. Word reaches her landlady that on an H family trip to Pennsylvania, Joann has "gotten drunk and was fooling around with a guy." The charge is not entirely true, but nevertheless, the older woman kicks Joann out of the apartment.

Without other friends to take her in, with no confidence that she could find a roommate, with no way to get to work because she does not have a car, Joann panics. She cannot simply go back to her family home—that would be admitting defeat. Not knowing what else to do, she phones an uncle, one of her father's brothers who never joined the church. He tells her she can crash at his place, across the state line in Michigan, and he arranges for her to get a ride to work from there—but he cannot otherwise look after her because he is out most of the time.

For three long weeks Joann is "on her own—like, 'nobody around.' " She works extra shifts at the restaurant just so she can "be around people." During this time, her father, perhaps alerted by his brother, telephones her every day.

Joann's father, the man who for years has argued mightily with his three older children to give up their wild ways, is no longer haranguing her! Now they are talking—holding daily one-hour conversations. They get into everything, discuss the residue of her childhood hurts and her anger at her parents misunderstanding her wish to try her wings for a while; her father apologizes for whatever distress he may have caused; she does the same; they forgive each other.

After that is "cleared up," Joann finds "the bitterness and the anger" are draining out of her slowly but surely. On the Saturday of the fourth weekend of being out on her own, at her father's urging she moves back into the family home.

The next morning she is welcomed at Amish church with delighted greetings—and no questions asked about where she has been for so many months. "Everybody just— I mean, I'm surrounded by people who *actually care*. You know, they actually care for who you are *now*, not for who you were yesterday; and they believe the best in you until it's proven otherwise."

Joann makes plans to be baptized. Her parents are elated, but the youth in her age cohort, the straight-arrow Amish who have gone to Sunday singings, not to parties, are dubious. She says, "They're, like, 'We know she used to do this and that.' Like, 'How can we trust her?' " She recognizes that she has to prove herself to them and to the rest of the community. Emblematic of her "healing" process is regret at having cut her hair, since she will not be permitted to join the church until it has grown in to a decent length and she can pin it up. But in other ways Joann eases back into the Amish life just as readily as she slips a long Amish dress over her torso. She misses jogging after work, but giving that up is a minor matter to her now.

In Joann's first meeting with the bishop in charge of the nine sessions leading to baptism, he tells her that living in the plain manner is not sufficient to help her get by—she needs more, she needs Jesus Christ. It is what Joann had longed to hear, and upon hearing it, she feels "a lot of joy and peace."

Reading more deeply in her Bible, she is struck by Jeremiah 29:11: "For I know the thoughts that I think toward you, saith the Lord, thoughts of peace, and not of evil, to give you an expected end." "If I'm having a really bad day, I just have to think, 'Well, hey, God knows the plans He's got for me, and they're going to be for my own good.' And it really helps me." She quits smoking, quits drinking. "I wish I could have said that I never opened a beer, but I couldn't." She and another former partygoer, "two girls from the wild side," bond, determined now to make amends and behave properly. They attend Sunday singings and volleyball games, no longer finding them too tame. They both hope that in time the straight arrows will get to like them.

Joann tries to warn her sister to get out of the party scene, but the sister's response is, "Well, I've got to go have fun." Joann explains, "You can't really tell somebody, 'No, don't do this, you're going to regret it.' " Knowing the signs of drink and drugs, Joann observes them in a few people in the prebaptismal class—notably in a former boyfriend, the one who was high on pot when he first asked her out. She is angered to learn from him that he is still smoking marijuana. She crosses him off her list of potential husbands.

Whether a prospective husband will come along and walk the Amish path with her is a concern, but not the most important one for Joann, now that she has embraced the faith of her fathers and mothers and is committed to yielding her life to God's will.

Joann looks forward to full church membership. "I'm realizing how much I need my family and the church. I'll be belonging to something. And that's really cool. When you have Christ in your life, you're going to be a quiet, submissive person, and just kind of think things through. You won't make as many rash decisions. And you'll be more sympathetic and compassionate."

. . .

Like Joann H, many Old Order Amish wholly and cheerfully do what Beachy Bishop Stephen Yoder would have them do, "commit their lives to Christ" and work toward gaining "peace with God." On a continuum ranging from horrible sinners to the impeccably upright, the Amish are far toward the latter end, a position attributable to the depth and intensity of their faith.

A social worker in Pennsylvania whose clientele includes Amish clients in emotional distress speaks for many others who work with and know the Amish well when he asserts that the vast majority of them are "quite happy with their lives" and quite religious, and that the two attitudes are interlinked. "There's a real attraction of the slower-paced, sheltered, religious-based life," he says. "It fulfills a spiritual yearning to reject modern conveniences and the consumerist way of life." Another counselor, born Amish, points out that "the Amish are not ignorant; they know what's out there, and they don't want it. They want to stay at home and be close to the church."

Dennis L, the Shipshewana grandfather who is a jack-of-all-trades, vividly recalls his mother telling him, when he was a teenager, that he had a guardian angel and must not take that angel where it ought not to go. One evening during his *rumspringa*, while he and his girlfriend were in a theater watching a movie, the film's unexpected violence made him uncomfortable. Recalling his mother's caution about endangering his guardian angel, he and his girlfriend left the theater. Soon after, they joined the church and married—and have never watched another film.

Vonda S, an Ohio Amish woman of thirty-five, the mother of five and the wife of a farmer, when asked about the joys of her religious view of life, told this story: "One summer afternoon I was standing at the window in my kitchen, doing the dishes, watching my middle ones playing and taking care of the baby, and the sun on the corn and all, and Elmer and little El coming over the hill with the mules—and I was just floored by the goodness of God. It was like everything we were doing and everything I was seeing was a prayer." Her husband recalls a similar experience in his youth, while cutting with a hand-held scythe through an acre of hay: "I was working in the same rhythm as the hay, as the wind and clouds, as my father before me and his before him. That was the moment when I knew I would do as God wanted me—be an Amish farmer."

A middle-aged Amish man in Illinois, Freeman H, described his father's death at eighty-nine as "a real Amish passing," because he "went out of this world with a secret smile," a contentedness that Freeman believes came from "knowing he did all he could in this world to prepare it for Jesus and to prepare himself for meeting Him."

6

Shunning: To Keep the Church "Pure"

Velda B, the spiritually troubled young woman who while in Florida had posed for a photo portrait in English clothes as her last memento of her rumspringa years, is seeking to join the Amish church, for romantic as well as for religious reasons. During the previous year, before coming home, she "developed a relationship" with an Amish-raised young man from a nearby community. They became "close friends." They will be baptized, and marriage will be the next step, the "expected thing to do."

It is contrary to Amish tradition to announce a wedding too far in advance of the date, but most weddings are held on Thursdays in November, and the decorations and fare feature celery, so when a celery patch appears in a family's yard, the secret is out. Velda begins sewing her wedding dress. As a young girl and teenager, she sewed all her own clothes, having been taught by her mother, a very good seamstress. Made from a silky fabric, the wedding dress is sturdily constructed and attractive, in addition to covering her body in the approved manner, and it makes her "feel like a queen." She imagines being the center of attention on her wedding day; it is a pleasant reverie. In the back of her mind, though, Velda knows that at the end of an Amish woman's mortal life, she will be buried in her wedding dress.

While attending Amish church regularly and preparing for her wedding, Velda realizes that her spiritual hunger has not abated. She has been seeing a counselor on the outside, and after several sessions of explaining her feelings and wants, the idea dawns on her that to find a career, interesting life experiences, and even spiritual contentment, she may have to go outside the Amish faith.

She continues to work at a job outside the community and there meets a young woman who has been raised Amish but has left the church and become a member of another Christian denomination. Having coffee each week with this new friend, Velda seeks answers to "all kinds of questions" because she is "just full of questions," primarily about spiritual matters.

The answers begin to help Velda in her "process of getting to know the Lord as a personal friend." On a Sunday when there is no church service in her Amish district, she secretly attends the friend's church, sitting in a back row so that she will not be seen. The non-Amish services feel "very strange," because Velda cannot help thinking "that these people should tell me what I should believe. Why aren't they telling me?" If she were in an Amish church just then, they would be telling her, "This is what you should believe and what you shouldn't believe."

After the English church's service, parishioners greet one another warmly and seem happy to have Velda in their company. Equally revelatory to her is this church's assertion that she can simply be baptized and will thereafter be in a state of grace, "saved," assured of a place in Heaven. She has always been bothered by the lack of such assurance in the Amish church.

The pastor at the non-Amish church is also a counselor, and she hints to him of her doubts about what lies ahead for her in the Amish fold and shows him the photo from Florida. He responds that she looks beautiful in the photo but asks, "What do those big earrings do for you?" Jarred, she tries to explain that they made her feel glamorous and exotic. He replies that he can "see underneath all that is a very empty, very hurting girl."

This is "very true," Velda acknowledges to herself; and it is a truth that she has not previously realized because she has "never looked at this picture before and thought that."

The hand-sewn wedding dress is finished, and Velda and her fiancé are choosing the menus for the wedding day meals and the gifts that the couple will give to the "servers," their young friends. Invitations have been sent out. The day for the marriage is just a month in the future.

Unable any longer to keep her qualms to herself, Velda informs her fiancé, begs him to leave with her. He has "mixed feelings about leaving the church." His concern is that if they go outside the community, they will be "rejected" by their families and will receive no "support," because they will be in the bann, shunned, a notion he deems "scary."

Velda's hopes that her fiancé would join her on the outside are dashed. She hesitates: they are still close friends, and she does want him for her husband, so for a while longer she goes on with the plans for the wedding. But one day, as she tries on her wedding dress, she feels as though it is "covering the girl I really want to be." In that dress, she realizes suddenly, she has "nowhere to go."

She informs her parents of her doubts about proceeding with the wedding and remaining within the church. They take it as "a slap in the face." Her parents feel they have raised her correctly, so her willingness to leave the community is "like saying to them that I don't believe that the way you brought me up is right."

She does not want to hurt her parents, and the realization that she will be doing so if she goes does give her pause, but finally she has to inform her parents and her intended that she will not walk down the aisle but instead will leave the community.

Velda's intended no longer objects. He understands that it would be useless for him to insist on their marrying if she is determined to go and he is content to stay within the faith.

Her mother is incredulous, unable to comprehend why Velda would throw over both the possibility of a marriage to a young man the family has come to like and a life within the church, and she implies strongly that for Velda to leave now will result in her damnation as well as her excommunication.

Though Velda is mortally afraid for her soul, and aghast at the problems she is causing for her fiancé and both their families, she leaves the community.

After an initial burst of exhilaration at escaping a stifling environment, Velda begins to feel wholly at sea. She has a job, she finds a place to stay, and she has a Baptist church to attend—but she is emotionally adrift.

Then she learns that the Amish church district, rather than waiting to see whether she will come back, has already placed her in the bann. She is shunned. She soon discovers that no one in her family will eat at the same table with her or hand her a dish at dinner; members of the community will not do business with her in any way, or ride in a car with her, or acknowledge her presence when they see her on the street. She is shocked by the extent and force of her shunning. She feels "abandoned."

Velda musters her courage and speaks with her former minister in the Amish church, who tells her that she is shunned because at her baptism she "made a promise to stay in the Amish church," a promise that she "was not aware of" because the question was asked in German and she did not know German, and in any event she had not understood all the implications of her promise.

Breaking with a man she loves has been difficult enough for her, but she is emotionally unprepared for the severity of the family and community actions brought against her because she has been put in the bann. Velda has known about shunning all of her life, has on various occasions been instructed by her family not to interact with this person or that. But now she is the object of the shunning. Old friends will not chat with her, former neighbors pass her by in store aisles as though she does not exist. Worst of all, her parents join in the shunning.

Velda knows that her parents have to shun her "because of the church," that as good members they must "abide by what is expected of them." She understands all this intellectually but still feels "very rejected." She tries to be "compassionate," but "it hurts" that her parents are choosing to uphold what the church wants them to do rather than to help her in her suffering.

The confusion of being in the outside world combines with the harsh treatment from her family and former community, and provokes Velda to attempt suicide.

"My brother and his wife have asked me very expressly not to come into their home, and not to be part of their lives or their children's lives, because I left the church and was shunned," the

young, formerly Amish teacher Margaret M says. "At first my father told me, 'If you walk into my house, you'll be wearing plain
clothes and a covering, and if you're not, you'll have to leave.'"
Later on her father relented, "but when I go home to visit, I cannot get the holy kiss of greeting," which is given, woman to
woman and man to man, at church on Sundays.

Loretta Mae H, a woman in her seventies, had had a hard life;
born and raised on an Amish farm in Ohio, she joined the church
but then left it to marry a non-Amish man; for this she was "put
in the bann," excommunicated and shunned. She and her husband
struggled to make a living; they raised several children, and then
he died. In middle age she remarried but did not get along with
her second husband, and they eventually divorced.

Alone in her old age, Loretta Mae was depressed to the point of
needing professional assistance. Her daughter and social worker
suggested that she put on a bake sale, not for the money but for
the activity, to brighten her life. She was a well-known baker, had
a wonderful time making goods for the sale, and was pleased
when a daylong stream of Amish and non-Amish neighbors
stopped in to buy the cakes and pies. Most of the Amish women
who came calling were a generation or two younger than Loretta
Mae.

Two days later, all the Amish women returned to her door;
apologizing to Loretta, they said that because they were younger
they had not known she was still in the bann, and consequently
they were required to give her back the baked goods they had
bought, as they were not permitted to take anything from someone who was being shunned. She offered their money back, but
they said they could not take that either.

"More than fifty years," Loretta Mae later exclaimed to her
daughter, after telling her this story, "more than fifty years and
they still have me in the bann!"

· · ·

Velda, Margaret, and Loretta Mae have been shunned.

Shunning, an important aspect of Amish life, is much misunderstood by outsiders. It is the most drastic of the Amish church sanctions, which are known as the *meidung*. In German, *meidung* means social avoidance in the sense of ostracizing someone. Ostracism is an ancient community-based punishment: in its most intense incarnation, the ostracized person is treated as though he or she were invisible or nonexistent; the person is walked past, not spoken to or interacted with at all until he or she either leaves the village permanently or dies. The Amish form of ostracism is not as extreme, but it shares with the more harsh form a basis in rural culture. In a big city, a former member of an in-group who opts out and lives a few hundred yards from the residences of others in the group can easily avoid those community members, the vastness and anonymity of the city assisting in this task. In the countryside, where population density is lower and everyone drives down the same few roads, shops at the same stores, and attends the same weddings and funerals, shunning has more potency.

Amish shunning is nearly as stressful for family and friends as it is for the "fallen member," because congregants are in danger of jeopardizing their own church memberships should they continue to associate freely with the ostracized person.

The historian of the Amish Paton Yoder observes that, although the *meidung* is couched partially in the language of helping the sinner to repent, its larger function has always been to strengthen "the authority of the church over the community." Shunning is not applied to youngsters who exit the community for *rumspringa* and never return, since they have not been baptized into the church. It applies only to baptized members who later leave the sect voluntarily or are kicked out.

At baptism, church members make an "absolute promise," referred to as "the given word," that is considered more binding than any written contract; it is a compact with God, witnessed by the congregation, who thereafter are equally responsible for the member's adherence to the compact, which includes obedience to the church's rules. Such a promise cannot later be shaded, amended, or neglected. It is designed to prevent a member from initially agreeing to abide by a church edict such as the forbidding of divorce and then later divorcing a spouse; members understand that breaking the promise will result in punishments leading up to and including shunning, punishments given not for the infraction but for breaking the sacred promise.

Shunning and banning are biblically seated. In Matthew 18:15–17, Jesus instructs his disciples to treat an unrepentant church member as though he were "a Gentile and a tax collector." I Timothy 5:20 states, "Them that sin rebuke before all, that others may also fear." I Corinthians 5:9–11, Romans 16:17, II Thessalonians 3:14, and Titus 3:10–11 are also cited as instructing the faithful that unbelievers should be cast away, to maintain the purity of the group and its commitment to God. Shunning and banning are also specifically referred to in the church's founding documents, such as this passage from the Dortrecht Confession of 1632:

> We believe in . . . the bann, or excommunication, a separation or spiritual punishment by the church . . . so that what is pure may be separated from that which is impure. . . . An offensive member and open sinner [must] be excluded from the church, "rebuked before all," and "purged out as a leaven," and thus remain until his amendment, as an example and warning to others.

Article 17 specifically speaks of shunning:

> If anyone, whether it be through a wicked life or perverse doctrine, is so far fallen as to be separated from God, and consequently rebuked by, and expelled from, the church, he must also . . . be shunned and avoided by all the members of the church.

Shunning is the ultimate Amish sanction, not the initial one. Chastisement of an errant person begins with informal admonishment, harassment, and minor punishment. Older children or adults find themselves scolded at the barn door or on the country lane, mocked by peers, the subjects of over-the-fence wives' tales. Such private in-family and in-community rebukes of members' inappropriate behavior are common in the course of daily Amish life. More important, the community expects and believes that these sorts of exposures, mild punishments, and words-to-the-wise advice will be sufficient to curb the unwanted behavior.

Kathryn L, mother of Jerry and Susanne, has felt a lot of that sort of pressure from the community lately.

While Jerry's Tourette's is under control and he has graduated and is out working in a restaurant, the Amish boys who tormented him in school have become his running-around pals—and this worries Kathryn. One of these pals is very overweight and overbearing, and the other seems to have no mind of his own. On the weekends, Jerry and these two sally forth in buggies—all the families are quite traditional and will not permit them to have cars.

But after six weeks of the boys running around together, the parents of the overweight boy show up at the L family residence and complain to Kathryn and Vernon that Jerry is a bad influence on their son because Jerry is working at a restaurant that caters to tourists. They tell the L's, "You're bad parents because you're letting Jerry run around with English girls."

Kathryn does not know what to make of this accusation; in an area where most Amish men work away from home, it had seemed unrealistic to attempt to restrict Jerry to taking only jobs that were within the community or to working only for Amish employers. But this situation with the other boy's family must be resolved before that family decides to refer the problem to the ministers of the church district, which might result in sanctions against the L's. Kathryn and Vernon never consider that their neighbors might be mistaken or lying about the accusations. "Have we done something wrong?" Kathryn thinks to herself.

"How come we didn't know about this? We must not have been paying attention." She asks Jerry for an explanation, which he provides: one night, after working late as a busboy, he had to take a van home and rode along as the van first dropped off an English waitress in Michigan before bringing him home.

Having heard this from her son, Kathryn acts boldly, using the telephone next to Vernon's shop to put questions to Jerry's supervisor at the restaurant and to other colleagues. She is relieved when they say, "He's a good worker and doesn't hang around with the English girls." She now realizes that the overweight boy has been "jealous" of Jerry for many years, envious of his artistic talent, and that is probably why he spread rumors about her son. Next, Kathryn and Vernon confront the accuser's parents in their home, but the meeting doesn't go well because Kathryn cannot bring herself to say to them that their son is lying.

Shortly, Jerry's tormentor and several other young males send him a letter saying that they will no longer allow him in their group. Kathryn notices her son feeling "very alone, very isolated," because "none of the other kids visit." Jerry soon decides to buy a moped to get him out of the house and around on weekends.

While Kathryn and Vernon are deciding what to do about Jerry trying to buy a moped—they fear he will harm himself on it—their daughter Susanne's situation erupts. Susanne has been paired in *rumspringa* activities with a daughter of one of Kathryn's sisters. That sister has been telling Kathryn that she is wrong to permit Susanne to go out with Joe, the Amish boy who dresses English and has his own car—but Kathryn, though she might have preferred a more traditional boyfriend for her daughter, has not interfered with Susanne's wishes. After all, Susanne has been quite forthright in informing Joe that she will wear only Amish dress when they are out on dates and will not drink liquor or sleep with him. And Joe is the son of a family in the same church district as the L's.

However, at a big family Thanksgiving dinner, Kathryn's sister tells her, "in front of everybody, that I'm not bringing up my children right, that Jerry is a problem and that Susanne is going around with English guys—that she's practically a harlot." The latter accusation, it is clear to Kathryn, has originated with her niece, and when Kathryn tries to tell that niece to mind her own business, she is yelled at by a brother-in-law and told to "go home and take care of the purity of your own children." Everyone is reduced to tears.

The threat of church-imposed sanctions was more openly used against Ruth G's family when she and her sister were growing up in Wayne County.

A sticking point between the family and the church arose because of their father's supposed overuse of a generator in his woodworking shop. To help their mother, who had a bad back, he sometimes hooked up an automated washing machine to a long cord from that generator so that she could wash the family's clothes without having to bend and stoop too much. Someone in the community "tattled to the bishop," who came to their house, Ruth later recalled, "in the middle of the night" to inspect this arrangement and tell the family to stop using so much electricity because doing so was contrary to the *ordnung*.

When her parents didn't want to stop, they were subjected to temporary sanctions; "there was a big to-do," and the family was "almost forced to leave the church." Unwilling to risk ostracism, Ruth's parents complied with the demand to stop using the generator to run a washing machine and were permitted to remain within the Amish community.

Some years later, virtually the same issue came up again, in regard to Ruth's sister and her husband, who was using a generator to run a heater in his workshop; the heater was kept on all night to prevent explosive powders from becoming too damp to be used in the brother-in-law's excavation business. The bishop once again decreed that too much electricity was being used. This time, though, "there was a misunderstanding," and the minor infraction became a major matter, eventually resulting in Ruth's sister and brother-in-law being put in the bann and forced to leave the sect.

The bishop visited Ruth's house once more—this time just after she and her husband, Junior, had completed building a home of their own. He took one look at the fireplace installed in their living room and told them it was "too worldly"—too ostentatious—and would have to be taken out or otherwise concealed. Though Ruth and Junior did not agree with the bishop's arbitrary evaluation of their fireplace, they thought it best to comply with the demand so that the matter would never have to be brought up to the whole community in a church meeting.

The artist Susie Riehl's encounter with potential sanctions dates back to her first gallery show. In the 1980s, with encouragement from her husband, John, and her family, she started working seriously as an artist and soon came to the attention of a non-Amish friend, who persuaded her to exhibit in a Lancaster County gallery that the friend had opened. In conjunction with the gallery's opening, Susie agreed to a few newspaper interviews and attended signings—which provoked the community's reaction.

"There was some criticism of the publicity efforts," she recalls. "You're Miss Important" is the phrase she uses to sum up the Amish community's initial response to her art and the hoopla surrounding its public display. The celebration of her as an individual contravened the traditions and rules of the community. The Amish credo rails against "egotism" in any form, which, as an article in *Family Life* explains, "needs to be laid aside" so that "humility and submission can find their place." Not only was being celebrated a problem that arose between Susie and the community, one that might earn her sanctions, but she herself was of two minds about it. Searching for words to convey her inner struggle on this matter, she says, after a long period of thought and with deep emotion, "I don't understand people putting other people on a pedestal. As a Christian, I believe that everybody is worth something, and that in God's eyes no one person is worth more than anyone else."

As an upstanding member of the church, Susie had no interest in behaving in ways that were considered beyond its boundaries. So she freely discussed the matter with church elders, and afterward informed her gallery and representatives that she would continue to exhibit her work for sale but would give no further newspaper interviews.

Today, Susie takes part in occasional events, such as signings of her artwork, because, she says, she enjoys meeting people she would otherwise not encounter. If her reduced participation in publicity has had a negative impact on sales, she is unconcerned, because commercial success was never the reason for her art. "There *are* other things in life," she asserts. She has had reasonable success anyway, her watercolors having been made into prints, posters, and postcards that have sold quite well. She believes that her neighbors and community are now "mostly comfortable" with her work as an artist. Asked about residual jealousy and envy, she responds, in the Amish manner, with a story: Her women friends used to chide anyone who did not arrive at a quilting by 7:00 a.m., saying it was evidence of her laziness, but they now tolerate without comment several of the women arriving at 8:15, after they have first attended to an equally important personal task, making sure that their children have been properly seen off to their Amish schools.

If a sect member's internalized vision of the rules, or pressure from neighbors and family, does not result in "correcting" behavior perceived to be contrary to the *ordnung*, the religious leaders are made aware of the situation and must handle it. Most try to do so informally at first, but if a visit by a minister to an errant member does not produce the desired results, the matter is presented on a church Sunday to the full membership. The accused is asked to explain his or her actions publicly. If the offense is remediable—overuse of a generator or wearing inappropriate clothing—and the wrongdoer expresses remorse and promises not to repeat the offense, no formal sanctions are decreed. This is sometimes known as the "sitting confession," in which the miscreant agrees to "correct" the behavior.

However, if the errant member denies committing the offense, or claims it was not an offense, or if the offense is irremediable, then that person may be placed in the bann. An Indiana bishop characterizes as irremediable offenses the "sins that can't be changed, sins that can't be made right." At a meeting of all church members, the offending member's church privileges are suspended; he or she is "put in the bann."

The banned person may not receive communion or participate in regular services. Family members may not eat at the same table with the ex-member; the banned person is not even permitted to serve himself or herself food from the common dish used by the others—food must be given to the person, usually through an intermediary who is not a member, such as a child. Church members also may not take anything—food, a gift, a ride in a vehicle— from a banned person, buy anything from or conduct a financial transaction with that person. A husband or a wife of a member in the bann is forbidden to engage in sexual relations with the spouse.

"The Bann punishes the evildoer not in the spirit of revenge, but to bring him to repentance," says an article in *Family Life*. "The Bann expresses in the strongest means possible the church's love and concern for the erring member's soul." If the banned member makes a "kneeling confession," acknowledging the transgression and asking for forgiveness, he or she can be reinstated. The objective of the bann is to shock and prod the errant member toward enlightenment, by making him or her want so earnestly to come back to the enveloping warmth of the family and the church that the person is moved to repent. Shunning is the Amish version of tough love.

Temporary banns are numerous, and in most instances they work. The return of the errant member to the fold after a temporary bann is regularly achieved. There are far fewer total banns, but nearly every family has a member who has been excommunicated for life.

"Judge not, that ye be not judged," Matthew 7:1 quotes Jesus as saying. But Amish ministers do not view excommunication as a judging of a person's behavior. "God alone is the judge," affirms an Indiana bishop, "but we have the right to say who can or cannot be in our church."

The punishment for heresy in the Catholic church when Anabaptism began was death, and although early Anabaptist leaders did not believe anyone ought to shed blood for falling away from the faith, they perceived a need for strong measures to force those thinking about leaving the new faith to reconsider. Shunning was a way to curtail heresy and desertion without bloodshed.

Jakob Amman, founder of the Amish church, broke with his more liberal Anabaptist brethren in part over use of the bann. He advocated frequent administration of the bann as necessary for the health of the church and insisted that members who would not abide by every church tenet should be shunned.

Shunning's purpose today remains the same. It is elucidated by a minister in an article for *Family Life*: "The church must be kept pure, and a high standard of holiness maintained. If sin is winked at, it will not only contaminate the church by its very presence, but it will spread and increase . . . The church is held accountable [by God] if false teachings are not dealt with."

All highly religious-based communities find that rigid sets of rules, accompanied by strategies for ridding themselves of people who do not follow those rules, are necessary, the sociologist Émile Durkheim stated in his 1915 book, *The Elementary Forms of Religious Life*. He explained that a sect's "collective representations," its rules and myths, have been put together by "immense cooperation" of generations of like-minded people who have "united their ideas and sentiments, . . . accumulated their experience and their knowledge"; so that if all the members of the group "did not agree on these essential ideas at every moment . . . all contact between their minds would be impossible, and with that, all life together." Durkheim insisted that a religious society cannot "abandon" its collective ideas "to the free choice of the individual without abandoning itself."

Despite the need for an excommunication ordinance to maintain the purity of the sect, shunning has not been uniformly applied at all periods in Amish history. According to the historian and minister Joseph F. Beiler, it was not much used in the American colonies before the Revolutionary War. But during that war, Amish families were unable to persuade "more than one son to remain in the old faith . . . Many sons who came to this land of freedom were overwhelmed with the air of freedom in America." To counter these losses, the bann was more regularly applied.

"Disciplines" written down in 1809, 1837, and on into the Civil War era blame "neglect of the bann" for excessive defections from the church. In 1909 and in 1966, while the ostensible reason for large splits in the church was the desire among some members to make use of modern technologies, the underlying source of friction was the *meidung* and the degree to which errant members were or were not being punished for infractions of the *ordnung* that dealt with the use of new technologies.

Today, while less conservative Anabaptist sects—Old Order Mennonites and Beachy Amish—still believe in excommunication, they mainly banish those who have openly controverted the Ten Commandments. In contrast, most Old Order Amish excommunications are directed not against those who commit mortal sins but against those who leave the church after baptism or who repeatedly resist the authority of the church leaders.

The Old Order Amish church leaders can apply the bann regularly because they have numbers on their side. After the splits of 1909 and 1966, when significant fractions of the total Amish population defected from the Old Order, the *ordnung* was modified to prevent further losses—but in those eras, the aggregate population of Amish was still low. These days the Amish could absorb such losses—of 20 to 25 percent—and not worry that they might precipitate the disappearance of the church, because the membership would recover in a few years thanks to the sect's fecundity and high retention rate.

While there is no doubt that shunning assists the church in surviving, and that the threat of shunning is a puissant deterrent to would-be defectors, it has a deleterious effect on individuals. "Shunning does no good for anyone," charges Emma M; two of her siblings have been shunned, and they have continuing difficulties in relating to nonshunned siblings and especially to their parents. Emma feels that shunning simply enforces the separation of the children from the parents and "does not contribute in any way to a person's reconciliation"—with family or with the church.

Others who have voluntarily left the church charge that, in addition to being unnecessarily hard on families, sanctions are wrongly applied—used, for example, to prevent members from broadening their understanding of what it means to be a Christian. Mr. and Mrs. B of Indiana had wanted to study the Bible individually and in classes; blocked from doing so within the church, they left, with their children, and were excommunicated. They found the religious study they desired within a fairly strict Mennonite church. But years later, at the funeral of Mr. B's father, he and his wife had to eat apart from his brothers and their wives, and were forbidden to ride with them to the grave site. "What good does that do?" Mr. B asks. "Who is it that is served by turning brother against brother?" Some of his relatives seem to agree with those sentiments, for when the B's attended another family funeral, farther away from home, his Amish cousins thanked the couple for making the long journey and apologized for the inconveniences made necessary by the cousins' having to observe the shunning prohibitions. And a bishop deliberately sat at dinner with the B's and engaged them in friendly conversation.

Ruth T, a twenty-three-year-old manager of a home furnishings boutique in Shipshewana, left the sect before being baptized, so she is not shunned. She is highly religious; her reason for not joining the Amish church was a conviction that it was inimical to the essence of Christianity as she understood that essence, distilled from lessons at an outside church and from her own reading of the Bible. As do the B's, Ruth believes that being a true disciple of Jesus Christ is not measured by a simplified lifestyle; rather, discipleship is an obligation to proselytize as well as to perform acts of compassion and kindness to others. "If you're going to properly imitate Christ, you have to spread the Word of God," both Ruth and the B's say, though the B's are Mennonites and Ruth became a Baptist.

"Most of the Amish are religious, but the church gets in their way, you know?" Ruth says. "Not letting you study the Bible on your own, not doing any outreach." While holding a full-time job, Ruth regularly attends her Baptist church and midweek Bible study classes, and she is a financial supporter of overseas missionaries. She works with members of other faiths in drug-awareness programs.

Since Ruth is not shunned, she continues to be very involved with her parents and siblings, who remain Amish. She contends that in the Shipshewana area, with its reliance on tourist trade and on jobs in the RV factories, young people choose to be Amish "more out of a sense of liking the slower lifestyle" than from deep religious conviction. Two of her brothers, both members of the Amish church, work in those factories.

Ruth T's notion about lifestyle being of greater importance to the Amish than religious belief is buttressed by the research of Daniel B. Lee, a sociologist who found that few Old Order laypeople are knowledgeable about the specifics of their religious tenets as opposed to the tenets of other Protestant sects, other than knowing about their own deep commitment to adult baptism. The beliefs of Old Order individuals are "fluid and unstructured," Lee concludes, but "faith becomes socially relevant through action," that is, through shared religious practices. In Lee's view, shared rituals have become more important to a sect member's faith than the individual's interpretations of Christ or of the church's teachings.

Some in Ruth T's age-group among the Amish, she points out, now say that they may have married and joined church too soon. Their misgivings focus on what she characterizes as the "arbitrary" nature of the church's rules and discipline. These members cannot leave now, because they do not want to be shunned. But had they waited longer before joining, Ruth implies, they might have gone the route she has chosen for herself. "I've been born again, and I've been saved," she announces. "And I believe it's easy to be saved—we can all be washed in the blood of Christ."

While some people admire the Amish religious tenet that no one can be assured of salvation before death, Ruth does not. She characterizes the Amish church's nonassurance of Heaven as "arrogance," just another way of insisting that "this church is right and that everyone else is automatically excluded from Heaven. That's not fair and it's not logical. The church of the real is not about right and wrong, it's about belief. Anyone who accepts Christ can go to Heaven."

Accept is a key word for Ruth, one that she uses frequently; to her it means agreeing to a challenge—she likes challenges—whereas to most Amish *acceptance* connotes yieldedness and submission.

At Ruth's instigation, two of her siblings who are adult members of the Amish church have been "born again," but they remain within the Amish congregation. Their second baptism was countenanced because their first was in the Amish faith. "I'm very happy for them, because [the second baptism] means they're saved," Ruth says, and she is convinced that in that blessed condition her siblings are better able to accept the Amish cultural way of life, with its slower pace, emphasis on home and hearth, and time for contemplation. Their unusual state, in the Amish church but already "saved," is consistent with Ruth's own understanding of Christianity. "Christ is the freedom to make choices," she asserts.

Though in many Amish church districts the act of being baptized a second time outside the church would result in being banned, in Ruth's home district the church seems to tolerate the twice-baptized, so long as they do not desert the Amish church. Similarly, in many districts in northern Indiana, former Amish who were shunned but who have since joined acceptably strict

Christian churches have sometimes had their banns lifted. But not in Intercourse, Pennsylvania.

About forty years ago, two young people from Amish families long resident in the Intercourse area married and began a family. Anna became a housewife and mother, and her husband, Jacob K, a mechanically adroit man who could fix anything, opened a machine-repair business in a shop just outside the community. Soon he felt that he must have a telephone in the shop, and electrically driven tools, in order to compete effectively with non-Amish competitors.

Having these things was contrary to their home district's *ordnung*. The church told Jacob he could not use them and threatened the couple with excommunication if he did not accept the restrictions. Anna was conflicted. She wanted to stay within the church, where she had always been content, but it was her duty as a married woman to follow her husband. With him and their small children, she left the church, and they were soon "put in the bann."

"At the time, I felt the bann was unfair," Anna recalls. She and her husband had not done anything awful, yet, she says, "my parents and grandparents felt we had betrayed them, and I knew we had hurt them, but I also felt that we had no choice. The church wasn't going to change the rules for us, so we had to leave."

Banishment proved very difficult for Anna to bear: her two sisters and her parents and grandparents were forced to shun her. The worst, though, was the treatment she received from her former best friends, the young women neighbors in whose company she had grown up. An Amish woman's social life revolves around her interactions with other female church members—the quilting bees, the communal dinners, the everyday interchanges. After Anna had been shunned, she could no longer partake in any of those activities with her chums. "You can't replace old friends," she says wistfully, recalling the days when she and her girlfriends would go "choring" from house to house in a bunch, singing and laughing. Back then she had more reason than people in the mainstream do to believe that her group of friends would walk together with her through all the phases of life. The bann exploded that dream.

After the K family became Old Order Mennonites, Anna's and Jacob's relatives worked out ways to accommodate them, by hosting family dinners on non-church Sundays and the like. But, according to Anna, the K family continues to be isolated by non-familial Amish, for instance, by their immediate neighbors on a country lane. "They're still friendly toward us," Anna explains. "They helped us when a storm blew down our roof—fixed it real quick—but we're not invited over there for supper." Even at her sister's home, the K's are seated at the far end of a double table covered with a single cloth, so that technically they are not eating at the same table with Amish church members. All the more upsetting for Anna is that in later years the part of the *ordnung* relating to the use of telephones in businesses has been relaxed; had the modification been permitted earlier, the K's might have been able to find a way to remain in the church; but even now that the *ordnung* has been changed, they are not retroactively pardoned or welcomed. "The church never admits its mistakes," one of Anna's daughters comments.

Lydia T, who discovered that the "brand-new buggy" she had been given was more a burden than a pleasure, has left the church and her family's home. She is relieved to learn that she has not been put in the bann immediately, even though, like Velda B, before fleeing she had become a baptized Amish church member. But her new mailbox fills with letters from relatives, old friends, and neighbors, some pleading with her to come back, some threatening, and all having a single theme: you have just a short window of opportunity, a six-month period, during which you can return without being permanently shunned.

Lydia pays the warnings no mind; she is too busy enjoying her new freedom. Six months go by, and she is informed by family members that she is now in the bann. Though expected, this news is still stressful. She goes home for some of her mother's cooking—which she sorely misses—and hands her a plate.

"Put it on the table so I can get it," Mrs. T says. "You know I can't take that from you."

This is "dumb and silly," Lydia thinks, but she obeys and apologizes to her mother. More difficult to bear is her sister's attitude; on one of Lydia's infrequent visits home, when the two are alone together, Lydia asks her only sibling, now fifteen, if she ever has any thoughts of leaving. Her sister asserts that she is perfectly content at home—then stops speaking to Lydia. So do Lydia's childhood friends from Wisconsin.

The venetian blind factory closes, throwing Lydia out of work. She finds other jobs—at an RV factory, at a metal parts factory, at a gas station. After several months, she obtains a position at a factory that makes air conditioners; the work is very physical, and she often comes home to her shared apartment with cuts and bruises, but she likes the job. When her task at the factory is done, Lydia, constitutionally unable to be idle, assists colleagues with their unfinished tasks. She also tries working after hours at the gas station, until she quits because she really does need to sleep now and then.

Ugly rumors circulate in the Amish community: that Lydia is a drug dealer, that she has been stopped by the police and put in jail overnight, that she is gay because she is living with a woman and that woman's children. She tries to laugh off the rumors and denies them to her parents, but when her father continues to be upset, Lydia arranges for him to phone the police barracks and stands by a telephone and waits while he ascertains that his daughter has not been arrested or jailed.

"You happy now?" she asks after the call.

"Yes, but I don't know who to believe anymore."

On Lydia's twenty-second birthday, her non-Amish friends throw her a party at a bar. In contrast to the too-tame Amish celebration at home for her twenty-first birthday, this one makes her "feel good," because, she says, she is able to "be myself . . . do what

I want to do." The "blast" does not end until morning, when the cook makes her breakfast and coffee so that she is sober enough to drive home.

Lydia is still in the bann but has become somewhat used to it. A card-size letter arrives in her mailbox; the return address is that of an old friend in the Amish community, a woman in her age-group. She opens it "really quick," she says, "hoping, hoping that she's not going to chew me out for something or make me feel bad." It is a birthday card and a friendly, "cool" letter. On the card, the old friend has written something that touches Lydia: "Friends are forever." Lydia is not sure if this comes from a poem the friend has read or if she made it up, but she understands it as conveying the sentiment "It don't matter what you do or where you are, we still care." This makes Lydia feel good, as does the card's closing line, "You're always welcome in my house and we still love you."

Maybe she'll "stop by and say hi" to the old friend, Lydia thinks. But on further reflection, she is uncertain whether to visit the young woman, who might not like the way Lydia looks now, or what she is doing, or the way she is living. As for herself, "I don't know what in life I want yet."

But Lydia does desire closeness to her family and works hard at achieving it. She accompanies her mother to a public Laundromat, where they both do their wash and chat in Dutch, the twenty-something with the pageboy haircut and jeans, the older woman with her smock, gray dress, black shawl, and hair covering—the conjunction is startling to some onlookers. Her father is a harder nut to crack, but one day, when Lydia is visiting the family home, he shows her a tool he has just bought and another one exactly like it that he bought years ago but had forgotten he owned; the demonstration is an apology for his past blindness to her needs, for the times when he used money she had earned to buy things for himself instead of for the entire family.

The T's edge toward greater closeness as a family and hold discussions with Lydia about what went wrong and resulted in her leaving the church. Their consensus is that if the elder T's had permitted Lydia, though baptized, to go through *rumspringa*, to get the wildness out of her system, she might have come back to the church but that, having been denied her teenage rebellious period, she was determined to experience it in her early twenties, even in the face of the terrible punishment of being shunned.

Very troubling to many Amish youth in *rumspringa*, as well as to outsiders, is that the Amish use shunning to protect older members, particularly male members, in their disputes with younger members, female members, or sons and daughters who have not yet joined the church. Such allegations have even been made, albeit obliquely, in *Family Life*, in two anonymously written articles about child abuse in 1999–2000, "Purity of Little Girls" and "Journey to Freedom." These provoked many letters, testimonies that the letter writers had experienced or witnessed similar abuse in their Amish communities. Charges about sexual abuse in plain communities have been made in several series of newspaper articles over the years, ranging from one published in *The Kansas City Star* in the 1990s to the most recent, a weeklong series in the *Lancaster Intelligencer Journal* in 2004.

Shunning has been a point of contention, as well, in a series of criminal wife- and child-abuse cases in a half dozen states in recent years. Common to many of these cases is that when allegations are first aired, the initial reaction of the church is to support the accused member, even if he is the obvious aggressor. Also common are church assertions to the court that the member should not be punished by the criminal justice system because he has already suffered the church's worst punishment, excommunication.

Psychologists, sociologists, and counselors from Pennsylvania, Ohio, and Indiana who treat the Amish are adamant that there is no greater incidence of wife or child abuse in the plain communities than in mainstream communities; these counselors' experiences lead them to guess that there is proportionately much less abuse in the plain communities than in the mainstream. The counselors' anecdotal evidence is buttressed by a recent survey which reported that familial abuse is significantly lower in Protestant families in which the men attend church regularly than it is in families where male churchgoing is infrequent or sporadic.

The Amish are taking action against abuse, too. Diane DeRue, director of community services for the Counseling Center of Wayne and Holmes Counties, has been meeting regularly, for the past fifteen years, with the area's bishops; these interchanges have led to an enlightened campaign against child abuse. "I used to have to go to a family and explain what was acceptable and unacceptable punishment," she recalls. Then, with her encouragement, a group of bishops raised the matter of child abuse at a semiannual meeting of the state's church elders, "even though they knew the subject was controversial and that others would be angry at them for bringing it up at all." The recalcitrant bishops were convinced that they and their congregations would lose nothing by availing themselves of the counseling services of the CCWHC. "After that meeting, the bishops became more aggressive," DeRue says, "identifying offenders and going to talk to them personally in their homes and after church, and involving us when that is helpful." The reported incidence of spouse and child abuse in the area served by those bishops, and by the CCWHC, has declined.

Amish elders in other states and church districts, when made aware of abuse in their communities, have taken action against it, but the problems persist. Even after headline-grabbing cases in Ohio, Pennsylvania, and elsewhere, the difficulties of the Amish's seeming inability to accept that shunning is not the appropriate punishment for certain abuse offenses is still with us. It is on display in a complicated but also typical case decided in Wisconsin in 2004. Three Amish men and a woman were charged with counts ranging from sexual assault and battery to a child, to failure to aid a victim and report a crime. The defendants were a seventy-seven-year-old man, his wife, and her two sons from a previous marriage, who were in their twenties at the time of their arrest. The complainant alleged that when she was between the ages of eight and fourteen, she was raped and beaten more than two hundred times, in bedrooms, bathrooms, and barns in various towns in

Pennsylvania and Wisconsin, and that her attempts to obtain redress from the church had been ignored.

Wisconsin Amish church elders asserted to the civil authorities that they had dealt with the charges years earlier. The older man's church punishment had been to spend six weeks in the bann, the next youngest man was forced to admit his errors in front of the community and to ask for forgiveness, and the third male, who had been underage and not yet baptized at the time of the alleged crimes, had been instructed to stay home until he showed some character improvement.

The courts viewed the actions of the offenders as meriting much more serious punishment. At the request of the civil authorities, the woman who reported the abuse had worn a concealed recording device to a meeting with her former tormentors. During that meeting they admitted their guilt on some counts. The stepfather was arrested and accused of beating the young woman until she had fallen unconscious. According to the official complaint, "he admitted that he had been violent with his children, but [said] he had asked for forgiveness and believed things had been taken care of."

The men and the woman of the family were tried and convicted, and in the fall of 2004 sentences against them were finally handed down. Only one of the males, the youngest of the three originally charged, was sentenced to a long term, of eight years; the next oldest male was to serve just one year in jail, plus ten years' probation, because he was the sole support of a wife and family. A third son of the family was brought back from a western state, where he had initially fled to escape prosecution, and was convicted of the same offenses—rape and molestation of a minor—in a case unrelated to the first victim. He was also sent to prison. The father, the man who appeared to have set the pattern of abuse for his sons and stepsons, was not incarcerated for his offenses at all because of his advanced age.

Farming: "The Ideal Occupation"

On a twenty-acre field between Paradise and Intercourse, Pennsylvania, not far from busy Route 30, the temperature on a sunny January afternoon is in the teens and is chilled further by a fifteen-mile-an-hour wind. The prediction is for the thermometer to drop into the single digits and stay there for at least a week. Most people are indoors, even in this warmest part of the day, but not the Amish farmer working a team of six horses.

On the horizon, suburban-type homes sit, carved out of a field that at one time surely belonged to the farm; these residences have electricity and phone lines—signs of non-Amish owners. Passing by them on the road is a middle-aged, bearded Amish man on a foot-powered scooter, carrying a bag full of household supplies obtained from a convenience store at the junction of the side road and the busy highway. As he scoots by, he nods to a walker.

The surprisingly youthful farmer in the field, also friendly, is one of the many people hereabouts named Stoltzfus; he confirms to a stranger that the ancient-looking wooden contraption his team is pulling is a manure spreader. He agrees that the big freeze is coming and will soon curtail work in the fields but opines that the temperature today is "just right" for the task he is performing: the cold firms the ground enough to give the horses *good traction and chills the manure to a consistency that enables even spreading. He has spent several previous days this week preparing for this fertilizing. By next summer, these acres will produce a bountiful yield of corn, he hopes.*

With "a few acres to cover yet before sundown," he nonetheless moves the team and spreader slowly, carefully backing and filling at the ends of rows, sometimes going over a spot missed on the first pass. He must stand on his apparatus to see the rows properly and to have more leverage with the reins, though being upright makes him even more of a target for the icy wind.

His work is laborious and painstaking, requiring more skill than it takes to run a tractor or a mechanical spreader; and certainly it is more frigid and taxing than if he were in the heated cab of a tractor, pulling power-assisted levers. He appears expert at maneuvering a large team, which is a more complex and delicate task than guiding a single horse pulling a buggy.

The spreader holds several hundred pounds of manure, enough for five minutes of spreading, a small fraction of the tons of manure each acre requires. After he has dispersed his load, he drives the team back to his barn, where he reloads. There appears to be no one in the barn to help. After a brief interval inside, he drives back to the portion of the field that he had been working, and covers some more rows. The round trip to the right spot on the field takes him longer than it does to spread the manure. At this rate, Farmer Stoltzfus will probably not finish the field by sundown.

Another Lancaster farmer, the stolid, fair-faced Tobias K—the young man who had come back to run the family farm only after working for years as a mason—says that "farming's not always the cleanest work" and that it is filled with "very hard, very long days," but he now likes it. "Farming is the best thing there is," he avers. "Hard to beat." The farm he has taken over from his father is in good shape; the dairy herd that his father had worked so hard to increase is profitable, and the fields yield enough alfalfa and corn to feed his animals without his having to spend money for that purpose.

In earlier years, when he was in *rumspringa* and had not yet joined the church, Tobias had not wanted to farm, in part because the church rules on farming seemed too restrictive—more encumbered than carpentry shops, shed manufacturers, or construction crews—with rules about which machinery was permitted and which forbidden. However, the rules for Amish farmers have been changing steadily, Tobias says, as part of the attempt to encourage Amish to continue operating their farms and young Amish to become farmers when there are other options for them to choose, particularly construction and factory work, which could put more cash in their pockets.

For instance, the bishops now permit dairymen to have manure pits into which to sluice the considerable amount of cow dung that the herd produces, rather than having to shovel the manure onto carts and haul it outside. They also permit the use of some other mechanized equipment, generally powered by gas or compressed air, that makes farming in the Amish way a bit less arduous and time-consuming than it used to be.

Tobias is grateful for such changes, but he did have a run-in with the church elders over his use of some other machinery. He recounts:

> I had the same power unit—the same motor—to run my hay baler as I did the machine I used to cut my alfalfa with, and the bishops said they don't want that, they need a separate unit for each one, because—it's just something they didn't want to allow me. So I had to change that around a little bit. I mean, they didn't show me a hard time about it; they just came up and said they'd like to change this around a little bit. They were nice about it. They didn't say, "Get out of here."

In general he is satisfied with the bishops' sensitivity to the farmers' needs. "Every year, we get a little something new."

Articles in *Family Life* regularly extol the virtues of farming as the ideal occupation for the Amish, because it is close to the earth. The Amish are never to lose touch with the earth, which is why their buggies' wheel rims and other farm equipment must not be separated from the ground by a rubber cushion. Farming involves a great deal of manual labor—another desired quality for the Amish, who believe that God intended them to toil in this way. And farming has historically allowed Amish families to be less dependent than mainstream families on the outside world for nourishment, shelter, employment, and training of the next generation. Moreover, on the farm there are always chores for the children to do and many activities that sustain values the Amish respect, such as the importance of hard work.

All Amish children, future farmers or not, are taught to revere farming as inextricably intertwined with the Amish heritage and way of life. However, though there are numerically as many Amish farmers as there were in previous decades, the past thirty to forty years have seen a steady decline in the percentage of Amish youth who take up farming, and a consequent decline in the percentage of Amish children who grow up on farms. In Ohio today, less than 20 percent of adult Amish males make their living from farming.

This means that the vast majority of Ohio Amish men work away from the farm; and the adverse effect on children when they do not grow up in a farm setting, or in a situation where the father is available to them during working hours, riles many Amish, among them the retired farmer and farm equipment manufacturer Gideon F. Stoltzfus. A tall, lank, middle-aged man with great bushy eyebrows shadowing deep-set eyes, Gideon encapsulates his concern in a story he recounts of chatting with a customer in Indiana, a man who had bought specialized planting equipment from him over the years.

During the conversation, the customer told Gideon—rather reluctantly and apologetically—of having stopped hiring Amish youth to plant, harvest, or sell his crops at retail, as he used to do, because the Amish kids were "lying and cheating" and he could no longer depend on them to do their work properly or to be worthy of his trust. Gideon and his customer agreed that the problem could be traced to these being third-generation-off-the-farm kids, who grew up in homes in which the fathers (and grandfathers) were out of the home most of the day and therefore unavailable to teach, train, or discipline the children during working hours. Thus, the abandoning of farmwork has had an unforeseen and regrettable consequence, one that underscores a main reason why the Amish had always construed farming as the ideal occupation—it held the family and the church together.

Anabaptism did not begin solely among farmers, but in the seventeenth century, those Anabaptists who felt most keenly the need for separation from the world were farmers or soon became farmers, and it was at this time that farming became central to the Amish worldview. By the mid–eighteenth century, residing in the mountainous country where Germany and Switzerland intersect, the Amish were almost exclusively farmers and developed a reputation of being very good husbandmen, able to convert the marginal lands to which they had been relegated into productive farms.

Liberal use of manure as fertilizer was one supposed secret of Amish horticultural success. Others include a strictly adhered to schedule of crop rotation and, in modern times, a refusal to use motorized tractors, which, the Amish insist, unduly compact the soil. David Kline, an Amish farmer who is also a writer, cites in a book a university study that confirms what he and other Amish farmers have always known, that soil tilled in the Amish manner can absorb seven times more water than mainstream farms can before it becomes saturated. Moist soil acts as a better germinating environment for crops.

The fertility of the soil, the many sources of water, and the cheapness of land in Lancaster County are what initially attracted the Amish to the New World, along with William Penn's offer to take part in the "holy experiment" of an area devoted to religious freedom. Land-poor in Europe, the Amish leaped at the chance to own good land.

The history of Amish farming in the United States is a story of

ever-increasing density, according to Samuel L. Stoltzfus, a retired
farmer. Seven years ago, he turned his family farm over to a son—
the young farmer in that cold field whom we met while he was
spreading manure. Now Sam, a compact man with large hands,
rimless glasses, and an air of insatiable curiosity, grows horseradish,
manufactures gazebos, and pursues his passion for local history.

Sam discovered from a perusal of church records that the
county was originally carved up into three church districts, each
quite large. In the 1830s, two of these faded, but the third—in
the "Lower Pequea" Amish triangle area of Intercourse, Bird-in-
Hand, and Paradise—continued to grow, not in terms of acreage
but in terms of number of occupants in the district. The increasing density meant that approximately every fifteen years, as more
Amish were born, took up residence in the area, and began farming, the number of church districts in the Pequea had to be doubled. Daughter settlements were also spun off to areas farther
west—the mid-Ohio Wayne and Holmes counties, the northern
Indiana counties, Kansas, Iowa, Missouri, and Illinois, all places
chosen for settlement because they offered good land at low
prices.

The Amish continued to work mainly as farmers in the first
half of the twentieth century, long after most of their rural neighbors had given up farming for other kinds of employment. At the
turn of the century, the distance between the ways of life of the
farming Amish and their non-Amish farming neighbors was not
very large. But as the century wore on, and fewer of their neighbors farmed while the Amish continued to do so, that distance
increased.

"In 1963," Sam recalls, "the price for land in the Lower Pequea
was a thousand dollars an acre; by 1967, it was two thousand dollars an acre. Made a big difference in trying to hold on to a farm
and make a living from it." From that period on, the percentage of
farmers among the Amish in Lancaster County went into decline.

Gideon Stoltzfus observes, "Today most of our young people
aren't interested in investing their time and money, and struggling
every day to make ends meet on a farm, when there is easy

money from outside jobs at their fingertips." Gideon was a farmer for decades before turning over the farm to a son, and his new business has put him in touch with a wide variety of farmers in a half dozen states. More than twenty years ago, while still a full-time farmer, he modified a planting machine to fit the needs of his small farm and of machinery that would be drawn by horses or mules; soon he was responding to the requests of other small farmers who needed such equipment; today, his full-time business is reengineering and repairing planters for hundreds of farmers.

Amish farms have several characteristics that distinguish them from non-Amish farms. They are usually small, they utilize mostly animal power, and, Gideon says, "Amish farmers do the labor-intensive crops that most non-Amish farmers don't want to do." Tobacco, which is more labor-intensive than almost any other crop, was long favored by the Amish for just that reason. The banks that provide mortgages and other loans to the Amish also prefer that the Amish plant tobacco, Sam Stoltzfus points out, since it can always be sold for cash to pay the bank loan.

Labor-saving devices, whether on the farm or in the home, according to the Amish church and to farmers (and fathers of large families) like Sam and Gideon, produce idleness, which becomes an invitation to temptations. Far better then, from the Amish point of view, to plow a field slowly, by means of a team, rather than with a mechanized tractor, even if the task takes longer, because there is value to the farmer's soul—and to his soil—in doing it this way.

But farmers, especially young farmers starting out, need cash. Gideon Stolzfus, always interested in keeping young farmers viable, recommends to them a mix of crops, livestock, and specialty items such as "organic" products that will cushion their income and protect them from vagaries in the weather and in the prices that can be obtained for their regular products. "To farm today, you have to be aware of what's going on in the marketplace," Gideon insists. Crops that in earlier years were appropriate for Amish farmers, such as green peppers, which used to be harvested by hand, can no longer be profitably grown and sold because mechanical pepper pickers have been perfected, enabling non-Amish mechanized farms to undercut the price to the point that the Amish would lose money if they planted peppers to sell for cash.

"Can't run a small farm today unless it's subsidized in some way," Gideon states baldly. "Somebody in the family's got to have a cash job off the farm, or you have to run a small business on the side, or have a low rent for the farm because a relative owns it, or you need a rich uncle helping to pay the bills." He points out that there are committees in various districts that, in effect, act as rich uncles, or as doting lenders, to encourage young Amish to take up farming and to shore up their farms financially during difficult years.

So much emphasis has always been placed on farming in Amish life that, a quarter century ago, both inside and outside observers of the Amish worried that if too many Amish ceased farming, the sect itself would vanish through assimilation into the mainstream culture. That hasn't happened, even though the majority of Amish males of working age in Lancaster, Wayne, Holmes, Geauga, La-Grange, and Elkhart counties now have jobs off the farm. But the pool of potential farmers is continuing to shrink.

"I suppose if my dad had been a farmer, I wouldn't be in the community right now," says Johnny Y, the Cleveland Indians fan and factory worker. "I'd've gone over the hill, done almost anything to get out of being a farmer. Quitting whistle never blows for them, y'know?"

Since his father was not a farmer, nor was his paternal grandfather, Johnny did not have farming in his blood and so had little reason—and no training—to take up the daunting task of starting a farm, or buying one that was already in operation, or even marrying a farmer's daughter and taking over her family's farm, as a few of his friends have done. "Takes two to run a farm," Johnny says. "Lots of girls aren't into that either, anymore."

Tobias K, the Lancaster farmer, agrees with the need to have a wife to help run a farm, but he remains single, his mother doing the chores more usually done by a wife and partner. Now in his late twenties, Tobias says he continues to pursue the ladies, hoping to find a wife, but he "mostly thinks about it now on weekends."

Finding an appropriately capable wife for an Amish farmer is essential, Sam Stoltzfus says. With tongue only slightly in cheek, he suggests that the farmer should evaluate a potential spousal candidate by how she performs on three key tasks. "Not cooking," he says; "anybody can throw something into a pot and cook—but you see how she keeps her garden. That'll provide you with vegetables and such." Number two, "You watch her saddle up a horse and hitch up a buggy." If the lady can master working with the buggy horses, she will presumably "not be bothering you when she wants to go marketing or visiting." Three, "You watch how she takes care of her sister's children, to see how she'll do with yours."

No wonder Tobias is still single.

Virtually no young men leave the Amish sect and take up mechanized—non-Amish—farming. "If you want to grow up to be a farmer, or for that matter, a farmer's wife, you might as well be Amish," said a semiretired Ohio farmer. "Fits in better with your work than trying to make your fortune at it and keep up with the Joneses." His observation is echoed by statistics reported by Ronald Jager in a recent book titled *The Fate of Family Farming*: 90 percent of the family farms in the United States earn incomes of less than $20,000 each.

The state of Pennsylvania, for instance, contains 58,000 farms, but only 10,000 to 15,000 of these "provide a living to the owners," according to a recent report; Amish farms, including the 2,000 in Lancaster County, make up a large percentage of the state's profitable farms. One must wonder if, in another few generations, a disproportionately high fraction of all America's remaining small, family farms will be Amish.

Amish family farms are able to stay afloat, while non-Amish ones struggle, principally because Amish farm costs are considerably lower than those of comparable-size non-Amish farms: the Amish farmer seldom has to pay employees; he uses equipment that is less expensive to buy and maintain—horses or mules to pull his manure spreader instead of a $75,000 tractor; he does not need to pay high insurance premiums for coverage that would replace his facilities if they burned or were lost to a flood or hurricane, since he has Amish "mutual aid" assurance at very low cost; and he tends not to be paying off a sizable mortgage for his grazing land. He does pay as much in real estate taxes as his non-Amish neighbors do. He tithes to his church, which most non-Amish do not. Finally, the Amish farmer has a lower personal overhead—he makes no payments for cars, televisions, or other electrically powered equipment, or for college tuition—which means that each earned dollar goes further in buying his necessities and small luxuries.

Non-Amish farmers sometimes charge that it is the lower overhead costs of the Amish, more than secrets such as liberal use of manure, that permit Amish farms to be profitable. But a recent study of Amish farms in Lancaster concluded that while young Amish could get started as dairymen if the price of milk was reasonable, and could pay off their investment in cattle and equipment in seven years, "no farm could make payments to also cover real estate debt in the initial years of the operation."

Tobias K, like other dairy farmers, Amish and non-Amish, has continual problems with his herd. Fifty cows produce about a million pounds of milk each year. Expenses for feed, for keeping the cows healthy, and for machinery to extract, store, and cool the milk can offset most of the money that dairymen obtain for their milk. Between December 2001 and July 2003, for example, the country's dairy farmers received, on average, less money for their milk than it cost to produce.

To make money, the cows also must remain healthy. If one cow in a herd has mastitis, a common bovine disease, this will show up in tests of the milk that are made by the driver of the tank truck. The samples cannot be analyzed until the truck's load is about to be poured into the milk factory's larger tanks. At that point, if the milk is even slightly compromised, it must be dumped, and the farmer must pay for the entire truckload, which may consist of his own milk as well as that of a couple of other farms.

Another problem for Amish farmers, especially those who have dairy herds and also raise some cereal crops, as Tobias does, has arisen because of their liberal use of manure. Some years ago the runoff from fields (and from privies, or outhouses) was discovered to be a contributing cause to the compromising of Chesapeake Bay. The federal government threatened to shut down some Amish farms unless they curbed their use of manure; a formula for how much manure a farmer could spread per acre was worked out. The regulating of manure use is an added expense for Amish farmers and brings more inspectors in to examine their operations, which they do not like. Privies are less of a problem today because the Lancaster Old Order Amish have willingly accepted indoor plumbing and have agreed to abide by regulations to put in septic tanks and clear the septic fields at regular intervals.

Recent studies by Ohio State University agricultural extension agents revealed that the Amish have not been as successful managers of their manure as they might be. OSU has worked out innovative ideas that yield better results and mesh well with traditional Amish methods—such as staggering the times at which manure is put on fields to be planted with alfalfa rather than corn, or with silage corn rather than corn for human consumption. Similar innovations include "intensive grazing" methods to direct cattle to particular pastures on dairy farms rather than simply turning them out to grazing land in random rotation.

The farming life is more complex than it used to be and still hard, but despite the hassles Tobias K continues to tend his farm and to remain within the church. Eventually, he is certain, he will find a mate and raise a family.

Sometimes he thinks of leaving the church. He believes that most Amish entertain similar thoughts, usually in their twenties, a few years after they have married and settled down. "They think, 'Well, what am I doing here? Maybe there is a better life out there than being Amish.' It wouldn't be hard to leave. You just pack your bags and go." Tobias says he would leave if he met the right girl, even if she was from a less strict denomination. He has two friends who did just that—followed their hearts to their intend-eds' non-Amish churches, much to the consternation of their families.

But Tobias has no inclination to escape the church or the farm, because every time heretic thoughts hit him, he recalls what he has heard from friends who left and joined other churches: that life in those new churches "comes down to the same thing, you still have your good days and your bad days . . . And I think, 'Well, if it isn't any better out there, why would I leave?' "

Sam Stoltzfus figures that his son, age twenty-four, has now, after seven years of being principally responsible for the family farm, accumulated enough experience to be a successful farmer—because he's been through thick and, more important, through thin. The latter category includes surviving an unexpectedly dev-astating hurricane named Isabel that in September 2003 severely damaged the area's corn crop, tearing stalks in two or twisting them into unworkable knots. Farmers had to act quickly to har-vest what corn was left in the fields or risk losing it all. The longer corn remains unharvested, the drier it becomes and the less prac-tical it is for use as feed for farm animals. Moreover, when farm-ers harvest less corn, there is less available to be bought, and the price of substitute feed for the animals skyrockets.

Non-Amish farmers were able to bring in the damaged corn by means of mechanical "croppers" that they either owned or could rent from others who owned the machines, which retail for upward of $200,000 apiece. But Amish farmers were constrained by the *ordnung* from using such mechanical assistance; they were permitted to harvest their corn only by means of horse-drawn "binders," which take much longer to work through an acre. Thus, the hurricane presented a crisis for the Amish farmers. A convocation of the bishops, after consultation with the farmers and a state agricultural service agent, decreed a one-time dispensation for Amish farmers to rent the heavy, mechanical croppers necessary to salvaging their corn crops.

A headquarters was set up in the Gordonville Fire and Ambulance Company building, about a quarter mile from the Stoltzfus farm, and a three-phone bank was established as the core of a new organization called Harvest Aid, tasked with matching up Amish and non-Amish farmers in need of the croppers with those who owned croppers and were willing to rent them out or operate them in someone else's field. With a limited number of croppers available, scheduling was imperative. Retired Amish farmers manned the phones, conversing in Dutch with their Amish neighbors and in English with other farmers. A cropper owner-operator, a non-Amish from Bird-in-Hand, worked around the clock, employing various crews to harvest the crops. Because the fields were in what the businessman described as "horrible condition," his cropper machines were able to clear only forty to fifty acres a day, rather than the seventy to one hundred that they could have managed if the corn had been less tangled. By mid-October, the close of the window of opportunity, most of the corn was in, though some was lost because the croppers could not get to it.

The Amish farmers were grateful for the dispensation that enabled them to rent the croppers but began to wonder why they could not regularly have access to such machinery. "Why couldn't it be like cars?" an Amish farmer asked rhetorically. "We can't own cars, but we can ride in 'em if they're operated by non-Amish. We could do the same with the croppers—rent 'em when we need 'em."

The church has been struggling with the problem of whether to permit more modern farm equipment. "Will sanctioning a few pieces of equipment so the farmer can make a living have as adverse an effect as having the fathers driven off the farm?" an Amish minister asks in *Family Life*. To him, the solution is clear: assist the farmer by permitting him to purchase the equipment with which to compete properly, and in the long run you will also help the church.

The community and its would-be farmers also have to contend with soaring prices for land in the long-settled Amish areas. When 80- to 120-acre farms are offered for sale in Lancaster, these days they can fetch a million dollars or more. "For that price," a farmer confided, "I could sell the old place, divide the profits among my three children, and give each a stake big enough to buy a farm in Kentucky or somewhere's more sparsely populated." Such a sale and distribution would probably also disperse the family, which is why he has not done it—yet. But others have. Old Amish farms are often carved up into 4- to 10-acre parcels, some of which are bought by young Amish couples. As a correspondent for *The Diary* observed, "It seems these 5 acre plots are ideal for an Amish day laborer looking for a home site." A farm sliced into smaller lots can bring as much as ten thousand dollars per acre.

To encourage continued farming in older communities, the church has had to help individual members purchase farms that might be otherwise sold off for development, and to assist in other ways. On December 30, 2003, there was an Amish barn raising on a modest-size farm in Baumgardner, just six miles from the city of Lancaster; it was picturesque, with what a reporter for the *Lancaster New Era* called the "controlled frenzy" of swarms of black-garbed men working on all phases of the project. The reporter also remarked that the "image" of barn raising, "cherished" in the area, had been "immortalized in the film *Witness*." But this barn raising was more than a quaint and picturesque event. Usually, barn raisings are done to replace structures damaged by disaster; in this instance, the Amish were helping one of their own transfer his operations from his old farm in Strasburg, three miles east, to this new location to prevent the sale into development of this prime acreage, which is within easy commuting distance to Lancaster City. The Amish in Lancaster County have helped rescue nearly two hundred farms since 1980, and the county leads the nation in percentage of total farmland preserved; between 1994 and 2001, for every acre lost to development there, two were preserved. However, Lancaster is still losing farmland five times faster than any other county in the state. Every farm saved by the Amish helps to preserve the rural character of the county and their own way of life.

The high price of farmland and the crowded nature of the long-settled Amish centers, along with their high tax bills, have forced young would-be farmers who have no acreage to inherit toward a new frontier: played-out land that can be bought for relatively low prices because it is too far from cities to be snapped up for development and because other, mainstream farmers seem unwilling to put in the work necessary to make the acres profitable.

"It's like being a pioneer," says Jacob R, a twenty-nine-year-old farmer from Holmes County who moved his family to a hard-scrabble relocation area, southeastern Ashtabula County, Ohio, near Lake Erie, and bought a small farm for a song.

Jacob is a large man with a ruddy complexion; his blond beard is still growing in. He points out that Amish who migrate from the long-settled areas do so for a combination of reasons, not just for the cheaper farmland. "Some want to get away from their old church districts," he says with a smile. This is not because those districts are too strict—rather, it is because they are too liberal, and some men want to begin life with their families in a new area, with compatriots who are determined that their district's *ordnung* will be less lax than it is back home. Tougher rules seem to go hand in hand with the more difficult farming challenges.

New Amish settlers have been arriving in Ashtabula since 1991, buying up old farms that had been deemed unprofitable or whose soil was exhausted. One man was able to trade in his 32-acre farm near State College, Pennsylvania, for a 207-acre one in Ashtabula; a second man, from New York State, was able to double the acreage he had been tilling yet cut his taxes by three-quarters.

Others, including some three hundred people from Lancaster, a dozen families, have more recently begun a similar migration to Grant County, in southwest Wisconsin. By early 2004, a weekly moving van and shuttle service between Grant and Lancaster had come into existence, and a realtor in Grant claimed to have fifty Amish buyers for additional farms—if he could find existing farms whose owners were willing to sell.

"I got enough acreage so's I can keep twice the number of dairy here that I had back home," Jacob says, "and my wife's selling strawberries and cherries for cash, too. Not as much competition here as there was back home for berries, either." For assistance with the cows, both the milking and the feeding, Jacob relies on his bevy of children, all still at home. "We're about breaking even," he confesses but adds, "This time next year, if everything works out like it should, we'll be buying a washing machine."

His farm is relatively primitive, like many of the Ashtabula farms that the Amish have taken over. Some were so backward that the county now has worries about whether they have adequate septic fields to take care of the "gray water" used in washing clothes and other farm tasks. But oats, corn, hay, strawberries, and other cash crops grow reasonably well, and the R's and the two dozen other Amish families in their neck of the woods are gradually improving their farms and their financial situations. "Everybody likes building something up," Jacob says. "Feels like you're doing the right thing by the land and by Jesus."

8

"Working Away"

An Amish boy of eight walks along the snow-banked, fairly narrow shoulder of a busy state highway near Spring Garden, Pennsylvania, in the late afternoon of a relatively mild January weekday, trailing a red wagon loaded with two spent propane fuel canisters. He wears a black peacoat, dark pants, mud boots, and a pullover cap; cars and semi tractor-trailers whiz by at fifty miles per hour, and he is continually buffeted by the strong gusts of wind they stir as they pass. It is a struggle for him to keep the wagon from upending into a ditch. He is unsupervised, quite alone on this errand, and in danger from the hurtling trucks, but he appears not to mind. He tells a stranger that his destination is about a mile away, beyond many acres of open fields and pasturage: a gas stove exchange and repair depot located in a roadside home, where he will trade in the spent canisters and receive two filled ones to haul back to his house. He says that he likes this chore and does it every Wednesday after school; the round trip will take him about an hour; he adds that if he did not do it, another family member would have to, and they all have a lot of other work to do.

In the early morning, before full light, the twelve-year-old boy lays his socks atop the gas-fired stove of the small farmhouse to warm before he pulls them on. Outside, snow covers the fields. Dark-haired, dark-eyed, fair-skinned, and slim, very much the prepubescent youth, he is reluctant to leave the warmth of the kitchen or his mother's side as she chats with a stranger, though the school day will be starting soon and he must be at the school on time. He wears suspenders to hold up his pants, which tells other Amish his age: he is not yet old enough to wear the same clothing as teenage males. He packs two concessions to modernity: his in-line skates—no help going uphill to the school but a pleasure to look forward to for the downhill-to-home ride—and a frozen pizza, which is put into his lunch pail. The heating stove at school, similar to the one at home, has racks on top so that he can defrost the pizza and the other students can warm their lunches.

He likes classes very much, he says, enjoys being a "scholar," and he has just one more year to go. What will he do after he graduates at age fourteen? "Don't know," he answers, his eyes displaying a faint hint of fear. Is there anything he would like to do? He shrugs negatively. He knows that he will not be going on in school and also understands that he will have to work, but he does not know at what trade or business. Though his family lives on a farm, farming does not provide the bulk of the family's livelihood. He has little interest in being a farmer.

"Maybe I'll work with my dad," the boy offers at last; the father has a business producing indoor furniture. If not that, what? He shrugs again. Does he find the furniture business interesting? "Yeah, I guess."

Matt E and Lorina L, the happy couple of teenagers who are enjoying their car and the party scene while they try to decide what to do with their lives, are counting up all the jobs they have had since they left school at fourteen. Matt has held four jobs at a tourist restaurant, "dishwasher, busser, stock boy, and host"; for two years he worked at the restaurant during the summer and at a furniture-manufacturing shop in the winter; then at sixteen he

"went full-time" at the furniture facility. He began at an RV factory before he turned eighteen; he was not permitted, then, to use
power tools because he was underage, so he "cut parts" until he
turned eighteen and could work on the line, where the salary is
much higher. He is amused that his father is now at the furniture-
making factory, and he has taken an RV factory job of the sort his
father held for thirty years: "He just started a little bit before I
quit. We just kind of switched actually."

Lorina also left school after the eighth grade, was not needed at
home to care for younger siblings, and had to find paying work
elsewhere. Employers in the Shipshewana area are used to hiring
Amish boys and girls in their midteens. Lorina found a job at
Tiffany's in Topeka, a buffet restaurant that caters to local Amish
and English families. After working at the register and doing
kitchen tasks for two years, she was asked to try waitressing. She
recalls, "I never wanted to be a waitress. I was scared. But then, I
wanted to be," because of the good tips, "and now I like it." Currently, she works as a cashier at a hardware store during the day
and at Tiffany's as a waitress in the early evenings. She has no idea
what she will be doing in two or three years, insofar as employment goes.

In north-central Indiana, along the huge interstate, U.S. Route 80,
which runs east-west in a straight line across the northern edge of
the state, are dozens of manufacturing plants for recreational vehicles (RVs), trailers, "towables," mobile homes, and prefabricated
"modular" homes. Located on the sides of parallel though smaller
state highways, five to twenty miles south of I-80, are more such
plants, as well as smaller ones that service this industry by manufacturing curtains and blinds for trailers, or plumbing or cabinets
specifically designed for the relatively small spaces in mobile residences. These facilities produce more than half of the RVs made
in the United States, and their brands are well known: Coachmen,
Sportsman, Redman, Double Eagle, Jayco, Haulmark, Forest
River. They sell for anywhere from a few thousand dollars for a

small "towable" that provides no sleeping bunks to rolling palaces that sleep eight people and retail for $80,000 to $100,000.

In these assembly plants, the Amish and the formerly Amish make up a large percentage of the workforce. Statistics on precisely what percentage are hard to come by, but the latest figures on Amish households show that 53 percent of household heads younger than age sixty-five work in factories; their number includes 71 percent of all the male Amish heads of households under the age of thirty-five.

In David K. Shipler's recent book *The Working Poor*, he pinpoints why many workers cannot lift themselves out of poverty: they lack a driving "work ethic" and the "soft skills [of] punctuality, diligence, and a can-do attitude." Amish-raised factory workers embody these soft skills and are enthusiastically sought by employers. A management supervisor at an RV plant says that Amish-raised employees "come in on time and work hard; they don't take sick days; and they show up on holidays when everybody else wants off."

One of those young, Amish-raised employees at an RV factory is Phil T, now twenty-one, the son of a factory hand legendary for his hard work, that father who regularly pitted his sons against one another in competitions while needling them that coming in second meant you were "first loser."

When at sixteen Phil left his home in Missouri, he made his way to northern Indiana to stay with an older brother. Shortly, with a third brother, they signed on as a construction crew and were sent to Texas to build hog barns. Phil and his brothers, plus a quartet of other men, were able to erect a several-story, 240-by-84-foot barn in three days, doing all of the various wood and metal construction tasks necessary. He and his brothers did good work, Phil says, until the boss's wife accused him of calling her a "bitch," though he hadn't done so. The realization that such a little thing—and a false thing—could set off the boss irritated him and his brothers, and they promptly quit and returned to Indiana. Their parents followed, by now disenchanted with Missouri or perhaps not wanting to continue to live so far away from their grown children.

The brothers rented a house in Middlebury and took up a lifestyle that included motorcycles and deer hunting. Phil walked into the RV factory, announced he was John's son, and the manager gave him a job. The work was assembly line but not uninteresting or overly repetitive; each worker had to perform multiple tasks within the cavernous assembly buildings and could feel that he or she had a real hand in the finished product. Phil worked hard, though at a relatively low wage level, in part because he had been promised a promotion to "swing man" if he remained at the factory for a full year. When that hiring anniversary came, he was told that there were no swing man positions available at the time. He quit and moved to Detroit, where, still a teenager, he found work "doing 'drop buries,' that's where we bury the cable underground for a satellite," he explains. He stayed six months, then moved to Atlanta for a similar job.

One brother was convicted of stealing and sent to prison, though the other stayed on the straight path, taking factory jobs and slowly climbing promotion ladders. In Atlanta, Phil deliberately stayed out of touch with his family for a while; then he phoned a brother and left a callback number, and within a few days his older sister reached him with the news that their father "had some sickness but nobody knew what it was."

Upon learning of his father's illness, Phil quits his job and immediately returns to Indiana.

John T is diagnosed with Crohn's disease, a digestive tract disorder in which the lower bowel is unable to metabolize certain foods, such as potatoes. "Of course, Dad being Dad—he's stubborn like the rest of us—he tries to eat potatoes and then he has to go to the hospital again."

Phil decides he can have a closer relationship with the family so long as his parents agree to tolerate his not yet having joined the church and the possibility that he may never do so. Several of the T sons and daughters have joined, but two left after joining;

the family is forced to shun them, which is hard on everybody. To avoid losing more children to the outside world, the parents are not too tough on Phil and the others who have not made up their minds. Nonetheless, Phil soon has the inevitable fight with his father, and they do not speak for many months.

But Phil is able to rejoin the workforce at the RV factory. Getting the job is easy; the family reputation still precedes him. As his father was a very good worker, so are his brothers—at one RV factory, Phil says, two people were fired and one of his brothers was hired to do the work of both former employees.

Since he is over eighteen, Phil is now eligible for more strenuous work and higher pay. As would any other new hiree, he starts at just above minimum wage, with the promise of more when he proves he can do the job. Most people, he says, take a few months to make the jump, but, like his brother before him, Phil does it in a few days and is then "put on rate," bumped up to a significantly higher hourly wage. Rate wages at the factory start at twenty dollars and can reach thirty to forty dollars an hour for the most skilled and productive workers. In other factories, the employees can also make as much as a thousand dollars a week but are paid on a different basis: by piecework, with everyone sharing in the pool of money allotted for a completed unit. The workers have a quota, and once they fill it, they can choose either to go home early or to continue making units and some added cash. These RV industry jobs, whether on rate or by piecework, are the highest paying ones available in a radius of a hundred miles; Elkhart County boasts in a brochure that more people commute into the county for jobs than commute out of it.

The work at the factory is exhausting, but Phil can do the tasks, and to the management, nothing else matters—certainly not whether he has a high school diploma or a GED. Alongside him in the factory are Mexicans who came to Indiana originally to work in the fields, and ex-convicts, some still on parole.

Phil knows that few workers continue at top rate at these factories when they are past fifty-five, because, while the work requires some skill, the most important assets are the strength and stamina to push those RV assemblies, on ball-bearing-wheeled platforms, from stage to stage, to sequence the supplies properly, and to do line tasks such as soldering and bolting on various parts. Many male floor workers wear broad weight-lifter belts around their waists to prevent their backs from failing.

Riding his motorcycle after work or on weekends, Phil at twenty-one finds that he is meeting increasing numbers of Amish young men going through *rumspringa* and learns that he has more in common with them than he does with the non-Amish who have made up the bulk of his pals since he left Missouri.

Over the next year, he allows his home in Middlebury to become a crash pad for visiting young Amish in *rumspringa*; Emma M, his childhood friend, stays for a while. Joann H knows where to find things in the kitchen. Faron Y is a frequent visitor. Phil's place turns into a choice location for weekend-long parties where roomfuls of Amish-born youth can sleep off their excesses before heading back home on Sundays or directly to work on Mondays. Phil is friendly with the local police—who generally are not very tough on Amish kids having a wild time—and alerts them to parties at his house that he will be supervising; he also posts signs explicitly forbidding drinking by minors, more to protect himself from liability than because he is opposed to underage drinking; he has "no problem" with kids drinking and using recreational drugs so long as the users keep themselves under control. Phil does forbid fighting at the parties, and if an English guest starts a fracas at one party, he is barred from attending the next. Another rule of Phil's forbids fraternizing between the houseguests, because he knows that Amish young men do not treat women well—he admits to not having done so well himself in that regard—and doesn't feel that his female friends "need to be put through that kind of situation."

These large parties are the furthest reach of Phil's rebelliousness; six months after the party period, he decides to marry the non-Amish lass with whom he has been keeping company for a while, and to settle down. He also plans a concerted effort to stay with one manufacturing company and rise in it, as his brothers did before they left to found their own businesses.

In five years, maybe ten, he hopes to be "living the good life," to have a home worth three-quarters of a million dollars, a child—he does not want more than one—leisure time, and the ability "to buy whatever I want to buy." To accomplish these mainstream goals, he will have to be successful in work, but he is fairly certain that he can be, thanks to the lessons his father instilled in him during his youth; whether or not those are Amish tenets he does not know, but they are a part of his makeup that he has no intention, and perhaps no possibility, of rejecting.

"To fear God and to love work are the first lessons they teach their children," Dr. Benjamin Rush wrote of the Amish in 1789, adding that they were an "industrial and frugal people." At that time, the fear of God was more common than it is among today's Americans, so that was not the aspect Rush found so notable about the Amish; rather, it was their love of work, an attribute that may be even more remarkable now than it was then, because the locus of their paid employment is no longer the family home and farm.

According to the sociologist Joseph F. Donnermeyer and the demographer Elizabeth C. Cooksey, whose research encompasses nine thousand Amish households in three of the largest Amish areas of the country, around three-quarters of all adult Amish males today "work away." Two generations ago, three-quarters were farmers. Now the most usual nonfarming job is as a woodworker, the second most usual is factory hand, and there are three to four times as many Amish factory hands and woodworkers as farmers.

In 1972, when the Supreme Court in *Wisconsin vs. Yoder* permitted the Amish to pull their children out of school after the eighth grade and to establish their own schools, which would not need to teach advanced subjects, the Court's decision was predicated on Amish boys and girls becoming farmers and farm housewives, careers for which rudimentary abilities in reading, writing, and arithmetic were deemed sufficient. Today an eighth-grade education is less adequate to the future tasks of an Amish life—a situation foreseen by Associate Justice William O. Douglas in his dissent. Douglas was "troubled" by the likelihood that an Amish child might have his or her "entire life stunted and deformed" if not permitted to obtain advanced education:

> He may want to be a pianist or an astronaut or an ocean-ographer. To do so he will have to break from the Amish tradition . . . If a parent keeps his child out of school beyond the grade school, then the child will be forever barred from entry into the new and amazing world of diversity that we have today.

Douglas's prescient observation sums up a major problem for Amish youth: the lack of advanced education leaves them unprepared academically and technologically for the jobs available, and it seriously hampers their chances of leaving the Amish sect should they desire to do so.

Employment problems for Amish youngsters commence upon graduation from public school eighth grade or from Amish school. They run smack into restrictions on the employment of children that date back to the Progressive era, when rules were imposed to prevent exploitation of children in factories and sweatshops. The Fair Labor Standards Act expressly prohibited children under fourteen from work in any manufacturing business (except farming), those under sixteen from operating heavy machinery, and those under eighteen from toiling in particularly dangerous workplaces, such as sawmills. In the wake of the *Wisconsin v. Yoder* decision, the Department of Labor relaxed the work rules for fourteen- to fifteen-year-old Amish, permitting them to work more hours than other teens and during daytime hours, when other teens were in school.

Apprenticeships used to be the norm in Amish communities. These were based on the farming way of life but more fundamentally on a style of learning to work that all civilizations had used for thousands of years. The Amish still like and use apprentice-ships, but with fewer farm jobs available, they must find other work for their teenagers.

Sam Stoltzfus of Gordonville has a handful of sons and only one family farm to run, which one son now operates. How to employ his other sons? On a hot August afternoon, I found two of them working with him on a new gazebo in his workshop, which is on the grounds of the farm. While his twelve-year-old mixes paint, Sam challenges his fourteen-year-old to choose the most appropriate spot for a latch that can hold the shed door open. After a moment of thought, the lad points to a spot, is re-warded with a curt nod, and then he uses the power drill to sink holes for the latch. Is the boy glad to have graduated from his Amish school this past May? "Yes," he says excitedly, "but this is the *real* school."

Not all teenage boys have such a fortunate apprenticeship awaiting them at home. "Suppose I have a fifteen-year-old," says Dennis L of Shipshewana, the grandfather who has toiled at many trades during his life but who now finishes furniture at a manu-facturing shop. "I have one acre here. There's no farm or house chores for a fifteen-year-old boy to do here, and if I'm working at the furniture place during the day, there's nothing to keep him here—so he goes out, and who knows what will happen." Dennis grew up on a family farm; in his teens he migrated seamlessly from chores to farmwork, then from farming to blacksmithing, and later to carpentry and construction, eventually becoming a general contractor. Most of the Amish kids around Shipshewana do none of those tasks, he points out. Rather, they "end up work-ing in the RV factories. But you can't take the good jobs in those factories until you're eighteen. So the years between the time you graduate eighth grade and when you start at the factory tend to be difficult."

Dennis has a possible solution for those difficult years: he wants the Amish community to offer vocational training classes, to "make the youth think about future careers, even when they're in school yet." Such classes would not contravene the Amish prohibition on higher learning because the knowledge taught would be not worldly philosophy or useless literary analysis but training in blacksmithing, dental technology (for the girls), bookkeeping, and construction trades. Classes would be succeeded by formal apprenticeships designed to help youth remain in those fields even after they reach eighteen and can seek work in the factories at higher wages. At the moment, however, Dennis's vocational training dream is still in the planning stages.

The farm equipment manufacturer Gideon Stoltzfus of White Horse, in Lancaster County, has also put thought into the problem. He acknowledges that certain Amish teens whose fathers do not have their own workshops may have trouble finding jobs because they lack the proper technical training. "Some of us are aware," he says, "that our kids don't get enough education [in the Amish schools] if they're going to go into business rather than into farming." He and other elders are reexamining the adequacy and relevance of current Amish schooling practices to a culture where most jobs are going to be off the farm.

Gideon believes strongly that teaching Amish children the value and the joy of work, and providing them with work at or near the home—where their fathers can be continually involved in their lives—is "key to the preservation of the Amish way of life." He argues that every task, no matter how small, drab, or menial, can reinforce the work ethic; in the workshop where he reengineers mechanical planters so they can be pulled by horses or mules, his fourteen-year-old daughter is often found, bagging spare parts.

Gideon "wonders why the United States has to resort to importing agricultural workers from Mexico when so many people here are unemployed." Part of the reason, he charges, is that some of our unemployed are unwilling to do the work that is available, the backbreaking, poor-paying labor of agricultural harvesting— the kind of work the Amish routinely do, and as routinely teach their children to do. This is part of his charge that mainstream America has a two-faced attitude toward allowing and encouraging young people to work. "They allow kids as young as sixteen to operate very dangerous machines—cars," he points out, "but yet they don't want to allow our Amish youngsters of the same age to work in our shops? I have a problem with that."

A young man who had an even more severe problem with just that is Daniel Smucker of Narvon, a town some twenty miles north of White Horse. Working at his father's harness-manufacturing business one day in 1998, as he had done all of his life, Daniel at age fifteen was disturbed by investigators from the U.S. Department of Labor. Acting on a complaint from an under-age worker who had been employed for a while at Smucker's Harness Company before being fired, the Labor Department soon charged Daniel's father, Moses Smucker, with violations of the labor law for having wrongfully employed not only the com-plainant but also Daniel, his thirteen-year-old sister, and a fourth teenager. Moses Smucker was fined $8,300 and ordered to stop employing underage children in the "dangerous" environment of presses and other machinery used to work leather.

Investigations into Amish manufacturing businesses had begun years earlier, after the reporting of a rash of injuries in sawmills. Sawmills, Amish or not, have always been among the most dan-gerous employment locations; injuries occur there at twice the rate of any other industrial facilities. In 1995, the Department of Labor forbade the employment in sawmills of anyone under the age of eighteen and had fined some Amish sawmill operators for employing their sons, nephews, and neighbors' sons. One was fined twenty thousand dollars for letting neighbors' sons load lumber onto a slow-moving belt. He paid the fine, and other Amish, the owners of woodworking shops and shed manufactur-ers, paid similar though lower fines. But Moses Smucker decided to fight what he characterized as "the government trying to take away my rights and my children's rights to be Amish."

Smucker is a bear of a man with large hands, a loud and deep bass voice, sparkling black eyes, a gray-flecked beard, and rather longish hair for an Amish man. He is a chain smoker of little ci-gars, and his tiny office in the harness company manufacturing and retail facility is impregnated with their scent; a dachshund near his feet is a favored companion; the phone console that he uses has several lines.

Daniel had been around the harness shop since he was a toddler, had worked there part-time when he was in school and full-time since finishing school at fourteen. He preferred spending time at the shop to being at home. Moses hoped someday to turn the business over to him and his younger son. His thirteen-year-old daughter worked as a cashier after school and on Saturdays, and Smucker's youngest child, four, was often in the shop, dragging her security blanket and a stuffed toy as she wandered among the leather-working machines, the honed knives, and other equipment.

Moses himself had been only ten in 1962, when his father began the harness shop adjoining the family farm near Churchtown, not far from the Pennsylvania Turnpike in the eastern portion of the state. "Nothing to it," Smucker recalls. "We simply opened our doors and started. Didn't put up a sign or anything—people started coming to us." In 1970, when his father died in a truck accident, the farm had to be sold, and Moses decided to try to make his living from the harness business. He did not like farming and felt he was not suited to it, although, he says, "I do like horses."

His harness products were good, his business sense was acute, and his enterprise expanded steadily; by the 1990s it was grossing several million dollars a year. It had become a fixture in Narvon, along busy Route 23, which courses diagonally across Lancaster County from northeast to southwest, through a district full of Amish farms and other small businesses. By this time, as well, most of Smucker's customers were non-Amish; his products dress the draft horses in Budweiser commercials and are in use at harness tracks and fancy riding stables across the world. He employs more than twenty people, about half of them Amish. Moses contends that he can hire only workers whom he has trained, since it takes a year to teach someone the various leather-working tasks.

Although at home Moses does not make use of electricity from the grid and has no telephone, in his business he uses most of the tools available to a mainstream manufacturer, marketing his products via an 800 phone number, colorful yearly catalogs, and an Internet Web site, the last of which is, as he puts it, "kept at arm's length"—as the *ordnung* insists—by having it maintained by their non-Amish auditing firm. The Smucker Harness line includes hundreds of products, from brass sleigh bells to the most intricate leather harnesses, some of which cost thousands of dollars.

When the government sued Smucker, he decided to hire a lawyer and seek publicity. Hoping to "shame the government into dropping the case," he told his story to local reporters, stressing his outrage that the government would attempt to interfere with training his sons in the family business and emphasizing his belief that this was threatening the entire Amish way of life. The stories ran, and, he recalls, "Next thing I know, I get a phone call from something called *Good Morning America*, wanting to know if I can come to New York City, stay in a hotel, and go on their ABC television—all at their expense. I told them I couldn't do that and hung up. No sooner do I get off than my secretary here tells me CNN's on the phone."

Shortly, the story went around the world; a friend sent Smucker an Australian clipping about it. What caught the media's attention was the notion of a case featuring religious freedom versus overzealous government regulation.

Representative Joe Pitts, a Republican whose congressional district includes most of Lancaster County, introduced a bill in the House of Representatives to exempt the Amish from some child labor law restrictions. "Teenagers use the same equipment in shop classes and vocational classes in high schools," Pitts argued. "Why shouldn't they be able to use them when being supervised by their fathers?" He gathered support from other members of Congress whose districts contained substantial numbers of Amish and Mennonites.

Now the federal government began to negotiate with Smucker. "Their first offer was that I should pay half the fines and they wouldn't keep after me. We said no. Their second offer was I should pay a dollar for each offense, and we said no to that, too, because that would mean I was admitting I'd broken a law."

Hearings on the potential exemption were held. Christ K. Blank of Gap, Pennsylvania, national chairman for the Old Order Amish Steering Committee, told a congressional committee, "We believe that forced idleness [of our teenagers] to be detrimental to our long-standing Amish way of raising our children and teaching them to become good productive citizens." Other Amish witnesses told stories of teens who had gone to work in Amish and non-Amish businesses and had been fired and sent home, in tears, when government inspectors threatened their employers with fines.

A Republican-controlled House of Representatives passed the exemption bill, but a companion bill ran into trouble in committee in the Democratic-controlled Senate, where Senator Edward Kennedy of Massachusetts emphasized points made by labor unions and others concerned with child labor, who contended that any weakening of the child labor laws would damage the government's ability to prevent exploitation of children in the workplace. The acting administrator of the Labor Department's Wage and Hour Division also testified that Amish employment of children gave Amish factories an unfair advantage over factories that strictly adhere to the existing labor laws and consequently have to pay workers more per hour than Amish teenagers are paid. Comparison pay charts showed that wages and fringes, the noncash benefits for workers, were indeed higher in non-Amish manufacturing places than in Amish ones doing similar work.

One young man, raised Amish in Ohio, sent a letter to the committee charging that he and other underage Amish teenagers had been forced to work in their relatives' commercial operations, in dangerous situations, at what he characterized as very low pay.

"One thing to operate a big business, another to make a profit," Moses Smucker grumbles in answer to a question about how his business is doing. As have other harness manufacturers, he has introduced a line of plastic products that look, feel, and perform like leather but cost less. The rising price of the leather he purchases in

bulk from a tannery in western Pennsylvania has made it necessary to create alternative products that customers can afford. The
cost of materials is one factor in his profit-and-loss picture, but, as
in most manufacturing and retail businesses, labor costs make up
the most significant fraction of the total.

Taking Smucker's self-report of his pay scale, $15 an hour, and
of having more than twenty employees, his labor costs would be
between $750,000 and $1 million per year. An increase in wages,
to an average of $20 per hour, would boost Smucker's labor costs
more than $250,000 a year. If he is, as he contends, barely prof-
itable at current wage levels, increases to those wages might put
his business into the red. Employment of teenagers at less than his
top hourly rate may be what makes the difference between a
profit and a loss.

While the exemption bill was dying in committee in the Senate, in 1999 and 2000, the suit against Smucker continued. He still
refused to admit wrongdoing or to pay even the smallest of fines.
"Finally, they just dropped the suit so I would go away and stop
making a stink," he recalls with a smile that conveys bemusement
at the situation as well as satisfaction at having beaten the government. The Labor Department did warn him that he was to employ only his own children in the harness shop, not those of other
Amish. "I didn't really agree to that," Smucker says, "but so far it
hasn't come up. The last fellow I hired was a retired farmer."

The issue of the exemption for Amish teens was reintroduced
in the House by Representative Pitts, and once more it passed but
was blocked in the Senate. The third try was in 2003, after Re-
publicans gained control of both Houses of Congress as well as
the presidency; Pitts's bill was matched in the Senate by one introduced by Pennsylvania's Arlen Specter, who told journalists that
he had worked in his father's salvage yard when young and that
Amish workplaces were no more dangerous than that. The bill
would permit Amish children aged fourteen to seventeen to work
in various manufacturing and retail enterprises, though only at a
"sufficient distance" from dangerous machinery, and only under
close adult supervision.

In committee hearings, critics of the proposed exemption pointed out that the First Amendment forbids Congress to make any law regarding the establishment of religion—and that a religious-based exemption for the Amish had the effect of the government favoring one religion over another, which, in their view, was unconstitutional. There was some sentiment that the Amish were unduly extending the notion of religious freedom to cover economic practices that had nothing to do with religion, that the freedom to worship was not at the heart of this matter. If the Amish chose to take their children out of school at fourteen, then whatever economic consequences flowed from that decision, such as the need to employ the children, were results of their own choices and thus not the responsibility of the government to redress.

The exemption legislation passed both Houses of Congress, and President George W. Bush signed it into law in January 2004.

Johnny Y, the Ohio factory worker who follows the Cleveland Indians, sees little likelihood of his employment changing radically in the near future, "unless the whole thing gets, y'know, sent overseas." That is a possibility, since he works at an automotive parts factory, but it currently seems remote. Although his is not the most interesting job he could imagine, it pays well, entails no more pressure than he can handle, and is allowing him to build up seniority. Not without ambition, Johnny thinks he could be a supervisor at the factory someday, and so does his girlfriend Becky, who, he says, is "getting on me to study for the GED, and then maybe I'll take a correspondence course in management, y'know? So's I can be ready for things up the ladder."

Johnny has seen the positive things that steady factory employment has put within the reach of his father, in terms of both the comfort level of his life and his ability to continue the family inside the Amish church. Johnny believes he too could do "thirty-and-out" with ease and retire from the factory at an even earlier age than his father did. He understands that if he becomes a member of the Amish church, he will be asked to sign an IRS form that says he is voluntarily opting out of Social Security and government health insurance plans, but he sees no danger to himself in that, because he will be essentially covered for health care and his old age by the community should he need its help.

On his agenda now is decreasing the number of road trips he takes on the weekends, principally at the request of—or possibly the demand of—his girlfriend. He explains, "Quit smoking, and I'm cutting back on the beer. Have to give it up eventually, of course. At least in public."

Johnny and Becky plan to marry in the not too distant future, a plan that evidently worries the four parents, who have protested to Johnny that they have not yet had a formal meeting, although the Y's have met Becky and Johnny has met her folks. He says, "Everybody's saying 'slow down,' y'know? Like, 'She's still pretty young.' " Johnny opines that Becky is very mature for her age and will be a "terrific" wife and mother. He looks forward to providing his parents with their first grandchildren. According to Johnny, Becky will continue as a schoolteacher even after marriage, until pregnancy makes it necessary for her to stay at home.

Though Johnny does not say so directly, it seems clear from the way he speaks about the future that he has already made his big decision. He has no interest in breaking permanently with his community of faith and admires those men like his father who are able to work outside the community yet still be "fully Amish." "Knowing you can punch that clock every day and still come home to the buggy, like my dad done for so many years—it ain't that hard. Little inconvenient here and there. But being Amish, it's like having the best secret of all, y'know?"

Is he fully ready to give up the pleasures of the outside world? The liquor, the parties, the road trips? "Well, I was getting tired of it all, anyway." He plans to sell his car to his younger brother, which will permit Johnny to continue to ride in it and not have to rely solely on horse and buggy. He can ride to the factory with a non-Amish co-worker, even pay the guy to take him if necessary.

As for his passion for the Cleveland Indians, Johnny says he can always follow the team in the sports pages of the *Plain Dealer*, and even if he became a church member, he might be able to watch a game on a neighbor's television should he happen to drop by at an opportune time. And what would happen, I ask, if he was a church member and the Indians made it into the playoffs or the World Series? Would he be able to refrain from watching the games? "That'd be a problem." He nods. "Might even have to risk a bit of a bann for that."

In 1950, nearly two-thirds of the jobs in the United States were in manufacturing; today manufacturing provides only around 20 percent of the jobs. Most people in the United States no longer make or produce anything; rather, we are engaged in process—we manage employees, accounts, or inventories; we move paper around; we provide governmental services or personal services such as health care or education. The United States has become a postindustrial, consumer-oriented economy whose major product is services. Through our consumer purchases, we hire other people to grow our food, make our clothes, cut the lumber for our houses, carry our messages, create our entertainment, and prepare our dinners so that all we have to do is pop them in the microwave. The seismic shift from making to processing has already brought about tremendous consequences for our society, though they have not all been acknowledged.

One way to understand the impact of the shift is to note that the Amish continue to be primarily producers, as were most people throughout recorded history, and that the Amish appear to take satisfaction from the kinds of work they do—while polls of the country's mainstream working populace consistently suggest that more than half of all working Americans are dissatisfied with their jobs.

The Amish satisfaction in their work stems in part from their religious attitude toward their toil but also from the very tangible nature of the products of their endeavors—whether they be pies and clean wash, or hundredweights of milk, or backyard swing sets, or RVs, and whether or not these products are produced at home, on the farm, in the shop, or at the factory.

Mainstream Americans may have lost a positive feeling about their jobs because they no longer make tangible things and must rely on the amorphous rewards of being involved in process.

"English people don't know how to work hard," charge Amish-raised young people such as Phil T the factory worker, Eli K the small-engine repairman, and Joann H the waitress, who come in contact with many non-Amish. Lydia T was puzzled by English co-workers in her factory who refused overtime in order to have the extra hours for themselves, or who held to the "silly" notion that a workweek was or ought to be limited to forty hours.

"Never could see the value of punching a clock," Dennis L says after more than forty years of working. In every job he has held, whether as an employee or as an employer of others, work has been a sunup to sundown aspect of life. Dennis and Gideon Stoltzfus and Sam Stoltzfus all say that a main task of fatherhood is instilling in their children a work ethic that will become as deeply ingrained as their Christian outlook and their need to be-have in a moral way. They and other Amish fathers (and mothers) are largely successful at the task of embedding that work ethic. Levi King, who owns a short-order restaurant in Shipshewana, prefers to hire Old Order Amish waitresses and counter people, even when he can find many non-Amish young ladies willing to make and serve pretzels. "What I like about the Amish girls who work for me," he says, "is that they come to work happy and they work hard." Other employers echo this sentiment.

To put this into perspective, we need to remind ourselves that Americans as a populace do work considerably more hours each week and year than Europeans do; our productivity is high and continues to increase. Yet most of us in the majority acknowledge that our working lives are easier than those of our grandparents in their prime, and that we do not toil as hard as people in the sweatshops or on the small farms of East Asia and other Third World areas. In comparison with the cultures that have come before us in the history of the world, and that of our own forebears, we middle-class, mainstream Americans have leisure-filled lives. Our progress as a society has been measured, in part, by the whittling down of the workweek, from an average of sixty hours at the beginning of the twentieth century to forty hours a week today.

The Old Order Amish work as hard and for as many hours as our ancestors did or as people in Third World countries now do, and the Amish do not acknowledge much of a demarcation between work time and nonwork time. Before and after spending eight hours a day at a factory job or a shop position, Amish men and women do chores, take care of siblings and farm animals, and so on for another several hours each day. "If you work as much and as hard as we do," Sam Stoltzfus teases, "you sleep very good, and you can eat anything you want and not get fat. What are we here for, anyway, if not to work and to pray?"

Work, the Amish contend, contributes to the inner strength and stability of the family and the community. Work is duty. Work is the essence of the human condition. For those reasons, hard tasks and "chores" have inherent value and are not to be complained about or gotten through for the sake of enjoying the consumer products or the leisure they may bring. If an Amish person does not take satisfaction from a day's work, the community considers that a sign of neurosis. To toil hard is to honor God; therefore, the ability and willingness to work are virtues, and not abstract ones of the sort only preached about but not lived; rather, those virtues are learned in the best way, from the example set by one's parents. The work ethic, when instilled early and at home, seldom seems a burden.

Working away, in addition to depriving the children of a father at home during the day, brings other dangers, among them the risk that a worker may become infected with the virus of pride. Signs in industrial buildings exhort employees to take pride in their work; company advertisements suggest that the workers should be proud of their achievements. The sort of pride the Amish call *hochmut* is a chief evil in their canon; it is a concomitant of worldliness, associated with the activities of Satan, who urges human beings toward unwarranted pride when they should be acknowledging that all their abilities are the products of God. Abhorrence of pride and a commensurate understanding and embrace of its opposite, humility, *demut*, stand in vivid contrast to the mainstream's excessive egotism and celebration of the most minor individual accomplishment. Pride may be endemic to the human condition, but, the Amish say, it needs to be fought, not burnished and celebrated.

A generation ago, a study in Lancaster County determined that children of nonfarming Amish fathers were five times more likely to leave the community than the children of farmers. More recent studies, done in Ohio and Indiana, have shown the opposite: that the children of Amish factory workers and shop owners and workers are no more likely to leave the sect than those of farmers, although they do migrate to other communities in larger numbers, perhaps because they have more portable skills, such as carpentry.

Working away is giving the children of nonfarmers a better understanding of the true differences between Amish and non-Amish ways of life, and a basis for choosing to stay within the community when they reach adulthood. These Amish youth are successfully rejecting contemporary mainstream America's usual context of work—one's employment as the defining aspect of life. For Amish young adults, the job is not the be-all and end-all of life; the wages earned are a means to an end, an attitude that allows the source of these youths' identities as individuals to remain their Amish faith and way of life.

9

"Women's Lib Would Have a Field Day Among the Amish"

The annual Gordonville Fire and Ambulance "mud sale" is in full swing. It is 8:30 a.m. on a blustery Saturday in mid-March. The two-lane road that runs between Paradise and Intercourse, a road that at all other times of day and night is a quiet, rural route, is jammed with cars, trucks, buses, buggies, and thousands of people, divided almost equally between Amish and English. A collection of auctions whose purpose is to benefit the volunteer service, many of whose volunteers are Amish men, the mud sale takes place in areas on both sides of the road, to the north in an open field below a culvert, and on the south in a paved area fronting the large fire station and associated smaller buildings. Farm and shop equipment are north, while quilts, furniture, bric-a-brac, and assorted decorative objects are south of the road. There is an enormous profusion of merchandise; some of it is donated, but a large proportion is on consignment—the Fire and Ambulance company will get about 10 percent of the proceeds of the consigned goods. The Amish like auctions, considering them a good way to buy and sell things at fair value.

The Amish at work for the sale, and the Amish customers, cluster in separate male and female groups, the males in small bunches in spots around the open field, wandering through the tent where the thoroughbreds and draft horses are tethered, standing in semicircles surrounding raised platforms at the odd-lot farm- and shop-equipment auctions, and strolling in threes and fours to inspect the hundred buggies; and the females gathering in somewhat larger aggregations in the paved area, where they work at several trailers selling pretzels, donuts, and coffee, and especially in the large basement of the firehouse, where dozens of them offer more substantial fare—slices of pie, whole cakes, corn soup, hot dogs, sandwiches that they have been making for days in their homes. A few young men and women work side by side on the firehouse floor and in adjoining buildings, acting as assistants to the older male auctioneers as they offer up quilts, wooden yard ornaments, and used furniture to mostly non-Amish audiences seated in folding chairs. In back of the firehouse, on a level with the basement, are trays of household goods for sale at reduced prices: clotheslines, flashlights, and shower-curtain rings.

All the Amish exude an air of suppressed excitement. They walk quickly, and not only because of the cold: the men have their hats pushed down on their heads and their hands jammed into their pants pockets; the women clutch their shawls or coats tightly around them to counter the stiff breeze.

The boys and men seem cocky, self-assured, obviously enjoying themselves; the competitiveness of the auctions appeals to them, and they have come to buy. The women seem to have come to be of service: they are not the ones haggling over harnesses, or assessing the quality of the horses that will pull their buggies or the salability of odd lots of garden furniture that they may be offering to tourists at a later time from their front-yard shops. Rather, the women are engaged in offering food, packing up quilts when those are bought, acting as cashiers.

A group of teenage Amish boys, going from one sale space to another, passes a group of similarly aged girls, but there is virtually no interchange between the two, no flirting or eye contact. The girls' eyes are cast down as they walk, as are those of their mothers, older sisters, and grandmothers. And like these older women, the girls appear plain, neat, well-scrubbed, and sturdy.

Each age cohort of females travels by itself, regiments on a parade ground distinguishable mainly by uniform, the younger girls with one sort of apron, the older unmarried ones with another sort and a certain type of hat, married women in their childbearing years wearing matronly dresses and coats, the grandmothers in versions of the same gear that are more uniformly drab. The girls and women seem reluctant to venture forth as individuals, as though needing the safety of their numbers, an impression intensified in the basement, at counters behind which a dozen women serve where one or two would suffice. A group of Amish men enter and purchase sandwiches, coffee, and pie slices; the women know them, serve them, and exchange a few words with them—but as soon as the men have left the counters to sit together at a table, the women gladly return to speaking among themselves.

Kathryn L's daughter Susanne, who told her suitor that she would not sleep with him, drink alcohol, or wear English clothes when they dated, is still working at the big flea market and auction house in Shipshewana during her *rumspringa*, as is her suitor, Joe, whose job is on the loading docks. Their relationship, and the L family, have survived the disastrous Thanksgiving dinner at which an aunt called Susanne "a harlot" for dating Joe.

Kathryn still has her worries about Joe, stemming from his wearing of English clothes and owning a car, but, she says, "we don't think we can tell Susanne not to date him," since he is Amish and his family is in the same church district as the L's.

One Sunday at 6:00 a.m., Kathryn opens the front door to find a state trooper there with a disheveled Susanne. She had gone to what she thought was a birthday party, but it turned wild, and she had drunk some alcohol—enough so that when the police came and broke up the too-raucous celebration, Susanne had been arrested, along with several other young Amish girls.

After a court appearance, the girls are sentenced to six months' probation. Kathryn takes Susanne to a first visit with the probation officer. Susanne professes herself "astonished" when the officer says, "I don't believe you," in regard to her assertion that she had never before participated in wild activities. As a van is bringing Susanne and the other girls back home, Kathryn listens to them saying nasty things about the probation officer.

This is the moment, she realizes, to give her daughter some instruction grounded in Kathryn's life experience as an Amish woman, mother, and small entrepreneur. "You have a bad attitude on that probation officer," she tells her daughter when they are alone. "You did something wrong, and he's trying to help you go right, so you better pay attention to that."

Under pressure, Susanne does begin to change her attitude, assisted by having to make monthly visits to the probation office and report her progress to a non-Amish stranger. By the end of the six months, she is, her mother observes, "more contrite—she knows what she's done wrong and wants to do right."

Kathryn has concurrently been pushing Susanne to find a different job, one that is more fitting with her age, eighteen, than the general assistant's position at the auction house. After a search, Susanne takes a job that fits her talents much better, as a "striper" in an RV factory—a person who paints stripes on, and applies decals to, the finished vehicle. The pay is also higher.

She grows closer to her mother and father, especially after Vernon closes his independent cabinetry business and takes a steady job at a carpentry establishment, which permits him more hours at home while lessening financial stress.

In the same period, Joe applies for and wins a job at another carpentry shop where all the workers, and the owner, are Amish and wear Amish garb. With these moves, Kathryn hopes, Susanne and Joe are on the verge of joining the church, renouncing the last vestiges of their wild ways, and preparing to marry and start their own family.

"The man is supposed to be over the woman, and they're not supposed to have equal rights, in our way of thinking," an Amish bishop explains. This is biblically mandated, the Amish insist, in I Corinthians 11:3, ascribed to the apostle Paul: "The head of every man is Christ, the head of a woman is her husband, and the head of Christ is God;" and in Titus 2:4, 5, where wives are instructed "to love their husbands, to love their children . . . to be obedient to their own husbands, that the word of God be not blasphemed." This bishop contends that women trying to have equal footing with men is the leading cause of divorce in mainstream society; if women would stay home, raise the children, grow food in the garden, make and darn the clothes, and do all the other jobs of a homemaker, he suggests, there would be "less need for trips to the Wal-Mart," which would make the family finances run more smoothly and economically.

Dave E, who is not a church leader, takes a milder stance. He agrees that while "there are probably some prejudices against women—I mean, women's lib would have a field day among the Amish"—in certain senses Amish women "are almost more esteemed than men are." He explains that, in the Amish culture, women are "more important, more valuable" than men because they raise the children, who are the future of the Amish sect, and they maintain the home, which is the locus of Amish life.

However, the collective portrait of women in Amish society that emerges from interviews with Amish men, women, boys, and girls is similar to that in the pages of *Family Life*: women as the objects of a reflexively misogynist culture which treats them as weak, dumb, and in need of protection from the world.

Husbands, fathers, ministers, and frequently the women themselves, write to *Family Life* to suggest that women are incapable of making important decisions on their own and continually require assistance in all sorts of endeavors. Many letters from Amish housewives tell of berating themselves for their perceived inadequacies as housecleaners, as disciplinarians of children, as cooks, and as family bookkeepers. An article entitled "Not Born to Be Tidy" provoked many such letters. One correspondent attributed her own ineptness in doing the housework to having had to help her father on the farm, rather than her mother inside the house, when she was growing up. As an adult, she tried hard. But she asks,

> Why then does there not seem to be any progress? Sure, I can clean the house, but the peaches don't get canned or the pants sewed. Why can't I do both like other housewives? There is this

constant battle to keep a cloud of depression from pressing me down. Just yesterday an aunt told one of the children: "We know your mama isn't a good manager." Yes, it hurts. How I long to be orderly.

Another responder wrote that she felt "smaller than dirt" upon realizing that she couldn't keep up with all the housework when the children were young and arriving every other year. A third woman, however, sternly insisted that "mothers need to teach their daughters that housekeeping goes with marriage," and that it is a wife's responsibility to be competent at domestic tasks.

An even larger flurry of responses was stimulated by a letter from an Indiana woman who described her husband as a good provider and gentle with the children, a man she told every day that she loved him—but a man unresponsive to her:

> I can bake his favorite cookies . . . not a word. I keep our house clean . . . not a word. (He will say something if it is not clean.) I take good care of the children . . . not a word. What I long for is an expressive and loving husband. Is it selfish of me to crave some recognition and words of gratitude? I feel at times more like his servant than his wife.

"I learned years ago that one can live without being thanked or praised or encouraged," wrote one of the many women who responded to this letter. Most of the other letter writers counseled the woman not to seek praise for doing her duty but to keep her complaints to herself and be grateful to her husband. One chided that the complainer's letter contained too many instances of the word *I*, and several more charged that the problem lay with the letter writer, not with the husband. "How refreshing to hear of your husband who is serious-minded, a hard worker and good provider, gentle with children, soft-spoken and uncomplaining about you."

Articles and letters in *Family Life* regularly emphasize how women benefit from submitting themselves to men's greater wis-

dom. A grandmother wrote that years ago, when her husband insisted they move from their home community to an outlying one,
hundreds of miles away, because the home church was "drifting,"
she wished she could "run away from it all." The "battle raged
within" her until she yielded to her husband; over time, the Lord
showed her that "peace and rest in submission far outweighed the
things that were left behind."

A reader told of her quandary when, during a drought, her
husband forbade her to water the tomato plants because he was
certain it was going to rain. The rain did not come, and she,
knowing the family would need canned tomatoes next winter,
disobeyed her husband and watered the plants. Grateful for the
plants' survival, for years afterward she was bothered by having
had to disobey her husband. Her worries were exacerbated by
having continually to read, in *Family Life*, "stories on husband-
wife relationships [that] ended by portraying the wife as having
been in the wrong." She wondered: "Were men ever sorry? Did
they ever apologize?"

In the proceedings of a conference about Old Order women,
the scholar Beth E. Graybill writes that the Amish cling to practices that emphasize the differences between men and women.
Men cut their hair regularly, women do not; men wear shoes
when working, women do not. Women are told not to wear pants
unless they want to be mistaken for men. They wear plain dress to
accentuate gender differences; moreover, Graybill found, their
dress has symbolically important meanings of submission, confinement, similarity with other women in the community and
solidarity with them, and it is the emblem of being at home and
of virtuous behavior.

The feminist scholar Anne Marie Pederson, another contribu-
tor to the conference, points out that Amish women are precluded
from becoming church officials, and from leadership roles on
safety councils and parochial-school boards, and in many other
ways have ceded to the men in the community the right to make
all decisions affecting the women's lives. The rules of the *ordnung*,
Pederson writes, "concentrate on control of women [and] prom-

ise the salvation of culture, community, and masculine identities through self-denial by women . . . Women's domesticity, piety, and submission to men are the foundation of moral order and male identity . . . Women's sexuality and women's voice must be denied in the interest of the traditional social order." She concludes that Amish men have structured a misogynist society because they are threatened by female independence. She rhetorically asks why Old Order women would acquiesce in such processes and gives her answer: "Presumably women collaborate in exchange for security, community, and cultural identity. Compliance yields the security of conformity."

Psychologists and other mental health professionals who work with the Amish, like Rob Schlegel of the Counseling Center for Wayne and Holmes Counties, who has been a social worker among the Amish for thirty years, say the Amish tend to be "more stressed out by the special requirements of their culture" than non-Amish are by the mainstream culture's requirements. He attributes this to the Amish needing continually to restrain their behavior so that it fits within the bounds of the *ordnung* and thereby avoids criticism from other community members: "Their dress pins must be properly done, their stray strands of hair in place."

Statistical studies have shown that mental problems are about equally divided in Amish culture between men and women. But LeVale Beiler, assistant director of the Family Resource and Counseling Center of Gap, Pennsylvania, which counsels Amish and Mennonite families, says that almost all the Amish who seek help from the center are women. "Problems that show up first as mothers having difficulties with teenaged children, or with personal depression, often reveal deeper or broader family issues." She adds that the depression can be traced to the heavy "pressures" put on the women by "having to perform" up to standards that are higher and more strict than those faced by non-Amish women.

Seeking help for any sort of mental problem is difficult for the Amish, according to Dr. James A. Cates, a psychologist, and the public health nurse Linda Graham of Fort Wayne, Indiana, who have worked extensively with the Amish. According to their recent article in a professional journal, mental health problems are stigmatized by the Amish community for "culture-specific" reasons. What might appear to outsiders as maladjusted behavior, ripe for counseling, may seem to insiders a manifestation of sin, which helps to explain why fewer Amish attempt to find help for mental problems.

The usual response of an Amish woman to mood swings, depression, excessive flirting, or bouts of anger, agrees Diane DeRue, director of community services for the CCWHC, is "working harder at being Amish, and working harder in general." If those cure-alls are not effective, the Amish will try "homeopathic remedies, faith healers, and in-church counseling—not necessarily in that order." Only after such remedies are exhausted, DeRue adds, will they seek professional counseling.

Marlys B, the tightly wound ball of energy who likes to wear all black—turtleneck, bell-bottoms, platform shoes—is having a problem not of her own making. She has taken a job at the RV factory where her boyfriend, Steve, is employed. Her salary is "terrific," but after a few months the work environment has become "awful." Her male co-workers, mostly English but some Amish, too, pinch her, try to fondle her, harass her. She has told them to stop it, but they won't.

She complains to the shift boss, who asks her to "give me some time to take care of it." She is quite willing to do so because she has been raised Amish, which means she is inclined to give people second chances, and to avoid becoming involved in fights to redress grievances. She endures the harassment for another month, but nothing changes.

She "goes up another level," to an assistant plant manager, and is again assured that action will be taken. She is patient: "We Amish know a lot about patience," she notes. After another few weeks, though, when nothing has been done by management to rectify the situation, she is faced with a decision. It seems clear that to

stop the bad treatment she will have to either institute legal proceedings or go to the press with her story, neither of which she is
inclined to do, or she will have to quit. The only course really
available to her, she becomes convinced, is to resign.

She does. It is shortly after this event that she and Steve break
up, and Marlys moves in with girlfriends.

Where can she work now? Not in any of the other RV factories, where the same sort of harassment might occur. Beyond that,
she feels limited by her schooling. It has been choppy at best. Because her family moved a lot, she went to public schools in various places in Indiana until the fifth grade, and when she arrived in
an Amish school in Shipshewana, she was "seriously behind the
kids who'd been there since Day One." She caught up eventually,
learning everything—"enough to get my GED if I wanted to"—
before graduating at fourteen. But she has never gone further,
made no attempt to obtain that GED.

Without some sort of high school diploma, many employers
will not even interview her for a job. Moreover, in her Amish
school there has been no training in computers, secretarial skills,
bookkeeping, or in any other trade that might qualify her for jobs
with salaries that are closer to the twenty dollars an hour she had
been making in the RV factory.

But with her friends' help she finds a new job, in a factory that
sews drapes and other coverings made of cloth for use in RVs.
"With overtime and bonuses, it comes to about ten dollars an
hour," she says bravely. In the drape factory, she works alongside
women who are mostly older, some English, some Mexican, not
many Amish. "They're all really nice people. Not threatening at all.
And they think I'm ultrahonest and sweet, which I guess I am."

Shortly after Marlys finds the new job, she and Steve "hook up
again," but this time they decide to do things differently: they see
each other at every opportunity but live separately. When she
turns nineteen and he turns twenty-three, however, they decide
that their "destiny is to be together in the church." They will end
their *rumspringa* periods, be baptized, marry, and eventually have
children.

It is for the benefit of these expected offspring that Marlys particularly wants to become an Amish adult. She envisions having no more than three children. "That's all I can handle, and I'd rather wait a few years to have a child, until we can put aside enough money for a home of our own." This means that she plans to continue working through the early years of her marriage, if possible at the drape factory, which for her is "much safer" than the other one. When the children come, she will quit that job, or maybe will find a way to do some piecework at home.

Another reason for becoming Amish is that she and Steve both desire "a slower life . . . out of the rat race." Steve has had some setbacks, too: a scheme for cutting out the middleman in buying big-ticket appliances has not generated as much money as he had hoped, perhaps because he and Marlys refuse to take any profit on appliances they sell to friends.

She realizes that when they are married, Steve will be expected by Amish tradition and the *ordnung* to be the head of the household, charged with making all the important decisions, but she feels that they have been equals in their relationship thus far and will continue to be after they join the church and marry. In this regard, she points to her father and mother, who after many years of marriage, now work in the same real estate firm and spend a lot of time together. "It's good for them, and a nice change for everyone." One of her brothers and his wife live in an apartment in the family home, and another and his wife reside in a second building on the same lot. When she was younger, Marlys found that environment "claustrophobic," but she no longer does. Family closeness is now very important to her.

The most exciting aspect of joining the church, Marlys says, will be having a strong moral surround in which to raise her children. In an era when public schools do not teach morality, when entertainments celebrate the "bad" over the good, and when there are obvious splits between what English parents say and what they do—"like with divorce," Marlys points out—the firmness of the moral fiber within the Amish community, and its potential benefits to her future children's character, has great appeal.

Another important feature for her is that inside the community, "nobody will lie to you," as her bosses regularly did in the RV factory. She appreciates the honesty and integrity of the Amish community, where doors are not locked, shopkeepers give you full value, promises are kept, and obligations are conscientiously fulfilled. It is one of those things that are taken for granted inside the community, so that you have to have been out in the world to appreciate its true worth.

More practically, Marlys touts "the trade-offs" in becoming Amish: "no car payments, no gas for the car, no buying expensive clothes, no insurance," which will translate into having low expenses and enabling her and Steve to save money for a home. Living within the community will mean lots of "learning to make do with what you have, and to celebrate what you are given by God," lessons that will also be invaluable to the children. She does not mention having to give up the telephone—on which, according to pals like Emma M, she gabs continually during off-work hours—or the likelihood that when she has a child she will have a reason to stop working for any outside employer who might harass her.

As for having to give up her silver hoop earrings, bell-bottoms, and platform shoes, Marlys says she is now ready for such "sacrifices"—as she was not earlier. She hopes that the church elders will still permit her, when she is on vacation in Colorado, where her father and mother own property, to wear her bikini, "because you can't very well swim in Amish clothes."

Marlys understands that by joining the church she will be putting herself under its authority, and that this will relieve her of many everyday decisions she would otherwise have to make alone or with her future husband: what to wear, what level of decorations to have in the home, what entertainment, what transportation, what schooling the children will have. She likes this arrangement, believing it will free her from fretting about the "small stuff" and allow her to concentrate on the more important aspects of life.

She also understands that before being fully accepted into the church she will have to make a confession, attesting that she and Steve lived together before marriage, something the church forbids. But she is certain they will be forgiven for that so long as they pledge thereafter to act within the church's rules. She is continuing to take birth control pills, to complete her course of treatment for her "female problem," but expects that in a few months she will go off the pills, because artificial birth control is not permitted. "I'm putting myself under the church's direction, and I'm okay with that."

Marlys's first big test of her willingness to be fully Amish comes next Monday, when she must cast off her English clothes, hoop earrings, and platform shoes, don the Amish dress that she has not worn in the past three years, and in all other ways prepare for living a plain and religious life.

Increasingly, young Amish women like Marlys, Susanne, and the others met in these pages have Amish models for their adult behavior who are more than housewives and mothers—women who also work outside the home. According to recent statistics compiled by the sociologists Donald Kraybill and Steven Nolt, more than half of all single Amish women now work full-time outside the home, and about 20 percent of all Amish-owned businesses are run by women, some of them married women with children.

Ruth G, wife of a carpenter in Fredericksburg, Ohio, is a typical middle-aged mother in that her main tasks include caring for her thirteen-year-old daughter and her aged mother. She worries about her beautiful child who has just graduated eighth grade, and who is employed babysitting for a three-year-old who adores her. Not all such jobs pass her motherly muster: "There's one English guy, he's got a four-year-old, and the parents are getting a divorce, and I thought the guy was getting ideas about my daughter, so I told her she couldn't do that one anymore." Ruth also has her hands full with her elderly and ill mother, who resides next door: the mother has Alzheimer's and frequently forgets to take her medication. But, Ruth says, even with such responsibilities, "you don't have to stay home all the time, and you also don't have to 'work away' in order to do something interesting."

She has what friends characterize as the perfect job to match her bubbly, outgoing personality, her responsibilities, and the requirements of the Amish community: "I'm an 'in-home Stanley demonstrator,' " Ruth announces. Stanley is the carpet-cleaning company whose major appliance is the Stanley Steemer; they also have a whole line of home-cleaning products. Stanley is also allied with the Fuller Brush Company and its line of beauty products. Ruth explains, "I like the job because of the money, but also because it gets me out of the house." Once or twice a month the company arranges "parties" in someone's home—"Amish and non-Amish homes"—and Ruth shows up to demonstrate the products and take orders; she is paid a percentage of the sale price on all the products sold at the parties. "It's like Tupperware or Avon, only better," she says, because the products "sell themselves, and people keep on needing new supplies," so she continues to make money after the initial sale.

Ruth seems not to be resented within the Amish community for her assertiveness or ingenuity; recently, in association with a few friends from the church district, she arranged a ninety-nine-dollar-per-person one-day "mystery tour" by bus to another state. The participants were mostly middle-aged men and women; they visited some scenic attractions and had a nice lunch, but the most fun was had on the bus, where they played endless hands of rook, a card game favored by the Amish, and rearranged themselves into separate groups of men and women to sing some songs from the *Ausbund* that everyone knew but that were not frequently used in church.

Ruth M, the ascetic-looking Shipshewana grandmother with firm opinions on combating peer pressure among teenagers, spent many years working in the local public school system, first in a grade school and then in a junior high. Now, after all her daughters have married, she no longer works for the school system, though she still attends board meetings. Constitutionally unable to retire, she has a new job, working with her husband, DeWayne, at the fabrication shop on their property. DeWayne, a barrel-chested man with a broad smile, used to own a construction firm; a few years ago he traded in his stake in that firm—he was tired of going up on roofs, he says—and bought a business that allows him to keep his feet firmly planted on the ground. He makes only one product, intricately machined wooden pedestals for dining room and other tables. Mostly, DeWayne toils at the big lathes by himself. He has as many orders as he can accommodate, from about a dozen steady customers. When Ruth is able to get away from her chores as a grandmother and sometime minder of her aged mother, she walks over to the woodshop and works alongside her husband, handling machinery that DeWayne says most women "have no idea how to operate."

A bicycle-riding young Amish woman in her married garb with a toddler in the infant seat eases off busy State Route 5 near downtown Shipshewana and into the tarmac driveway of a retail quilt shop located in a private home. She parks the bike, dismounts, leaves the sleeping child in the secured seat, and goes in. No more than two minutes later, she returns to the bicycle, bearing a basket full of fabrics, which she stashes in a holder at the front, and rides off again.

Edna and Wanita M, who are mother and daughter, operate the quilt shop in a front room of the family's home. It is separated from the living quarters by a privacy curtain, and by the shop having its own outside entrance. Across the driveway, in a converted garage, is another shop, where the men of the family do upholstery. The M ladies offer quilted furnishings in rich colors and interesting patterns; these range from pillows, good for decorating a couch, retailing at twenty-five dollars, to immense spreads for beds or for use as wall hangings, at around a thousand dollars.

The owners say that the young woman who just rode in has been working for them for some years, as has her mother. With one baby and expecting another, the young woman can no longer work away from the home, but she needs to do something to help meet family expenses. She sews by hand and with a machine that is operated by a foot pedal. In payment for her quilting at home, she will receive a dollar amount based on the number of yards of thread she has used. The spools of thread are 250 yards long, and each pillow requires only a little thread, so the bill for the work is usually toted up when a spool is exhausted. According to the shop owners, to quilt a pillow takes one person about half a day and to complete a large quilt, about four weeks of full-time work.

Assuming the usual 100 percent markup of a retail store on materials and labor, the young woman will receive from the quilt shop, for four hours of work on a pillow, about twelve dollars, or three dollars an hour.

Though jobs such as those filled by Ruth G, Ruth M, and Edna and Wanita M give newer generations of Amish women a purview beyond the old one of *kinder, küche, kirche*—children, cooking, and the church—Amish men still have wider horizons than Amish women do, and more freedom to interact with the outside world. Kraybill and Nolt, surveying Amish entrepreneurs, found that while women make up about 20 percent of the entrepreneurs, their enterprises are usually far smaller than those of the men and pay the workers significantly lower wages. Amish women still have far less say in the ordering of their own lives than do Amish men; the women react rather than act, support and sustain rather than initiate, and are more dependent than independent.

These concomitants of the Amish patriarchy provide to some young women of *rumspringa* age a powerful motive for wanting to leave the sect: to have more options for their futures.

Lydia T, who felt she had been baptized too young and has burst out of her Amish home to work at a factory and live with a woman roommate and her children in White Pigeon, has been having a running dialogue with a favorite uncle, a thirty-seven-year-old who has also left the sect.

"Go back to school, will you?" he usually needles during their monthly phone calls, implying that more schooling will result in her being eligible for better jobs.

"I don't have to," she just as regularly retorts. "You didn't, so I don't have to. I'm not going back if you don't."

Then one day he telephones to say, "Hey, guess what, Lydia? I'm going back to school."

"You are not."

"Yes, I am. Talk to your aunt if you don't believe me."

After Lydia confirms with her aunt that the uncle is attending GED classes—how "awesome," they agree—she becomes a bit jealous and wants to do the same. She imagines a future in which she'll telephone and ask him, "What did you learn today, uncle?" then dazzle him with what she has picked up in her classes.

Velda B, the young woman who made the heart-wrenching last-minute decision not to go through with her wedding and was then banned and shunned, survives her suicide attempt but falls into a deep depression and tries with the help of a counselor to understand its roots. She has always "desperately wanted to know the truth" but feels she has only now begun to have a better shot at knowing the whole truth—the reality of the world—because she is permanently outside the sect. Some evidence of progress is in her current dreams. These differ "totally" from those confided to her years ago by her Amish girlfriends; they dreamed, as she did when she was inside the community, of "getting married, having a couple children—limited dreams that revolve around the little things that you could have . . . that are invested into material things like decorating your house or sewing."

With the pastor of the Baptist church, Velda B finds a verse in Romans that becomes her mantra: "We should rejoice in our sufferings for they bring forth perseverance." She explains, "Perseverance brings forth character, and character brings forth hope, and hope is something that keeps me going." The pastor encourages her to "keep seeking, keep walking the journey," when many times she wants to "just give up." She estimates that on a journey of many miles she has gone only a quarter mile.

As she continues to work at an office, Velda and her counselors try to resolve the central question, what she wants to do with her life. To generate more options, she decides to take classes, complete her GED, and at the same time to go for secretarial training. She keeps in touch with her family, although, she says, the bann is "a huge wall between my family and me," preventing them from "reaching each other." When she goes home, she abides by the strictures because it is "important for me to respect them."

Shortly after leaving the sect, Velda had gone to the bishop of her district and argued that since her defection was motivated by a need for deeper faith she was not a transgressor and therefore should be treated more leniently than those who left for worldly gain. The bishop said that a rescinding of the bann might be possible in six months, if her pastor would write a letter to the church saying that she was a member in good standing, had a good attendance record, and was proving herself to be a good Christian. The pastor should also include evidence that would permit the Amish to conclude that his church's practices were reasonably strict. Her pastor willingly sent such a letter to the bishop, but there has been no response.

Her former fiancé becomes engaged once more, to a woman within the community; Velda cannot blame him for moving on.

She completes her GED and her secretarial classes, and obtains a job as a secretary at an RV plant, a job to which Amish women cannot even aspire, she knows, because they lack the training with computers and other electronic equipment that is necessary for secretarial tasks these days.

She is invited to an Amish wedding of an old girlfriend. With some trepidation, she goes to it in her English clothes. She asks her sister-in-law to sit beside her and serve her, since she will not be able to serve herself from the same bowl that others are using. Her sister-in-law informs Velda that she is no longer in the bann and can serve herself. Velda is "so overjoyed." The feeling is "like a big load of coals taken off my back."

Now she can work to restore those relationships that were broken when she left the fold—with her family, and with her former girlfriends who are still in the Amish faith—though she recognizes that her life and the lives of these young women will diverge more and more as the years go on. An instance soon arises: Velda applies to and is accepted by a college program.

On the eve of her departure, while packing her clothes, Velda sums up her new dreams: "to become something, to have a career of some kind. And another one of my dreams is to someday have a ministry," perhaps go into the field as a missionary. Now that she no longer has to remain within the Amish fold, she sees no limit to her career possibilities.

Seventeen-year-old Sara S and her mother push Sara's younger brother D in his wheelchair out of the rain and into the main building at the Leola Produce Auction on a Saturday in September that is buffeted by the sort of intense rain and wind that the previous evening brought tornadoes to some nearby Lancaster County areas. They position the wheelchair at the back edge of the folding chairs, to get ready for the start of an auction for the benefit of D's doctors, the Clinic for Special Children.

The clinic, located in Strasburg, identifies and cares for Amish and Mennonite children with genetically based diseases. There are many such children, because inbreeding and other isolating factors have produced a population in which the odds of a child being born with one of three dozen genetic-defect conditions are much higher than they are for the general population. Also, since the "plain people" permit no abortions, even when expecting parents know, from tests the clinic performs for them, that they may birth a child with severe problems, such children are brought into the world with the expectation that the family will care for them. Moreover, the Amish and Old Order Mennonites will not countenance putting even the most severely disabled family member in an institution.

The clinic's founder and medical director is the pediatrician and geneticist Dr. Holmes Morton, who, with his wife, Caroline, and other members of the staff, is walking around the auction hall, talking to friends and supporters. Several hundred volunteers from Amish and Mennonite communities have made quilts and solicited, collected, and transported other items for the sale, and they are now preparing and serving food and in myriad other ways assisting the auction process. They do so because the communities are acutely aware that this event raises nearly a third of the clinic's annual operating budget, and the clinic has become an important resource for them.

About two dozen other filled wheelchairs are near D's, all of them attended by women—mothers, sisters, grandmothers. Mrs. S leaves Sara to oversee D and goes to work in the food area, where volunteers are making and serving traditional delicacies such as pulled pork, rhubarb punch, and donuts—a goal this year is to sell more than the eighteen thousand donuts bought at last year's auction.

Sara appears young, voluble, and vulnerable. She is the eldest daughter of a family of five, and near her, at the rear of the seating area, gaggles of young ladies from her age-group walk around, conversing among themselves, having a good time. But she seems content to sit in a chair alongside D, who is severely disabled and needs frequent attention.

Her brother is "one of God's special children," Sara says, and "is here to teach us how to love." She believes that she is learning more about that every day from him.

Sara is in *rumspringa* and attends Sunday singings and the occasional party, but sometimes she cannot go to such events because she is "needed at home." As the relief for her mother, Sara is principally responsible for her brother in the evenings, after she returns from work at a bakery during the day. But she says she does not feel especially tied down by having to care for D. "There's time for everything," she insists.

Sara does not currently have a boyfriend but does expect to find one in the next year or two, and eventually to marry. She expects to have children and is knowledgeable enough about the possibilities of genetic inheritance to recognize that a child of hers may be at risk for the same disease that has affected D—though there are treatments now that are able to prevent the sort of permanent damage he sustained when he was young. Any prospective husband, she says, will have to understand that and also "will have to accept D," by which she means that he will agree that her brother is one of her responsibilities, and that when her parents pass on, D will come to live with her for the rest of his days.

Seeking Solutions

It is when Ruth M has a house full of kids in rumspringa *and is running out of activities for them that she conceives a partial solution to what is a community problem. At home are her own adolescents, plus a visiting one from out of state—all "good" kids, not inclined just to go out and drink and party—yet if they want to have fun, they have few alternatives to gallivanting in the outside world. Ruth knows from her work in the public school system, and from long experience in the Amish community, that her children and their close friends are the sort of youth from proper home environments who are most likely eventually to join the church, but she also senses that if they cannot find ways to enjoy themselves, as well as to meet teenagers with similar backgrounds from neighboring communities, their chances of "coming home" to the church will diminish.*

The church itself sometimes seems to contribute to the problem. During the period that Ruth is ruminating, some of the boys in the rumspringa *age-group, and also some of the young married Amish men, have been playing softball in a Shipshewana town league, in afternoon and early evening games at diamonds near a public school complex. The ministers decide that too many of the young males are getting "carried away" by the excitement of sport, spending so much time playing softball that they are neglecting their families. The church officials make them give up this secular recreation.*

Ruth M's idea is that the community should establish a recreation center where teenagers can go to spend time in approved activities, such as volleyball, singings, perhaps roller skating, fashioning gifts for shut-ins, and just being together with minimal supervision from parents. Ruth finds enthusiastic support for the idea among like-minded Amish parents, who are willing to do all the work of organizing, raising the necessary funds, supervising the kids. But before going ahead with the center, she and the other parents decide that they must ask the ministers and bishops whether this could be permitted.

To her consternation, the church officials say no. In their view, the rec center would mean, she says, "too much sports, too much competition, too much organization."

With reluctance, Ruth drops the idea.

A few years later, a similar idea occurred to the minister Norman Y of Shipshewana, his wife, and a half dozen other couples from three different church districts, all parents of children of *rumspringa* age. Norm recalls, "The question was, what can we do?" He and his group felt that they "could not stand by and let the kids slide into trouble." They had to try new ways to help "even if we couldn't predict all the consequences."

Norm believes that while a "strength" of the Amish is "that we respect tradition and are slow to change," that strength can function as a drawback when the community and its families must deal with a rapidly changing world and escalating bad influences.

The best thing for Amish youth, Norm argues, is "more witnesses from among us who grew up and never did drugs, alcohol, premarital sex." But plenty of parents in the community "strayed" when they were young and so are afraid to be too tough on their kids now. However, the community has "plenty of youth that understand the value of purity," and Norm and his group of parents believed that those youth needed a place to go to let off steam, a place where parents could be assured that the kids would be protected and led in the right direction by concerned shepherds.

Norm had been planning to erect a new warehouse and showroom building for his business, and he had the facility redesigned so that the rear part of the building would be a gymnasium with space for a full-size, high-ceilinged basketball court, a kitchen, bathrooms, small meeting rooms, and a lounge. The complex could be used for basketball, volleyball, Ping-Pong, suppers, singings, and other activities.

Without seeking approval from church officials, Norm and his group underwrote and built the rec center. This was a "risk" for him, as a minister as well as the prime mover of the project, Norm says, but one that he was willing to take. The center opened in the fall of 2003 and has been busy ever since.

Only those over sixteen are permitted, and on some weekday evenings, as well as Friday and Saturday nights, crowds of sixty to eighty Amish youth show up for activities that are supervised by one of the founding couples. Norm says, "That's not a great many youth, compared to the many hundreds who go to one of those big parties, but it's a start."

The kids arrive by "bicycle, buggy, rented van, roller skates, and on foot." The location is central, near the confluence of two major roads. "They come from about a ten-mile radius" that includes the towns of Topeka, Middlebury, LaGrange, and Goshen, and some from across the state line in Michigan. Horses are tethered to hitching posts outside the rec hall, and the parents even clean up the manure so that the teenagers will not have to. Each young person pays three dollars to attend and modest prices for refreshments. The rules include proper attire—full-length pants and shirts for the boys, full-length dresses and hair coverings for the girls—and no drinking, cursing, or fighting. The original plan called for the center to open twice a week, but some weeks it is open every evening. Now that the center is thriving, some ministers and bishops have become admirers and supporters.

And the parents' group is going further than providing a facility. "If the problem comes from outside, we can use outside help to solve it," Norm says, and so, even though the Amish have traditionally solved all their challenges on their own, he and the group have engaged outside counselors, such as the psychologist Jim Cates of Fort Wayne, to work with the parents and advise church officials about drugs and the psychological problems of teenagers.

The community is more willing now to try such things because, as Norm says, "we became more aware of drugs and of other evil influences that are all around us. They are part of the world that our kids live in, and we can't ignore them or wish them away." Aside from drugs, the major threat is premarital sex, which can result not only in out-of-wedlock pregnancies but also in cases of AIDS and other sexually transmitted diseases. But drugs are the greatest evil. Norm explains, "Abstinence can be taught, and alcohol you can wean yourself off of, but drugs are the worst, because you become addicted and don't get rid of 'em easily—maybe never."

Amish communities first became acutely aware of possible drug problems in their midst in June 1998, when the case of the two Abner Stoltzfuses in Lancaster County made headlines all over the world. Abner King Stoltzfus of Ronks operated a roofing business; an employee who was a close friend (though not a close relative) was Abner Stoltzfus of Bart. Both were raised Amish but had not yet joined the church. And both had five-hundred-dollar-a-week cocaine habits, acquired from the Pagans, a violent, non-Amish motorcycle gang whose members attended Amish parties and gave "free" tastes and sold drugs to the Amish. To feed their habits, the two Abners became middlemen, reselling drugs from the Pagans to their Amish buddies.

The FBI heard the Stoltzfus names on wiretaps of the gang and sent an informer named Cianci, who rode with the Pagans, to apply for a job with Abner King. Since the roofing firm always needed workers, Abner hired Cianci, whom he knew from the parties. "I took him as a nice, quiet guy who never asked questions, who minded his own business," Abner would later tell a reporter.

With evidence from Cianci in hand, the authorities notified the Abners in late 1996 that a case was being built against them and, in July 1997, told them they were about to be indicted. By that time they had kicked their habits.

The Lancaster attorney John F. Pyfer, Jr., of Pyfer and Reese, was hired to defend Abner Stoltzfus, though not Abner King Stoltzfus. "I grew up in Lancaster, and we'd handled many matters for the Amish in the past—mostly real estate transactions, public sales, and the like," Pyfer recalls. "Once in a while an Amish kid would get in trouble, drunk behind the wheel, keg of beer in a barn, minor property damage." Though his firm's bread and butter is matrimonial cases, Pyfer had plenty of experience in drug cases. He quickly realized what the family had not yet understood, that Abner was accused of participating in a ring that sold cocaine and methamphetamine with a street value of more than $1 million—which put the offense into the top category, subject to very severe penalties.

Visiting the Stoltzfus home, Pyfer was astonished to find there more than two dozen family members and neighbors. "Usually, in a drug case, you're lucky if both parents show up," he explains. He gleaned something of his client's character from stories of how Abner had stuck by a girlfriend who had taken ill, and something of the family environment from quizzing the parents on their ignorance of their son's drug habit—"When Abner started sniffling, they thought he just had a cold." Such naïveté, in Pyfer's view, was also the reason the drug dealers had seen the Abners as "big fat targets . . . The Amish are known for having money in their pockets, for paying their bills in cash, and for having absolutely no education at all about drugs. My daughter, who was in fifth grade at the time, knew more about drugs than these two Amish guys in their twenties."

A few days later, in Pyfer's town-house office, FBI and state police convinced Abner to wear a wire against one of the Pagans.

"They told him how and where to conceal the transmitter, under his black hat. He had absolutely no idea of how dangerous this was, and neither did his parents." Cooperation was necessary in order to avoid a long jail sentence. Pyfer was petrified about what might happen if the Pagans discovered that Abner was wearing a wire, but his taping went off without incident and provided the authorities with precisely what they needed to start the dominoes toppling, to force one Pagan to incriminate a higher-up, and that man to incriminate others, until there was enough evidence to charge eight members of the gang. Had Abner Stoltzfus not tape-recorded the first Pagan, the entire case might not have been made, since the Amish generally do not testify in court cases. The Pagans had likely been counting on the Amish refusing to testify.

Helping make the case against the Pagans would not necessarily assist the Amish community to fight the drug scourge in its midst. But that process could begin with the shock of the indictment of the two Abners, announced by the U.S. attorney in Philadelphia during a news conference on June 23, 1998. That press conference birthed a media storm, typified by the six-column headline in the *Lancaster New Era*: AMISH, PAGANS ARRESTED IN TWO-COUNTY DRUG RING.

Most reports featured the gang nicknames and reputed violence of the Pagans, who referred to themselves as "one-percenters . . . the baddest of the bad." As David Remnick would shortly suggest in *The New Yorker*, to the media "the juxtaposition of Harley-Davidsons and buggies, of Abner and Twisted and Abner and Fat Head . . . proved irresistible." The case became fodder for late-night comedy routines. David Letterman's Top Ten list of "signs your Amish teen is in trouble" was soon on the Internet, its authorship claimed by several dozen would-be wits.

More sober reporting in *The Philadelphia Inquirer* suggested that "the indictment is evidence of the increasing vulnerability of the Amish and their ways to the modern world they shun." Many young Amish and English people in Lancaster, interviewed by reporters, said they had personal knowledge that drug dealing and drug abuse had been going on in the area for some time.

The impact of the indictment was heightened because it was handed down at the peak of the summer tourist season, when throngs of visitors flood the main roads of the "Amish triangle" formed by the small towns of Intercourse, Bird-in-Hand, and Paradise, which had become an Amish-themed Disneyland built by outsiders around the area's twenty thousand Old Order Amish residents. Dozens of non-Amish enterprises used the attractiveness of Amish culture as drawing power—the Dutch Haven crafts and shoofly-pie emporium, the Amish Country Homestead, the Amish Experience theater, the Dutch Wonderland amusement park, the Good 'N Plenty restaurant complex, a Christian experience theater. With the news of the big case hanging in the air, Lancaster tourists were looking at the Amish with even more curiosity than usual.

As part of a plea-bargain arrangement, the two Abners agreed to participate in a drug-education program for the Amish community. Seeking permission from the Amish for such a public program, Pyfer and an FBI agent met with the Old Order Amish Steering Committee. "They turned us down flat," the lawyer recalls. "Said there was no drug problem in the community, just an isolated incident or two, and that a drug-education program was not needed."

However, a groundswell arose from Amish parents of teenagers, and a general meeting was held one summer evening in the Gordonville Fire and Ambulance Company building at the center of the triangle of Amish-dominated towns. "There was no publicity for this meeting," Pyfer recalls. "We didn't want the media showing up, so it was just word of mouth." Several hundred Amish appeared on August 15, 1998. "The girls sat on one side, the boys on the other; the elders were down front, the parents were in the back," Pyfer recalls. The arrangement echoed the usual church seating plan. The FBI agent on the dais told Pyfer that he recognized many kids in the audience as drug users from the community, "and when he spoke to them, he looked them straight in the eye, as though to say, 'I know who you are and what you've been doing.'"

The audience was aghast to learn that the federal government had five years from the moment of an infraction to indict someone for a drug offense—which meant that even if a user stopped cold now, he might be liable for past offenses for years to come. The notion that the government would not forgive and forget as the Amish do was worrisome to the kids, and parents were equally heartsick to learn about "forfeiture"—that if drug offenses were traced to their children, or had taken place on their property, the parents could lose their farms or homes. All of this astonished people who had never watched *Law & Order* on television and until then had taken very little interest in the justice system. The most powerful speakers were the Abners, telling friends and neighbors what signs of drug abuse parents should look for in their children, and how drugs had affected their lives. Abner King, an asthmatic, said he had ruined his fragile lungs with cocaine. "Basically, my life is on hold," Abner Stoltzfus chimed in: he could not marry his girlfriend until he learned if he was going to jail.

In the middle of the meeting, dozens of beepers went off—the Gordonville company was called to respond to a fire, and a lot of the males had to leave—but enough people remained so that an important divide could be crossed. "It really took off during the question-and-answer session, when one young man stood up and said he was also abusing drugs, and wanted out, and didn't know how to get out. After that it became like a revival meeting, with everybody wanting to give their testimony," Pyfer recalls.

After this successful community meeting, the bishops jumped in, nineteen of them authorizing a letter from "Concerned Parents of Our Youth Today," sent to 125 Amish districts in four counties in Pennsylvania. The letter warned parents to "beware of evil changes which your children could or might be going through," such as jittery nerves, needle marks, "watery, blurred or staring eyes, appetite changes . . . lack of communication with parents . . . lack of good workmanship on the job," and to realize that "our bodies are a temple for the soul to live in . . . There is still time to change, and the time is now." Over the next year the Old Order Amish Steering Committee helped organize a dozen meetings in barns and Mennonite meeting halls attended by more than ten thousand Amish and Mennonites. The two Abners became impassioned proselytizers for drug awareness and abstinence.

As had been planned by the defense attorneys and the prosecutors, the Abners changed their pleas to guilty in exchange for the prosecutor's written promise to seek no more than five-year sentences. Over a hundred Amish loaded into ten rented vans for the trip to Philadelphia for the sentencing hearing. Television cameras hounded them at the courthouse. Supporters of the Abners had already written extraordinary letters to the judge. "Most people, when they write to the judge, say they know the defendant and that he's a good guy and the judge should be lenient," Pyfer points out. These letter writers took the opposite tack: they admitted not knowing the young men personally and opined that the Abners had done wrong and that the judge had a difficult job; they encouraged him not to treat the Amish offenders differently than any other defendants but pointed out that the Abners had shown the community they realized their mistakes and were ready to take their punishment and make amends; therefore, the writers concluded, they have our support.

The judge was a former Lancaster County prosecutor. Citing these letters, the Abners' work in drug awareness, and Abner Stoltzfus's having worn a wire to help crack the conspiracy, he ignored the federal sentencing guidelines for offenses involving heavy drug weights and dollar values, and sentenced the Abners to a year in federal prison and five years' probation, with a recommendation for immediate work-release status and confinement to a halfway house for the first six months. The sentences were light, and the Amish community was relieved. Seven members of the Pagans received jail terms.

A year after the arrest, crime statistics and an informal poll by the Lancaster *Sunday News* showed that drug use was rapidly dropping among the Amish, almost certainly as a result of the public meetings, as well as the outcry about the case.

· · ·

Faron Y., the nineteen-year-old, foulmouthed "prince of crank" in the Shipshewana area, followed the details of the Lancaster drug case but believes that what happened to the Abners will never happen to him. He has been caught with drugs many times—is "on probation in three counties"—but he's still mixed up with drugs and still free. Now and again he goes home, to the house where his preacher father and mother live. He has not really resided there for years, not since he began to run away at fourteen.

His parents have tried everything, including "tough love" tactics, to straighten him out, but none have worked. They do not like Faron smoking and drinking in the house, but he does it anyway. He says,

> I guess I don't show them much respect—for all the [expletive deleted] they did to me they don't deserve much respect from me. True, they help me out a lot, I do respect them for that, but—it's very complicated: they help me out so much, yet at the same time they just . . . it seems like they did everything in their power to piss me off, you know?
>
> My parents could have done some things differently. Like my older sister—well, she didn't even use my name, Faron, but most of the time she used to call me Devil . . . and my mom and dad would just let it go on. When people first started calling me a troublemaker and a druggie, I wasn't a druggie, and I was, like, well, you know, I'll earn the [expletive] name if I got it anyway—and [expletive] like that, I think my parents could have helped me some with that.

Similarly, Faron continues his tormented relationship with his Amish, Christian faith:

> I think we all, like, have a certain path in life, you know: I mean, sure, you can control a lot of the small stuff, but the major stuff you can't control; I mean, it's all planned out, I think. I really do believe in God. I believe each of us has our own path to walk.

Shortly, Faron's life is pulled mightily in two directions. His drug selling becomes so desperate and overt that it piques the attention of the police, who document his dealing, then threaten him with prosecution and decades in jail. To avoid prison, he wears a wire against two Amish dealers who run a local methamphetamine lab. Later the dealers will find out he has "snitched" on them and let it be known they will pay to have him killed.

But it is also in this period that he meets and falls heavily for Emma M, the sixteen-year-old, willowy Amish beauty, raised in Missouri and Wisconsin, who came to Shipshewana to escape her own home. Emma has stayed on at work at the Blue Gate in Shipshewana as a cashier and hostess for several months more than she had intended in order to continue her affair with Faron. And for her sake—as well as to help himself in court when it comes time for sentencing—Faron goes cold turkey and attempts to lead a quieter life, working for his father in the lawn furniture business. Now he tries hard to convince Emma that they should both be baptized, marry, and live forever as Amish.

Emma is already certain that she never wants to become an Amish adult: two of her siblings did join the church and then left, resulting in great difficulties for themselves and the family. She is also scared of "commitments," of agreeing to any lifelong obligation when she is, as she understands, still quite young.

She flees to Florida, where another sister lives. This sister has borne twins without marrying their father and now lives with her small children; to earn money she cleans houses and waits on tables. The father of the twins is courting the sister again, and she may marry him but is not sure about that. Emma finds many commonalties with her older sisters. She says, "We like taking care of ourselves, we're capable of earning our own living, and we don't like having someone else take care of us—watching my back, making sure I'm getting my sleep and getting home on time." Attractive and competent, Emma has no difficulty finding a job as a waitress. Or finding new suitors.

Without her, Faron disintegrates and returns to drug use. His parents kick him out. He crashes at his friend Gerald's trailer.

Once again he tries, on his own this time, to go straight. After several months without drugs, he is accepted back by his family and then, with their blessing, goes to visit Emma in Sarasota, where there is an Amish enclave.

Faron reunites with Emma, albeit tentatively on her part, and meets new people who, he says, "don't expect me to be a badass . . . Here I do not have to be anything that I don't want to be. I can be like this nice person, and funny, and everything . . . a normal person without the whole town knowing who I am." He defines normal as someone who does not get into fights or conduct affairs with five girls at the same time, and who obeys the law but can get drunk with a small group of friends once in a while "without it controlling their life."

But while driving to an interview for a job as a gardener, Faron has an accident and nearly comes to catastrophe. Yet as he waits at the hospital for the passenger in his car to be treated, he talks himself into a job as a parking valet.

His liaison with Emma grows more tenuous. When the high season ends in Florida, there is less money to be made as a parking valet, and Faron tries to sell expensive vacuum cleaners door-to-door. Soon it becomes clear that Emma will not return to Indiana with him, because, among other reasons, she "hates winter" and wants to "see other guys." Faron's father attempts to lure him back with the promise of a much higher salary for making lawn furniture—equal to what he made in the factories—and the possibility of Faron taking over the business in the not too distant future.

Not knowing what else to do, Faron returns north without Emma and at home continues to abstain from drugs. But several months later he admits that

> I was staying clean for her. Well, for me also, but, you know, well, I thought if I'd stay clean, I'd be like this perfect guy and she'd stick around, but evidently I wasn't perfect enough, so now I don't give a [expletive]. I don't know. I'll probably end up, like, at the age of twenty years, twenty-five years, die at the

age of twenty-five years a crackhead, burned-out [expletive]. I don't really give a [expletive].

Bored by making lawn furniture, Faron slides back into drugs. This is the last straw for his parents. His father turns him in to the police for possession of drugs and of a loaded gun whose serial numbers have been filed off. Faron is convicted and sentenced to two years in jail, some of it to be spent in a work-release program that allows him to work daily in an RV factory, plus five years' probation.

Emma has always wanted to see the big cities, and she goes to New York and Chicago. Unlike other Amish who dread the idea of so many people in one place at one time, Emma decides she likes urban life. But because she hates winter and wants to be an actress or model, she decides to move to San Diego. She takes a share in a house full of college students, finds work as a nanny that allows her time to pursue modeling and acting opportunities, buys a car and a cell phone, passes her GED on the first try, takes Spanish lessons, searches the Internet, and finds a job that will take her to Spain and back before she starts college.

When she learns that Faron has gone to jail and says he is happy to do so, she cries, believing he has at last given up hope.

Shortly after Emma turns nineteen, her grandmother dies, and she flies to Missouri to take part in the funeral. A thousand Amish from a dozen states attend. She has a good time catching up with her numerous cousins, some of whom were her closest childhood pals. Those teenage girls, the daughters of her mother's sisters, now appear relatively unsophisticated and without much varied life experience when compared with Emma's college-going roommates. At the funeral, Emma's father acknowledges her presence, and she and her mother have a good conversation and make plans to phone each other at regular intervals.

"It would be nice to be able to go to your parents if you have a problem, or for help with car payments," Emma says, but she is proud of her ability to make do without anyone's assistance. That self-assurance, she posits, is also what allows her to remain single and not to waste her time looking for a husband.

After the funeral, Emma has some wistful thoughts about being Amish and living the religious life, which, she says, would be "easy" for her because it is familiar and uncomplicated. She could do it—but she no longer wants to. Being on the outside, a single woman bent on a career, is going to be a struggle, but she prefers struggling to returning to the confines of the Amish life, where she would likely have no career but wife and mother.

"I'm not Amish anymore," Emma concludes. "I'm just a nineteen-year-old, female, Amish-American, and there's a whole lot of things in life that I'd like to experience."

Some Amish blame the drug problem on the automobile. They argue that because the Lancaster Abners were in the construction business and dealing with outside customers, they had to have motorized transport, and that their trucks took them out of the community and into frequent contact with evil influences. Similarly, in their view, Faron's factory job and drug dealing were dependent on his motorized wheels. Had such young men found jobs that kept them in the community, interacting mostly with other Amish and using buggies, they would not have gotten into trouble.

A linked target for blame is the skyrocketing price of land in older Amish communities, so prohibitive that it has forced young men off the farm and into occupations that put them in continual proximity to English workers or into businesses that deal more with non-Amish customers than with Amish ones. These circumstances, some Amish say, encourage kids with too much money and leisure time to get overinvolved in the excesses of the English world.

A perhaps more legitimate target for blame, frequently cited by the formerly Amish and by non-Amish neighbors of the sect—rather than by the Amish—is the *rumspringa* process itself.

Alvin Miller, a Shipshewana businessman, was born into the Old Order, the son of a minister, but is now a member of a Beachy Amish congregation. He and his wife left the Old Order when their older children were approaching the *rumspringa* period because he did not want them having unlimited access to the world when they turned sixteen—an age, in Miller's view, at which children who have previously been very sheltered are not ready for unregulated and unlimited encounters with English culture. To him, the Old Order's *rumspringa* process is "dishonest," because the church, in allowing children to run around at sixteen, is "tacitly approving behaviors that it knows very well to be sins," such as alcohol and drug abuse and sexual license. "If adult church members engaged in such behaviors, they would be punished severely by the church," Miller points out. "Allowing their kids to go and do these things, on the supposition that they will get them out of their system and then settle down, is morally indefensible as well as strategically and tactically wrong."

Miller's criticism of *rumspringa* is offered not in bitterness but in the spirit of neighborly advice. He retains good relationships with his family and his wife's family, who are Old Order Amish, and because the Millers have joined a sufficiently strict church, they are not in the bann. He explains his differences with his Amish neighbors and family members on the subject of *rumspringa* by reference to Aleksandr Solzhenitsyn's *Gulag Archipelago*: "Solzhenitsyn discovers in the prison camps that he isn't good and the other inmates bad, as he previously thought—he finds out that the dividing line between good and bad runs right through him." Miller feels that the Old Order Amish have yet to acknowledge this basic truth about the human condition, and that is why they have for the most part refused to accept the existence of a drug problem in their midst, or to adequately address it.

Gerald Y, the factory worker with his own trailer who has been trying hard to kick his cocaine habit, initially tried drugs, he says, when he was "already drunk" and had no idea what he was getting into. Faron Y offered him some, and he quickly became addicted. All his income went for his car loan payment and his cocaine. Nothing scared him off drugs, not even the visions of being excluded from Heaven that used to haunt him and push him to fall asleep quickly to escape them. What did it was the threat voiced by Joyce, his seventeen-year-old, non-Amish girlfriend—of leaving him, flat, if he did not quit. Now "clean," he refuses to label drugs as evil, recalling the "awesome" highs and the camaraderie of the stoned. But he knows that drugs adversely colored his entire lifestyle. Hanging around with guys like Faron, Gerald "cussed" too frequently, as they did, and is now trying to stop that, because, he says, "it makes you sound dirty."

He projects a slightly truculent attitude toward Joyce's pushing: "Wouldn't even let me smoke a joint. Didn't even let me explain that I like to do it every now and then. 'It's illegal. You're not doing it.' " Relationships, he has been learning—to his astonishment—are "hard work," almost more than he is willing to put in, but he "loves the commitment." However, he is not ready to marry, since he feels a man needs ten to twenty thousand dollars in the bank first, and also that he should wait until he is closer to age thirty.

Gerald's time in *rumspringa* has made clear to him an essential difference between those Amish teens who eventually return to the fold and those who never do. Those who stay out are "more self-conceited." He believes he has never fitted into that category, because he is "more interested in other people" than in himself; he sees his life as "boring" and enjoys working at the task of making the people around him "comfortable." He says he is "truly happy" about those of his peers who are becoming baptized in the Amish church, not out of inertia or blind following of tradition but because they "really want to go Amish, and join from the heart."

This reminds him of one more insight derived from his use of drugs: he avows that they "opened my mind" to being with other people in a casual way and contributed to leaching the anger of his early teenage years, which had been expressed in occasional fits of rage and had made him quit school. "Since I've done drugs, I know what it is to be judged, and it's easier for me not to judge people, just to get along with them."

That understanding contributes to Gerald's finally being able to meet his father on the street, "look him in the eye and talk to him," rather than run away and hide, as he has done in the past in vain attempts to prevent his father from recognizing that he was high. It is a relief for him to be able to say to his parents at home, "I haven't done anything in I don't know how long," and to have them respond that they believe him and are glad for him.

Gerald has also been affected by the plight of his younger brother. He can see what phase of the journey through wildness his brother is in, and realize that he himself has passed that phase and is closer to the end of the journey. He says, "Everybody settles down after a while. If they don't, you look at them walking down the street and say, 'Grow up,' you know?" What he admires about the Amish way of life is the relative absence of temptation. "I mean, like, in my trailer I got DIRECTV—you know, I can rent porn on there. You can't tell me that's healthy." Afraid of his weaknesses, Gerald feels that he needs the assistance of others to prevent his yielding to those frailties and to provide boundaries. Being in the Amish community, he is certain, will also provide spiritual backbone: "If you believe in Jesus and want to serve Him, you're not going to be tempted to go down the wrong road as much."

His own sense of "morals," Gerald increasingly realizes, after four years on his own in the wider world, is much the same as that of his parents and of the Amish community: he does not believe in divorce or in violence against others; "don't believe arguments settle anything . . . don't believe in cheating people." He admires his parents' commitment to the church and to each other, and his father's nonjudgmental attitude, "straightforward" conversation, and directness of speech, and he hopes someday to reach that level of forthrightness. He could use an apprenticeship in that, too.

One Saturday, after a particularly grueling week at work, and

after he and his girlfriend have broken up, Gerald moves back in
with his parents. At twenty he is still not ready to commit to joining the church at any specific time, but he is no longer insistent
on having a life outside the community.

Jerry L, son of Kathryn and Vernon, is approaching eighteen and
is tired of his dishwashing and busboy job at a tourist restaurant.
He also knows he doesn't want to work in a factory. Bright and
wanting to do something connected to his intellectual capacities,
he is casting around for a venue that will permit him to use his
mind to bring in money.

His Tourette's syndrome is under control, and he has stayed
clear of the former classmate who told lies about him (and his job
at the tourist restaurant) that upset him and his mother. Jerry sup-
poses he could work with his father, but Vernon's carpentry business is having enough problems without adding the tensions of a
father-son relationship. Kathryn also opposes Jerry's working with
his father.

One Saturday night Jerry is mildly distressed when his new
rumspringa buddies want him to go out cruising, because he can
find no one at the restaurant willing to trade shifts. So he works
while the buddies party, then comes home and falls asleep.

The next day he learns, from Kathryn, that after the buggy was
brought back the previous night, one of the partygoers, somewhat
drunk "and all hopped up," stole the keys to his brother's car and
took the others out driving. About two in the morning, they
pulled into the family's driveway and "gazed in at Jerry's window"
but did not wake Jerry to take him with them. "Five miles further
south, it was foggy and the boy missed a curve, veered off the
road, got himself killed," Kathryn reports. Jerry would have been
in the seat right in back of the driver and probably would also
have been killed.

"The job saved him," Kathryn marvels—the job that had
caused his earlier *rumspringa* pals and their families to turn on
Jerry.

The fatal accident is a sign from above that neither Kathryn nor Jerry can ignore. On turning eighteen, Jerry applies for a position as a teacher in an Amish school and easily wins the post—there are very few male teachers in Amish schools. The pay is not good, less than he has been making washing dishes, but he readily gives up his restaurant job. Since he will live at home, he will continue to have very low expenses.

It is "a good job for me," he tells a visitor a few months into the school year, a job he likes, and one that other people say he is soon performing quite well. "He has a gift for teaching; the children love him," his mother reports. "He had such a hard time in school himself, he wants to help these kids, and he is."

During his year as a teacher, Jerry joins the church, ending his *rumspringa*. Perhaps as important for his career decisions, he acquires a girlfriend, properly Amish and several years younger. He knows they are both too young to get married, but they like each other, and the possibility of marriage looms pleasantly for some time in the future.

At the close of the school year, thinking about that future marriage and the responsibilities it will entail, Jerry tells me he has to consider seriously once more taking a factory job, which will allow him to put away money toward owning his own home. His pay as a teacher is too low to support him and a wife, not to mention any children they might have.

In the late spring of 2004, Jerry takes his case for a substantial raise to the board of the Amish school. Unwilling to lose a good teacher—and a male teacher—the board agrees to the raise. It still is not nearly as much money as Jerry could make in a factory, but it is good enough, especially if he supplements it with the income from summer employment at a nearby carpentry shop and a part-time job when school is in session. He accepts the deal and eagerly starts preparing for the classes in the fall.

11

"Coming Home"—An Essay

The vast majority of Amish-raised youth in *rumspringa*—80 to 90 percent of them—end up "coming home," being baptized into the church and thereafter molding their lives to fit within the boundaries of the community and its demanding faith. "I think if you join church, you're a lot more comfortable with yourself, I mean, be more involved with God, and stuff," said a young man named Marty. Many, like Marty, come home because they believe in the Amish faith and its way of life. Others do so because they feel they will have a better chance of salvation if they are in the Amish church. As one young man put it, "It's in the back of my mind every day: if I don't change my ways I might not get to Heaven." Intertwined with religious-faith reasons is the sense of purpose that being Amish can provide, and that seems to re-turnees much more difficult or impossible to have, or to sustain for long, on the outside. Some come back for more practical rea-sons, such as liking the slower lifestyle or the comfort of a famil-iar surround, or because they are uncomfortable on the outside. And, of course, some do not come back.

Looking for ways to categorize and understand why most Amish come home and certain ones do not, I found helpful the theories of the psychologist Abraham Maslow. Maslow sought to explain all of human behavior through what he labeled a hierarchy of needs, with the more elemental needs at the broad base of a pyramid, supporting, as it were, the more advanced ones nearer the slimmer top. Any theoretical approach brings some baggage with it, but Maslow's pyramid and its levels provide an insightful framework for identifying precisely where Amish "needs" differ from those of the majority—a key, in my view, to identifying why most return and why certain individuals do not.

At the base of his pyramid, the largest and widest part of the structure, Maslow sited the "physiological needs," for food, water, shelter, sexual activity, and sleep. These needs are recurrent and can never be totally satiated, but they can be kept in proper equilibrium—what Maslow termed "homeostasis." But "what happens to man's desires," he asked, "when there is plenty of bread and when his belly is chronically filled?" His answer is that when any particular needs are satisfied, they disappear as motivators—or at least they retreat into the far background and are replaced as motivators by needs that are higher up on his pyramid.

On the second level are the "safety needs," a long list: "security; stability; dependency; protection; freedom from fear, from anxiety and chaos; need for structure, order, law, limits; strength in the protector; and so on." These needs are readily observable in infants and children, and only somewhat less accessible in adults. "The average adult in our society," he wrote, "generally prefers a safe, orderly, predictable, lawful, organized world, which he can count on and in which unexpected, unmanageable, chaotic, or other dangerous things do not happen, and in which, in any case, he has powerful parents or protectors who shield him from harm." The Maslow description and list of safety needs echoes strongly what many Amish adults, as well as Amish teenagers, describe as the strengths that the Amish community provides to its members: safety, orderliness, predictability, lawfulness, concrete and obvious organization, and the sense of existing under the protection of powerful parents. Maslow contends that all religions offer to their members the satisfying of safety needs, through philosophies and rules that "organize the universe and the men in it into some sort of satisfactorily coherent meaningful whole."

Maslow wrote in an era in which psychology routinely sought to explain away religion or to shortchange its power, so I must point out that satisfying safety needs is not the sum total of what religions do, and that certain important aspects of what the Amish faith provides to its faithful go beyond those needs.

Continuing up the pyramid: When the "safety" needs are satisfied, "now the person will feel keenly, as never before, the absence of friends, or a sweetheart, or a wife, or children. He will hunger for affectionate relations with people . . . for a place in his group or family . . . Now he will feel sharply the pangs of loneliness, of ostracism, of rejection, of friendlessness, of rootlessness." This description of needs, too, resonates with Amish community life, particularly with those aspects frequently emphasized by the Amish as being their joys: family life, group life, rootedness. Maslow thought these needs very important and rued what he saw around him: an American society being "torn up" by an

> unsatisfied hunger for contact, for intimacy, for belongingness and by the need to overcome the widespread feelings of alienation, aloneness, strangeness, and loneliness, which have been worsened by our mobility, by the breakdown of traditional groupings, the scattering of families, the generation gap, the steady urbanization and disappearance of village face-to-faceness.

Surely these unsatisfied hungers are even more prevalent today than they were fifty years ago, when Maslow first articulated them; and those "hungers" are precisely what the Amish slake by working hard to maintain familial and group cohesion, in-person communication, and the small-village way of life.

Beyond the needs for love, affection, and belongingness are what Maslow called "esteem needs," for self-esteem and for the esteem of others, and for "strength, achievement, mastery and competence, independence and freedom." He explained that these esteem needs translate into "the desire for reputation or prestige . . . status, fame and glory, dominance, recognition, attention, importance, dignity, or appreciation." Maslow insisted that the satisfying of these "esteem" needs was common to mainstream Americans, since our culture had provided us with the satisfaction of all the lower needs.

But my experience among the Amish demonstrates that, at least for this group of Americans, "esteem" needs are not universal. Adult Amish, and youth returning to the fold after *rumspringa*, frequently express their utter disregard for whether or not the outside world esteems them as a group or as individuals. They claim to be uninterested in personal fame, glory, dominance, or attention from strangers.

A hint that Maslow might accept the Amish prickliness on this issue comes from a note he wrote about his contemporary the influential psychologist Carl Rogers, who, Maslow pointed out, harped for years about "the dangers of basing self-esteem on the opinions of others rather than on real capacity, competence, and adequacy to the task." Many Amish express ideas consistent with Maslow's and Rogers's conclusion that "the most stable and therefore most healthy self-esteem is based on *deserved* respect from others rather than on external fame or celebrity and unwarranted adulation."

Finally, beyond the needs for esteem, Maslow identified the ultimate need, for what he labeled "self-actualization." Even the name that Maslow applied to this category of needs is enough to make an Amish person shudder with disgust. But Maslow was adamant that when all other needs were satiated, "unless the individual is doing what he, individually, is fitted for," there would emerge in that individual a "new discontent and restlessness."

In order for people to be truly at peace with themselves, Maslow argued, they must realize all of their personal potential. Realizing that potential, he believed deeply, is a basic human urge; and he hastened to explain that "realizing" one's potential is not tied to great achievement—it does not have to mean fulfilling the promise of one's talent by becoming an artistic star. One could realize one's potential, be wholly self-actualized, by becoming "an ideal mother," or creating a minor invention, or expressing one's athleticism in a race or a ball game.

Maslow contended that in an advanced, Westernized society, where the needs for physiological comfort, safety, love, and esteem are more or less satisfied, each individual must try to become self-actualized—or else suffer mentally. Not to attempt to be the best one can be, in Maslow's view, forces the person to remain on a lower level of human existence, at considerable psychological cost to the individual.

Since today's counselors of the Amish contend that the sect's adherents have no more psychological problems than other Americans, and possibly fewer than mainstreamers, Maslow appears to have missed something here. In my view, the missing factor is that for some individuals in the wider society, and for almost all of the Amish, having a genuine and all-encompassing sense of purpose in life becomes as psychologically important and as necessary to mental health and well-being as realizing individual potential.

The young Amish who return to the fold after a period of *rumspringa* do so for a variety of reasons, some more obviously connected to the sense of purpose than others. The reason most frequently cited by our interviewees is the desire of the young man or woman to marry a particular girlfriend or boyfriend who also seeks to join the church. That reason is given by diverse individuals such as Marlys B, Johnny Y, and Eli K. Sometimes, as with Velda B, the applicant's sense that his or her future happiness depends on the intended spouse overwhelms any doubts the partner might have about taking up the Amish way of life and its obligations.

The desire to marry someone may not equate in our minds to seeking a sense of purpose, but for Amish youth it is, because it is accompanied by the thought, expressed by many of the young people aiming for marriage and baptism into the church, that having a properly Amish spouse will enable the applicant more easily to live the Amish way. With a partner, one's ability to stick to one's sense of purpose is augmented, even magnified.

Another frequently cited reason to return is that the young person already knows how to live in the Amish way. "If you're not used to having electricity or TV, you don't miss it," said Christine, a sixteen-year-old in *rumspringa*.

> Sometimes, when you're in a hurry, you think, Man, if I had a car, I could go jump in the car and go, but most of the time, it doesn't bother me. I've been going bowling, and I've been to the movie theater. And your Amish heritage really teaches you a lot. And I miss it. I mean, I've been out, I've done stuff, I've seen the world some, and—you miss not being Amish. So I've pretty much decided that I'm going to be Amish, that's what I want to do with my life.

The promise of the simpler way of life is also a frequently cited reason for coming back to the church: young people mention as attractive the Amish way's slower pace, closeness to nature, and avoidance of the dictates of fashion.

That this is so attractive to many Amish suggests there may be many youngsters in mainstream society who also would like not to have to struggle daily with the fast-paced, fashion-forward, nonnatural aspects of modern life. They just don't have a way of avoiding it that is as readily available to them as the Amish way of life is to Amish-raised youth. Prospective returnees who speak of wanting the slower pace can also reel off a litany of bills they won't have to pay—electricity bills, insurance bills, clothing bills, car bills—obligations that lumped together make for financial worries that they see overwhelming their non-Amish peers. For returnees, the grass is not greener on the outer side of the fence, it is more expensive.

"I'd like to join the church for, you know, for my mom's and dad's sake," young Marty said. Most Amish youth, even during the depths of their rebellion, continue to have and to express tremendous respect for their parents, as we heard from Gerald Y and Joann H, among others. Amish parents' standing in their children's eyes is high because the parents are able to point to themselves as models of what can be done within the restrictions of the Amish way of life: they can legitimately say to the children, "Do as I say, and as I do," and their suggestions carry more weight with the children than do those of mainstream parents who cannot claim that high ground. Many Amish-raised youth give as a partial reason for joining the Amish church the equal desire to avoid hurting their parents, which they would do if they strayed from the faith.

Less usually voiced is the companion motive, a wish not to hurt themselves by becoming cut off from their parents. Based on what has happened to friends and relatives, they have reason to believe that they could be marginalized in the family if they do not join the church. Emma M and others who chose not to join were conflicted about their decisions because of their fear of being cut off from their parents if they did not come home to the church. These are kids who would not be shunned, but they know that the parental bond with a nonjoining child will likely be frailer than with one who joins.

The desire not to hurt one's parents by a refusal to come home is a significant factor in the sustainability of many cultures, according to Daniel Offer and his associates, who studied patterns of teenage behavior in ten cultures around the globe. The Offer research shows that most young adults in these cultures have no wish to injure their parents by leaving the surround in which they spent their childhoods but that this motivation has a more powerful deterrent effect on the children of close-knit, highly religious families, where it is reinforced by the threat of church sanctions against those who leave.

Amish parents are not shy about pushing this emotional button in their children; Emma M, Lydia T, Velda B, and DeWayne C report their parents lambasting a potential leaving of the family for an "independent" life as abandonment and defection—as a rejection of the parents' values and how they have brought up the children. Since most Amish-raised children go out in the world for the purpose of gaining experience and finding a mate, not to reject their parents or to risk losing familial affection, they are very responsive to parental emotional pressure. Even Faron Y, whose rebellion was a specific rejection of his family, shows quite a bit of vulnerability on this point.

Another reason for joining the church, allied to not wanting to hurt the family or suffer emotional damage by leaving, is the positive expectation of enjoying terrific family and community support. Youngsters like the idea of this kind of support and speak in celebratory terms of future receipt of various forms of assistance from the community and the family, aid of a quality and quantity not available to them on the outside. They feel keenly the peace of mind of being able to count on communal help in times of difficulty. It's more than money, said one young man. "They'll do a special church service for you, and everybody stays, and you feel better after that."

What is reinforced by such scenes is the individual's sense of having chosen the right path in life, of having a proper purpose, and of being supported in that purpose by relatives, neighbors, friends, and coreligionists. Thus, those wanting to return also speak fondly of the camaraderie that goes on over back fences and at the many community events, the sense of sharing moral values and religious beliefs with everyone around them, and the understanding that they as individuals will be taken care of by family and community when they become aged and unable to care for themselves.

For those of us who are not Amish, this yearning for support raises an interesting point. It underlines the degree to which people in their late teens and early twenties, while trying mightily to establish their independence from their parents, also have a strong need for support from them—perhaps stronger than most mainstream twentysomethings are usually willing to admit. A similar point is brought to the fore by the Amish youngsters' desire to have the resources of the community available to them as they age. Most young mainstreamers believe they are invincible and act accordingly, giving little thought to any future need for assistance—for that matter, to any aspect of what might happen to them when they are older.

This is not just the usual disregard of youth for aging; in my view, it is almost unreasonable for mainstream young people to give much weight in their thoughts to what may happen to them several decades hence, because they live in a world whose future is unpredictable and in which plans frequently have to be altered. It isn't unreasonable for Amish youth, though, since they have grown up in multigenerational households, in a tradition that emphasizes caring for the less able and the aged, and in a way of life and community where the shape of an individual's future can be minutely known and predicted.

The split between Amish and non-Amish kids' motivations on this matter reveals a far deeper divide between the two groups. Mainstream American youngsters have a basic sense that the world is changing rapidly, and a belief that planning for the future is less important than living fully in the present. Amish youth have the opposite view: their own society is changing only slowly and has withstood changes very well. Mainstream adolescents are not blithely ignorant that they will have a future in which they become older; rather, they recognize (because of their wider and longer exposure to mainstream culture) that as they age they will have opportunities to join or develop support systems to pay for medical expenses and their retirement years. For mainstream kids to consider carefully such matters when young and without responsibilities is, in their eyes, to act as though prematurely aged.

Amish youth have had no experience with outside support groups such as unions, fraternal organizations, YMCAs, YWCAs, Chambers of Commerce, or the Social Security Administration, and they have been warned since childhood about relying on them. But they need support and structure as much as anyone does—perhaps more than mainstream youth, because young

Amish have grown up with a great deal of structure, provided by the church, the family, and a tight-knit community, and on the outside they sense keenly the absence of that traditional support.

There is another facet of coming back to the church that Amish youth do not talk about very much, though it is fairly obvious to an older outsider, and that is the returnee's sense that he or she might never achieve much on the outside. More girls speak glancingly of the adverse consequences of not having advanced education, mainly that they are ineligible for remunerative and interesting jobs. The young men, who can obtain high-paying jobs in factories, do not mention this as much.

Those who do mention their lack of potential tend to clothe the observation in the more-acceptable-to-the-Amish explanation that they do not have—and do not desire to have—the driving ambition that they construe as necessary to making it in an ultracompetitive outside world.

Which brings us to the ones who do leave.

According to several longtime outside observers of the Amish, the 10 to 20 percent of each generation who leave the fold are of two types. The first consists of the more intellectually and the more artistically inclined who yearn for what Marlow calls self-actualization. While there are dozens of formerly Amish artists whose products are sold in galleries, only Susie Riehl and one or two others remain within the church. The second group consists of those at the other end of the spectrum: the disgruntled, the angry, and those who chose a more materialistic lifestyle than the Amish will countenance. The factory worker Phil T is in the latter category. Most of those in either category who leave require years to integrate themselves fully into non-Amish society, and plenty of them also require counseling to do so.

An important factor in both groups' unpreparedness for life on the outside is that they have not had adequate schooling, having been removed from classes at fourteen. Even observers sympathetic to the Amish charge that taking children out of school at an early age is bad for the children and not salutary for the sect. For the children, being denied schooling in the late teenage years is akin to being deprived of basic nourishment for their minds. Harsher critics suggest that this deprivation of children by the Amish ought to merit the same degree of disapproval from the outside society as would physical malnourishment.

Some Amish elders do acknowledge that cutting off schooling after the eighth grade limits the children, but that it benefits the continuity of the sect for the kids to have less ability to make it on the outside and hastens their return to the fold.

Do those who return home have a sense of limited horizons or of inadequacy? If they do, they don't express it. Rather, they affect an attitude of "been there, done that," of having seen enough of the outside world so that they are now ready, willing, and able to reject it in favor of an Amish life. These young people do concede that by spending the rest of their lives inside the Amish community they will miss out on some possibilities in the wider world, but they do not accept the notion that they are retreating before they have made themselves aware of all the outside possibilities or of their potential for realizing such possibilities.

"Been there, done that" is a rationale frequently voiced in tandem with the desire for the religious certainty attendant on being in the church when rejecting mainstream culture. Virtually all Amish-raised youth are religious, whether or not they attend alternate churches during *rumspringa*, and whether or not they eventually return to the Amish church. They want to be good Christians. Many, while on the loose, attend non-Amish churches just to sample different ways of worship, and a few join those churches. Those who are baptized in outside churches prefer evangelical denominations and their more exuberant brand of faith. Regina E, the shopgirl enjoying her *rumspringa*, was counseled by her mother that even if she did not eventually join the Amish church, she must not "leave God." Regina had no intention of doing so, and neither do most Amish youngsters.

A new notion in psychology, called "terror management theory," suggests that concern for the fate of our souls is more central to all of us than we are usually willing to admit—and more important in adolescence than we might have imagined. The theory argues that as children mature and become more conscious of their own mortality, they grow fearful and anxious, and turn for support and for management of their terror to cultural systems that make the reality of an eventual death more bearable. In most tests of this theory, mainstream youngsters were judged to be fighting their fear of death by clinging to youth culture as an "anxiety buffer." But the sociologist Denise Reiling, in her decade-long studies of Amish youth, discovered that Amish kids do precisely the opposite: when confronted with the realization of their own eventual mortality, Amish-raised youth do not cling to mainstream youth culture; rather, they rush home to embrace the culture of their parents. Their fear that they could die while outside the church, and therefore be condemned to Hell, Reiling found, motivates many to join the church.

Reiling's observation meshes well with what our interviewees mention as what they look forward to when they join the church, being enveloped in a community of like-minded believers, each striving for the common goals of salvation and Christian service to others. A frequently cited memory for many Amish youth in *rumspringa* is the comfort of communal worship with close friends in a neighbor's home or in their own home, and it is something that they want to replicate as they become adults.

This sense and their religious conviction also fit seamlessly with the satisfaction they derive from knowing what the future will hold. The shape of their lives will be quite certain—their lives will be very much like the lives of their parents.

On this point, too, Amish kids' views are opposite to those of the mainstream. Most American youth are determined *not* to live in ways overly similar to those of their parents, and they embrace uncertainty—they desire to be different and like the challenge of frequent change and the opportunities that change affords to reinvent themselves in the future. Amish youth have been taught since birth that change is generally undesirable; and during their time out of time, away from the community, one of the most significant lessons they learn is that a principal component of the wider world is rapid change. By choosing the Amish way of life, they are rejecting the notion of continual change and embracing the safety, security, immutability, and sense of purpose that come from knowing the shape and content of their own futures.

Those who return acknowledge that in joining the church they will cede to the community the power of making many adult choices, in terms of careers, companions, venues, and rules for behavior. But most do not see this as a loss of freedom or as an undue constricting of choices, and even those who do construe it as a necessary component of their religious obligation.

Yet their willingness, at a relatively young age, to yield their independence and to agree to having continual constraints on their lives is startling. It seems a stark contradiction of the larger society's tenets of liberty and free will, an attitude that evokes memories of one of the most famous chapters in literature, in Fyodor Dostoevsky's *The Brothers Karamazov*—the scene between the Grand Inquisitor and a "foreigner" who appears in the streets of medieval Seville and is thought to be Christ.

The foreigner arrives the day after one hundred heretics have been burned at the stake in an auto-da-fé. The Grand Inquisitor, a ninety-year-old monk, has the foreigner arrested and imprisoned, then visits him in a dungeon. The monk tells Christ—if the foreigner is indeed Christ—that He must have come (as He came once before) to make men free, but that He is wrong to have done so, because "man is tormented by no greater anxiety than to find someone quickly to whom he can hand over that gift of freedom with which the ill-fated creature is born." The Inquisitor demands that the visitor go and not return to earth, where the freedom that Christ once preached and represents is neither wanted nor needed, and to leave the governance of man, and man's spiritual guidance, in the hands of the Catholic church, which will give man the illusion of freedom while not permitting its realization.

Are Amish youth so unable to handle the "gift of freedom" that they leap at the chance of handing that freedom over to their church? The time that Amish youth in *rumspringa* spend on the outside, before returning, is short; the portion of the outside world they explore is narrow; and the experiences they have on the outside are usually shallow, most of them involving minor excursions into sex, drugs, and rapid transport. Amish youth from Lancaster, Holmes, or LaGrange county do not travel to Katmandu to experience a wholly different culture. They do not trace their roots in Germany or Switzerland. They do not move to Chicago or Cleveland or Philadelphia and study biology, art, or engineering. They do not start Internet businesses on a shoestring. They do not take three months to hike the Rocky Mountains.

Part of their reluctance to explore interesting avenues in the outside world fully is attributable to their truncated educations, which disqualify them for the sorts of interests that might take them further afield or set their hearts afire. It is nearly impossible to conceptualize becoming a great painter if you know too little about art, or a computer programmer if you have never logged on.

Amish youth are also psychologically ill prepared for complex, open-minded interaction with the larger world. Since early childhood they have been continuously instructed that the world outside is replete with snares set by the Devil; and they have been taught that their main worth is not as individuals but can be realized only when they are part of the group of believers within the church.

This combination makes them overly subject to the slings and arrows of fortune in the outside world, such as the near-inevitable personal betrayals of the late teenage and early twenties years. Young adults have been complaining about betrayals by friends and lovers for thousands of years; Aristotle commented that adolescents "are changeable and fickle in their desires . . . cannot bear being slighted, and are indignant if they imagine themselves unfairly treated." But few mainstream youths construe as a major benefit of marriage the assurance that there will be no future intimate betrayals, while many Amish youngsters cite this certainty

as an important reason to marry within their church. As young
Mel Y put it, "You never hear of Amish people getting divorced.
That'd be the main reason [for marrying an Amish woman], because I wouldn't be afraid of her running off on me, maybe finding a better man than me. Because Amish is just— They stick
together through thick and thin."

Avoidance of betrayal as a main reason for marriage hints at a
truncated psychological development process. In the course of a
more usual mainstream life, the accumulated hurts and experience
of adolescent betrayals eventually permit a person, as he or she
ages, to make wiser choices of mates and to adopt modes of behavior that steady the newer relationships and allow these to develop into mature partnerships. Mainstream youth also manage to
resolve their need for other kinds of structure: they slake their
thirst for religious meaning by joining a church, temple, mosque,
or ashram that they find amenable and expressive of their variety
of faith; they satisfy their yearning for rigor and discipline by devoting themselves to career and social goals and parenting; and,
last but not least, they put their fear of dying on a back burner
by construing life as a series of current and future challenges to
be met.

Psychologists have defined the major task of late adolescence as
"self-emancipation," taking control of one's life from parents and
exercising it for one's self. This emotional development does not
happen in one stroke and generally is not complete by a person's
early twenties. Many of the behaviors of Amish youth in returning to the church after a *rumspringa* period of only a few years—
and the rationales they offer for doing so—suggest that they have
not mastered this major emotional development task. In "coming
home" before emancipation is accomplished, many Amish youth
delay, and sometimes obviate altogether, effective separation of
themselves from the control of their parents, and from their
larger-compass parents, the church-based community.

What stage of development are they in then? Some insight
comes from Lawrence Kohlberg, whose theories are based on
Jean Piaget's pioneering work on the stages of human moral de-

\t. Kohlberg suggests that all human beings ascend a lad-
ᴗn which there are a handful of identifiable developmental
rungs, the first two reached during childhood, the middle two
reached in the early teen years, the last ones coming into possible
reach in late adolescence. In Stage 3, the individual believes that
"good behavior is that which pleases or helps others and is approved by them." In Stage 4, the mantra is "Good behavior consists of doing one's duty, having respect for authority, and
maintaining the social order for its own sake."

At these stages, a teenager conceives the social contract "in
terms of general rights and standards agreed upon by society." But
as he or she matures further, "there is an increasing orientation
towards internal decisions of conscience," and the reaching of
Stage 5, in which truly individual decisions are made. (Stage 6 is
reserved for Mother Teresas.) Tests conducted by Kohlberg and
others in various countries around the world have demonstrated
that in less well-developed countries, most adults score low on the
"moral development" ladder. Psychologists theorize that they are
stuck at lower stages or have never advanced to the "individual
decisions" of Stage 5, or that they reached Stage 5 during early
adolescence but regressed from it to Stage 3 or Stage 4 as they at-
tained adulthood.

A set of adolescents giving up on individual decisions and
embracing the idea that good behavior has to do with duty, up-
holding the social order, and respecting authority: this is a fair description of Amish youth who choose to return to the church
after a relatively short *rumspringa*. In coming home, they are opting to abide by the decision-making processes of the group rather
than to continue to struggle (and to have to make decisions) as
individuals on the outside. This pattern is not unique to the
Amish. It has also been identified through testing of groups that
have few external similarities to the Amish, such as Muslim Mo-
roccans and Turks residing in enclaves in Amsterdam and in other
cities of the Netherlands. Studies of the behavior of adolescents
who chose to function within those encapsulated communities,
rather than to assimilate into the outside culture, revealed that

they returned to the Stage 3 and Stage 4 formulations of moral development, in part because "obedience and respect for parents" were more important to them than "individualism and independence."

Amish elders insist that there is a lot of freedom within the picket-fence walls of their communities; that the members, freed from the need to meet the obligations of the outside world, are well able to fulfill their destinies. Those destinies are largely subsumed in the tasks of continuing the church and Amish culture, and are frequently detrimental to the self-actualization of some church members—of how many, or of what percentage of the total, it is impossible to tell. While some Amish are, indeed, able to realize their full potential within the structure of the community, a fair proportion are not.

But does the loss of "self-actualization" possibilities matter to individuals inside the Amish community? Most newly adult Amish will decide to live as their parents have—with a puissant sense of community and religious purpose, and they will take considerable satisfaction from doing so. That is a remarkable achievement for any society.

Looking at the decision to return to the community in a different way, we can posit that what these young Amish are doing is in effect agreeing to make their future decisions with reference to a rationale that is often overlooked in mainstream society but that is a counterbalance to Maslow's psychological hierarchy of needs—a more philosophical "hierarchy of values." All religions and ethical formulations develop hierarchies of values, according to the philosopher Alfred North Whitehead. For example, a reverence for life is consistently placed above a reverence for property in the Judeo-Christian heritage. According to Whitehead, each of us constructs our own ranking of values. Consciously or unconsciously, we regard certain values as being of greater (or more central) importance to us than others, and when we are in a crisis, or simply in a situation where we must choose between actions that uphold one value rather than another—say, respect for parents versus individualism—we choose the value that is the higher-ranked in our personal hierarchy. In the *rumspringa* contest between the siren call of individualism and the duty call of fulfilling parental and community wishes, Amish youth raised to revere and obey their parents almost always choose the latter. Rather than pursue individualistic enterprises in an outside setting more conducive to independence and uniqueness, they choose to return to the community and take up the responsibilities of a church member; and they make that choice because they value more highly their religion and their sect's way of life than they do personal independence.

Amish youth know very well that joining the church is an irrevocable act having multiple weighty consequences. They may actually join because they seek that irreversibility, because they want to end the stress and ambiguity that will otherwise continue for them in the outside world. By joining, they acquire and affirm an already existing set of values—a hierarchy of values, set by the church but with which they agree—that enables them to eliminate possible confusion about value choices, such as whom to marry, how to worship, where to live, and what degree of independence from parents to exercise. Making the one big decision of returning home and being baptized in the church releases Amish youth from the need to agonize over many other decisions.

Modern mainstream American adult life is chock-full of decisions and choices about where and how to live, what path to follow, whom to associate with, and so on. Some of the choices in the mainstream world come with pleasant alternatives, some do not, but many of them lead to consequences that are reliably unpredictable.

Tremendous predictability about the future is gained by the Amish youth who opts to live within the framework of the church. And the consequences of that predictability include contentment with one's lot, a relatively serene surround, clear direction and purpose, assured community involvement, and a high degree of certainty that he or she is living a proper, and a properly religious, life on earth that is the best preparation for eternal life.

Most Amish are satisfied with their lives; most mainstream Americans express a significant degree of dissatisfaction with theirs. Advertisers and politicians are continually telling us that we must aim at complete satisfaction in every aspect of our lives and must not settle for anything less. But is satisfaction with one's life the ultimate good? And is dissatisfaction with it inherently bad?

Satisfaction and certainty are at the heart of the Amish experience—and in acknowledging their centrality there we do several things: we recognize that these are positive attributes that many young people, Amish or not, want in their lives; we acknowledge that religious faith can bring these attributes to the faithful; but, equally, we recognize that a fundamental characteristic of modern American experience is uncertainty.

Americans are uncertain about the future, and none are more so than our youth. The threats of terrorist attacks, war, and epidemics, as well as of economic disasters and personal-life tragedies such as divorce and familial chaos, hang over them, as do unknowns such as success in personal, professional, and community endeavors; happiness; opportunities for great varieties of experience; and so on. American youth, with good reason, believe that the future is both unlimited and unforeseeable.

Is this belief incompatible with their also wanting and working for a sense of purpose, religious or secular? I think not. Most young people in the mainstream are not immobilized by the understanding that the future is less predictable than they might like it to be. They feel able to handle the risk. They may suffer because of life's chronic uncertainty, but they also surely gain from having to deal with its manifestations rather than pushing aside the risks and fleeing to safety; they gain control by understanding that the world is changing and will continue to change, and that if they adapt to the changes, they will survive and grow.

Can mainstream society make it possible for larger numbers of its young people to experience more of the senses of purpose, contentment, satisfaction, belongingness, community coherence,

religiosity, and commendable passion exhibited by the Amish—
without giving up the possibilities for progress, innovation, and
achievement that are regularly birthed by creative dissatisfaction
with the status quo, embrace of uncertainty, and commitment to
individual growth?

This writer hopes so. The Amish model of those positive aspects derivable from sense of purpose is, at least, available for
study, even if we don't want to emulate every aspect of it.

The Amish are going to change, whether they want to or not. The
trend away from farming and toward factory work and the nurturing of their small businesses is unlikely to be reversed. Left
unchecked, these changes in vocation will produce a somewhat
different Amish culture of the future. The signs of change are already there, for instance, in the statistic that families who do not
farm have fewer children than those who do, and that women
who work at their own small businesses—an increasing number—
also have fewer children than those who do not own businesses.

These trends highlight resemblances between the Amish and
another black-hatted, ascetic, highly religious, and successfully entrepreneurial group: Hasidic Jews. Despite vast differences in religious beliefs, there are plenty of similarities. The Hasidim follow
hundreds of biblically based directives and restrictions in their
daily lives, rules that govern their appearance and their behavior.
They are quite religious, live in enclaves, speak a language at
home that differs from the English language they speak to the
outside world, and have no intention of assimilating fully into the
mainstream. They, too, await the coming of a messiah.

But in contrast to the Amish, the Hasidim are integrated into
the business communities of the outside world; many of them live
in big cities, where interaction with people in the mainstream is
constant; and they do not reject the use of electricity, automobiles, cell phones, or any other technologies. Also, they are believers in education, students of the written word. As the Hasidim
prosper, some move out of their inner-city enclaves into more

amenable circumstances in the suburbs, and they do so without sacrificing their religious tenets or changing their ritual-based daily practices. A significant number of them achieve interesting individual goals—economic, artistic, political, and social—without defecting or living apart from the community.

In a study of diversity within the plain Christian communities a generation ago, Leo Driedger suggested that when urbanization and industrialization beset a plain community, maintaining a "structured rural ethnic enclave" becomes increasingly difficult, and the emphasis shifts from "structural" factors—the enclosed community, the use of horse and buggy, the nonuse of electricity from the grid—to factors that are more symbolic. The symbolic factors are shared beliefs, an awareness of shared history and social status, and, in some sects, charismatic leadership. Driedger documents how this route has been traveled by certain Mennonite sects and suggests that the Jews' adherence to symbolic factors is what has permitted them to survive as a religious people despite wars, genocide, and dispersal to many lands.

In fifty years, because of the shift to an off-the-farm, entrepreneurial culture, the Old Order Amish will certainly have closer integration with the mainstream society and greater participation in it, and they will likely maintain their separate identity principally by means of shared religious tenets rather than through the rural lifestyle. This shift will mandate, and perhaps make possible, more avenues for individual growth within Amish society. The examples of other, similarly religious cultures that permit individual growth show this is achievable without sacrifice of the community-first ethic. In fifty years, *rumspringa* will likely be redefined in broader terms, such as permitting the finishing of high school or of a stint in college before the young person has to make up his or her mind to become an Amish adult. The holding of a high school or college degree will not automatically exclude the degree holder from fitting into the Amish community. More interaction with the outside world will be permitted, because adult members of the community will feel secure enough in their shared faith to recognize that by itself it can serve as a shield against external pressures, as the Hasidim's shared faith does for them.

The Amish will move in the direction of the mainstream. The challenge for the mainstream is how to move toward the Amish. The Amish sit lightly upon the earth and upon American society in ways that we could readily adopt: their reverence for life, for the land, for neighborliness, for family matters, for hard work, for caring for the elderly and the infirm, and their judicious disdain for conspicuous consumption, and for not stopping to smell the roses. We in the mainstream need to find ways to incorporate these behaviors and attitudes into the goals and actions of the larger society, to help us raise our culture to higher standards of communitarianism, of appreciation of what we have, and of the pursuit of purposes larger than our appetites.

Notes

The listings in these notes are cumulative; references cited for the first chapter have also been used in later chapters but are not separately cited for those chapters. All Bible citations are from the King James Version of the Old and New Testaments.

Any outsider seeking to understand the Amish culture should begin with the work of Donald B. Kraybill and his associates, in *The Riddle of Amish Culture* (Johns Hopkins University Press, 2001); Kraybill and Marc A. Olshan, editors, *The Amish Struggle with Modernity* (University Press of New England, 1994); Kraybill and Steven M. Nolt, *Amish Enterprise* (Hopkins, 2nd edition, 2004); and Kraybill, editor, *The Amish and the State* (Hopkins, 2nd edition, 2003). Two other indispensable books are Steven M. Nolt, *A History of the Amish* (Good Books, 1992), and David Weaver-Zercher, *The Amish in the American Imagination* (Hopkins, 2001).

Family Life, the monthly magazine published by Pathway Publishers of Ontario, is a primary source for information about the Amish, conveyed in thoughtful articles and letters written by the Amish, frequently unsigned. A more widely available and accessible compilation from *Family Life* is Brad Igou, *The Amish in Their Own Words* (Herald Press, 1999).

David Luthy's most recent census of Amish districts was published initially in *Family Life* and separately as a booklet, *Amish Settlements Across America* (Pathway, 2003).

1. "GOING AWAY"

The quotation on adolescence is from S. C. Feinstein, editor, introduction to volume 14 of *Adolescent Psychiatry*, 1987.

Scholarly articles about the Amish are often published in the *Mennonite Quarterly Review*, abbreviated here as *MQR*. Among those consulted in regard to the "retention rate" are Thomas J. Meyers, "Population Growth and Its Consequences in the Elkhart-LaGrange Old Order Amish Settlement," *MQR*, July 1991; Meyers, "The Old Order Amish: To Remain in the Faith or to Leave," *MQR*, July 1994; Lawrence P. Greska and Jill E. Korbin, "Key Decisions in the Lives of the Old Order Amish: Joining the Church and Migrating to Another Settlement," *MQR*, September 2002.

John Howard Yoder's translation of *The Schleitheim Confession* (Herald Press, 1977) is essential, as is Pathway's version of the Dortrecht Confession, *Confession of Faith* (1998). These confessions are put into perspective by Karl Koop, *Anabaptist-Mennonite Confessions of Faith* (Pandora Press, 2004). Modern understandings of the confessions began with a reinterpretation titled "The Anabaptist Tradition," by Harold S. Bender, in a speech given in 1943, printed in *MQR*, April 1944.

Figures on the ages at which the Amish marry and bear children, and at what point in the couple's relationship, come from Joseph F. Donnermeyer and Elizabeth C. Cooksey, "The Demographic Foundations of Amish Society," paper presented at the Plain Communities Conference at Elizabethtown College in Pennsylvania, June 2004. In addition to the 12 percent of babies born to couples married less than nine months, the authors report that 5 percent of babies are born out of wedlock.

2. "A GLORY OLD TIME"

Donnermeyer and Cooksey recently determined that the average size of a nonfarming Amish family in mid-Ohio is 4.7 children, while the average size of a farming Amish family is 6.2 children.

Mainstream adolescent mental development and behavior is discussed by George H. Orvin, *Understanding the Adolescent* (American Psychiatric Press, 1996); and by Julia A. Graber and Jeanne Brooks-Gunn, "Transitions and Turning Points: Navigating the Passage from Childhood Through Adolescence," *Developmental Psychology* 32 (1996). Psychological and sociological factors affecting Amish youth in *rumspringa* are analyzed by Denise M. Reiling, "The 'Simmie' Side of Life: Old Order Amish Youths' Affective Response to Culturally Prescribed Deviance," *Youth and Society*, December 2002.

Diane Zimmerman Umble's thoughtful meditation is *Holding the Line: The Telephone in Old Order Mennonite and Amish Life* (Johns Hopkins University Press, 1996).

The critique of changing water-drawing practices is from E. Stoll's "Views and Values" column, *Family Life*, July 1973. Laurence R. Iannacone's interesting article, "Why Strict Churches Are Strong," is in *American Journal of Sociology* 99 (1994).

3. "STRAIGHTFORWARD CONVERSATIONS"

The articles in *Family Life* come from a collection of ten letters called "Leading the Lambs," in the April 1998 issue, and eighteen letters collectively titled "Protecting Our Teens," May 2000. The anonymous "Willing Submission" article is in the April 1998 issue, but nearly every issue contains an article or a letter attesting to the centrality and importance of willing submission in Amish life and education. Two articles by an Amish minister titled "Preserving the Moral Purity of Our Children" are in the issues of October and November 2002.

The minister Joseph F. Beiler's thoughts on the *ordnung* are in Beiler, "Research Note: Ordnung," *MQR*, October 1982.

David Wagler collected many years of his columns from the newspaper *The Budget* as *Stories Behind the News* (Brookside Publishers, 1993). His "Why the Amish Can Live Without Television" is a chapter in *The Plain Reader*, edited by Scott Savage (Ballantine, 1998).

The work of the psychiatrist Jerry M. Lewis and associates, comparing a range of families in the United States, is summarized in Lewis, W. R. Beavers, J. T. Gossett, and V. A. Phillips, *No Single Thread: Psychologic Health in Family Systems* (Brunner/Mazel, 1976); in Lewis et al., "The Impact of Adolescent Children on Family Systems," in *Adolescent Psychiatry*, volume 13, edited by S. C. Feinstein et al. (University of Chicago Press, 1986); and Lewis, "For Better or Worse: Interpersonal Relationships and Individual Outcome," *American Journal of Psychiatry* 155 (5) (May 1998).

Victor Stoltzfus's article "Reward and Sanction: The Adaptive Continuity of Amish Life" is in *MQR*, October 1977.

4. EDUCATION: "PREPARE FOR USEFULNESS"

The basic reference for information about Amish schools is John A. Hostetler and Gertrude Enders Huntington, *Amish Children: Education in the Family, School, and Community*, originally published in 1971 (revised edition, Harcourt Brace Jovanovich, 1992). I have written previously about schooling in early America in *The Inarticulate Society* (Free Press, 1995).

Wisconsin v. Yoder et al. is 406 U.S. 205, 1972. Contemporary reaction is reported by William R. MacKaye, "High Court Hears Amish School Case," *Washington Post*, December 9, 1971. An exhaustive study of the case and its implications is Shawn F. Peters, *The* Yoder *Case: Religious Freedom, Education, and Parental Rights* (University Press of Kansas, 2003).

Daisy Spangler's book, *Good Morning Teacher Daisy* (Gordonville Print Shop, 1994), is an important source of firsthand information. A similar book, though lacking the perspective provided by Spangler's many years in the public school systems, is *The Amish School*, by Sara E. Fisher, an Old Order Amish woman who taught for seven years (revised edition, Good Books, 2002).

Two important pre–*Wisconsin v. Yoder* studies of the efficacy of Amish education are Wayne Edward Miller, "A Study of Amish Academic Achievement," Ph.D. dissertation, University of Michigan, 1969, and Arthur A. Martin, "An Investigation of Amish Schools in Lancaster County, Pennsylvania," master's thesis, Millersville State College, 1965. The best recent roundup about Amish education, Thomas J. Meyers's chapter, "Education and Schooling," in Kraybill, ed., *The Amish and the State*, 2nd edition (2003), has few references to post-1972 studies. The Iowa 1987 study was reported in Hostetler and Huntington's revised edition, 1992. According to an oral presentation (Plain Communities Conference, 2004), Donald Kraybill has seen similar results in more recent Indiana studies, but these have not yet been published.

Melvin R. Smucker's study, "How Amish Children View Themselves and Their Families: The Effectiveness of Amish Socialization," is in *Brethren Life and Thought*, Summer 1988. Andrea Fishman's study is *Amish Literacy: What and How It Means* (Heinemann, 1988).

Dr. Ralph Gemelli's book is *Normal Childhood and Adolescent Development* (American Psychiatric Press, 1996).

Erik Erikson's ideas are summarized in *Identity: Youth and Crisis* (Norton, 1968).

5. FAITH AND DOCTRINE: "STAND FAST AND BELIEVE THE WORD AS WRITTEN"

David Wagler's comment about the "lively hope" is from his compilation of his articles for *The Budget* called *Stories Behind the News*.

In addition to English translations of the *Martyrs' Mirror* and the *Ausbund*, I have used abridgments and commentaries, including James W. Lowry, *The Martyrs'*

Mirror Made Plain (Pathway Publishers, 2000); Amish Brotherhood of Holmes County, *Light from the Stakes* (Amish Brotherhood Publications, 1983); and Benuel S. Blank, *The Amazing Story of the Ausbund* (2001).

Werner Enninger's article is "The Social Construction of Past, Present and Future in the Written and Oral Text of the Old Order Amish: An Ethno-Semiotic Approach to Social Belief," in *Literary Anthropology*, edited by Fernando Poyatos (John Benjamins, 1988).

The Amish elder's letter on persecution is in Joe Wittmer, *The Gentle People* (Educational Media Corporation, 2001).

Bishop Stephen L. Yoder's book is *My Beloved Brethren* (Evangel Press, 1992). In a prefatory note, he writes that the book is designed to be read by fellow Beachy Amish and not by outsiders. I have left unchanged his emphases in capitals and italicizings.

One of the formal questions asked at baptism is: "Do you confess this to be a Christian order, church and congregation of God to which you now submit?" *Hymn and Prayer Translation from Ausbund and Lieder Buch, Plus Prayers Used in Church, Marriage, and Baptismal Vows*, a pamphlet published by Isaac Stoltzfus (Aylmer, Ontario, 2000).

Denise Reiling's conclusions are stated in her article "The 'Simmie' Side of Life" and are based on interviews conducted for her dissertation, "An Exploration of the Relationship Between Amish Identity and Depression Among the Old Order Amish," Michigan State University, 2000.

6. SHUNNING: TO KEEP THE CHURCH "PURE"

Paton Yoder's book is *Tradition and Transition: Amish Mennonites and Old Order Amish, 1800–1900* (Herald Press, 1991).

The anonymous Amish minister's article on *meidung* is "The Church's Duty to Confront Error," *Family Life*, May 2002.

Émile Durkheim's *The Elementary Forms of Religious Life* (1915) was reissued by the Free Press in 1995.

The minister Joseph F. Beiler's note "Revolutionary War Records" is in *The Diary of the Old Order Churches*, March 1975.

Daniel B. Lee's paper, "On the Social Meaning and Meaninglessness of Religion" was presented at the 1998 meeting of the American Sociological Association.

"Purity of Little Girls" and "Journey to Freedom," and responses to these articles, in various issues of *Family Life*, 1999–2000.

The *Kansas City Star* articles are the "Plain Prey" series, published October 20–23, 1996. Other similar cases, such as that of an article on an Amish "elderly rapist" in Ohio are reported in Associated Press stories from September 19 to October 30, 2001. In July 2004, the Lancaster *Intelligencer Journal* ran a series of articles, "Silence by Shame," an exposé of "domestic abuse among Amish and Mennonites," which, the paper charged, was "often ignored, even tolerated, by church leaders," July 11, 2004 *et seq.*, chiefly written by Linda Espenshade and Dee Drummond, "Amish Won't Seek Outside Help for Abuse," *Toledo Blade*, May 8, 2001. For the Wisconsin case, see, *inter alia*, Ed Hoskins, "A Question of Justice in Amish Community," *La Crosse Tribune*, March 28, 2004.

Statistical survey study on abuse in families of churchgoers, cited in W. Bradford Wilcox, *Soft Patriarchs, New Men: How Christianity Shapes Fathers and Husbands* (University of Chicago Press, 2004).

7. FARMING: "THE IDEAL OCCUPATION"

Figures on manure spreading and soil absorption are from David Kline, *Great Possessions: An Amish Farmer's Journal* (North Point Press, 1990). Samuel S. Stoltzfus's articles include "Our Changing Amish Church District," *Pennsylvania Folklife*, Spring 1994. Other figures on Lancaster County agriculture are taken from "Lancaster County Farming Facts," a Chamber of Commerce and Industry publication. A source for comparisons to non-Amish farming is Ronald Jager, *The Fate of Family Farming* (University Press of New England, 2004).

The two cited papers on Amish farming, "Manure Management Strategies for Amish Farms," by Randall E. James, and "Economic Potential of Amish Dairy Systems in Lancaster County," by Roland P. Freund and Mary Beth Grove, were presented at the 2004 Plain Communities Conference.

The *Family Life* article "Our Choice of Occupation," anonymously written by an Amish minister, is in the July 2000 issue.

General information on the Ashtabula County Amish is in a series of articles by Carl E. Feather in the Ashtabula *Star Beacon*, 2004.

8. "WORKING AWAY"

The statistics on Amish working in factories in Indiana come from Meyers, "Education and Schooling," in Kraybill, editor, *The Amish and the State*, 2nd edition,

2003; and from "The Transformation of Amish Society," a chapter in Kraybill and Nolt, *Amish Enterprise*, second edition, 2004. I have found no published figures on the substantial number of ex-Amish who also work in these factories.

David K. Shipler's book, *The Working Poor*, was published by Knopf in 2004.

The controversy over an exemption for the Amish from the child labor laws was the subject of many newspaper articles, among them Steven Greenhouse, "Foes of Idle Hands, Amish Contest a Child Labor Law," *New York Times*, October 13, 2003. Figures on accidents were provided by Thomas M. Markey, Acting Administrator, Employment Standards Administration, Department of Labor, in his May 3, 2001, testimony to the U.S. Senate Subcommittee on Labor, Health, and Human Services.

An Amish person's inability to take satisfaction from work as a sign of neurosis within the community is noted in Hostetler, *Amish Society*, and in Lisa Colbert, "Amish Attitudes and Treatment of Illness," *Pennsylvania Folklore*, no. 1 (1980).

Discussion of what it means to have a father "working away" is in *Family Life*, March 2002, in letters responding to a January issue article entitled "Not Everyone Can Be a Farmer."

9. "WOMEN'S LIB WOULD HAVE A FIELD DAY AMONG THE AMISH"

References about women's lot from *Family Life*, all anonymous, can be found in issues such as June 2000 and February 2002.

Both Anne Marie Pederson's delineation of the antifeminist tilt of the *ordnung*, from her chapter "Anabaptist Women and Modernism," and Beth E. Graybill's chapter on Amish and Mennonite dress, "To Remind Us Who We Are," are in *Strangers at Home: Amish and Mennonite Women in History*, edited by Kimberly D. Schmidt et al. (Johns Hopkins University Press, 2002).

Web sites, brochures, and other materials detail the work of the Counseling Center of Wayne and Holmes Counties and the Family Resource and Counseling Center of Gap, Pennsylvania.

The work of James C. Cates and Linda L. Graham is summarized in their article "Psychological Assessment of the Old Order Amish: Unraveling the Enigma," *Professional Psychology Research and Practice*, April 2002.

The work of the Clinic for Special Children is outlined in D. Holmes Morton et al., "Pediatric Medicine and the Genetic Disorders of the Amish and Mennonite People of Pennsylvania," *American Journal of Medical Genetics*, vol. 121C, 2003; in various issues of the clinic's newsletter; and in my article in *Smithsonian Magazine*, February 2006.

10. SEEKING SOLUTIONS

Many articles in the Lancaster and Philadelphia newspapers dealt with the "two Abners" drug case of 1998–99, among them Joseph A. Slobodzian, "Pagans and Two Amish Accused of Selling Cocaine to Youths," *Philadelphia Inquirer*, June 24, 1998. David Remnick's article in *The New Yorker*, "Bad Seeds," July 20, 1998, thorough and fair, covered the story only to the point of the Abners' indictments. Later coverage includes Jon Rutter, "Gentle People Heed Drug Alarm," Lancaster *Sunday News*, July 4, 1999.

11. "COMING HOME" — AN ESSAY

The discussion of Abraham Maslow's hierarchy of needs derives from its formulation in his 1970 book, *Motivation and Personality*, published by Harper & Row.

The study of teenagers across many cultures is by Daniel Offer et al., *The Teenage World: Adolescents' Self-Image in Ten Countries* (Plenum, 1988).

The Grand Inquisitor scene makes up chapter 5 of Dostoevsky's *The Brothers Karamazov*, first published in 1879; quotations are from Constance Garnett's classic translation, 1895.

The quotations from Lawrence Kohlberg are in John C. Coleman and Leo B. Hendry, *The Nature of Adolescence* (third edition, Routledge, 1999). See also the Festschrift edited by S. Mogdil and C. Mogdil, *Lawrence Kohlberg, Consensus and Controversy* (Falmer, 1986).

The study of Muslim ethnic enclaves in Dutch society, and the moral judgment of adolescents in them, is Langha de Mey et al., "Ethnic Variation and the Development of Moral Judgment of Youth in Dutch Society," *Youth and Society*, September 1999. Its testing reflects Kohlberg's thesis and methods.

Alfred North Whitehead's ideas are presented in books such as *Science and the Modern World*, first published in 1925.

Leo Driedger, "The Anabaptist Identification Ladder, Plain-Urbane Continuity in Diversity," *MQR*, October 1977.

Selected Bibliography

Beiler, Joseph F. "Revolutionary War Records." *The Diary of the Old Order Churches*, March 1975.

————. "Research Note: Ordnung." *Mennonite Quarterly Review*, October 1982.

Bender, Harold S. "The Anabaptist Tradition." *Mennonite Quarterly Review*, April 1944.

Cates, James C., and Linda L. Graham. "Psychological Assessment of the Old Order Amish: Unraveling the Enigma." *Professional Psychology Research and Practice*, April 2002.

Donnermeyer, Joseph F., and Elizabeth C. Cooksey. "The Demographic Foundations of Amish Society." Paper presented at the Plain Communities Conference, Elizabethtown College, June 2004.

Dortrecht Confession. *Confession of Faith*. Pathway, 1998.

Driedger, Leo. "The Anabaptist Identification Ladder, Plain-Urbane Continuity in Diversity." *Mennonite Quarterly Review*, October 1977.

Durkheim, Émile. *The Elementary Forms of Religious Life*. 1915. Reprint, Free Press, 1995.

Erikson, Erik. *Identity: Youth and Crisis*. Norton, 1968.

Fishman, Andrea. *Amish Literacy: What and How It Means*. Heinemann, 1988.

Gemelli, Ralph. *Normal Childhood and Adolescent Development*. American Psychiatric Press, 1996.

Graber, Julia A., and Jeanne Brooks-Gunn. "Transitions and Turning Points: Navigating the Passage from Childhood Through Adolescence." *Developmental Psychology* 32 (1996).

Greska, Lawrence P., and Jill E. Korbin. "Key Decisions in the Lives of the Old Order Amish: Joining the Church and Migrating to Another Settlement." *Mennonite Quarterly Review*, September 2002.

Hostetler, John A. *Amish Society*. 4th edition, Johns Hopkins University Press, 1993.

Hostetler, John A., and Gertrude Enders Huntington. *Amish Children: Educa-*

tion in the Family, School, and Community. 1971. Revised edition, Harcourt Brace Jovanovich, 1992.

Iannacone, Laurence R. "Why Strict Churches Are Strong." *American Journal of Sociology* 99 (1994).

Igou, Brad. *The Amish in Their Own Words*. Herald Press, 1999.

Kauffman, Daniel. *Timely Talks with Teenagers*. Timely Publications, n.d.

Kline, David. *Great Possessions: An Amish Farmer's Journal*. North Point Press, 1990.

Koop, Karl. *Anabaptist-Mennonite Confessions of Faith*. Pandora Press, 2004.

Kraybill, Donald B. *The Riddle of Amish Culture*. Johns Hopkins University Press, 2001.

Kraybill, Donald B., ed. *The Amish and the State*, 2nd ed., Johns Hopkins University Press, 2003.

Kraybill, Donald B., and Steven M. Nolt. *Amish Enterprise*, 2nd ed., Johns Hopkins University Press, 2004.

Kraybill, Donald B., and Marc A. Olshan, eds. *The Amish Struggle with Modernity*. University Press of New England, 1994.

Lewis, Jerry M., W. R. Beavers, J. T. Gossett, and V. A. Phillips. *No Single Thread: Psychologic Health in Family Systems*. Brunner/Mazel, 1976.

Luthy, David. *Amish Settlements Across America*. Pathway, 2003.

Maslow, Abraham H. *Motivation and Personality*. Harper & Row, 1970.

Meyers, Thomas J. "Population Growth and Its Consequences in the Elkhart-LaGrange Old Order Amish Settlement." *Mennonite Quarterly Review*, July 1991.

———. "The Old Order Amish: To Remain in the Faith or to Leave." *Mennonite Quarterly Review*, July 1994.

———. "Education and Schooling." In Donald B. Kraybill, ed., *The Amish and the State*. Revised edition, Johns Hopkins University Press, 2003.

Morton, D. Holmes, et al. "Pediatric Medicine and the Genetic Disorders of the Amish and Mennonite People of Pennsylvania," *American Journal of Medical Genetics*, vol. 121C, 2003.

Nolt, Steven M. *A History of the Amish*. Good Books, 1992.

Offer, Daniel, et al. *The Teenage World: Adolescents' Self-Image in Ten Countries*. Plenum, 1988.

Orvin, George H. *Understanding the Adolescent*. American Psychiatric Press, 1996.

Pederson, Anne Marie. "Anabaptist Women and Modernism." In Kimberly D. Schmidt et al., eds. *Strangers at Home: Amish and Mennonite Women in History*. Johns Hopkins University Press, 2002.

Peters, Shawn F. *The Yoder Case: Religious Freedom, Education, and Parental Rights*. University Press of Kansas, 2003.

Reiling, Denise M. "The 'Simmie' Side of Life: Old Order Amish Youths' Affective Response to Culturally Prescribed Deviance." *Youth and Society*, vol. 34, December 2002.

Remnick, David. "Bad Seeds." *The New Yorker*, July 20, 1998.

Smucker, Melvin R. "How Amish Children View Themselves and Their Families: The Effectiveness of Amish Socialization," *Brethren Life and Thought*, Summer 1988.

Spangler, Daisy. *Good Morning Teacher Daisy*. Gordonville Print Shop, 1994.

Stoltzfus, Gideon F. "Where Are We Headed?" *Family Life*, November 2001.

Stoltzfus, Samuel S. "Our Changing Amish Church District." *Pennsylvania Folklife*, Spring 1994.

Stoltzfus, Victor. "Reward and Sanction: The Adaptive Continuity of Amish Life." *Mennonite Quarterly Review*, October 1977.

Testa, Randy-Michael. *After the Fire: The Destruction of the Lancaster County Amish*. University Press of New England, 1992.

Umble, Diane Zimmerman. *Holding the Line: The Telephone in Old Order Mennonite and Amish Life*. Johns Hopkins University Press, 1996.

Wagler, David. *Stories Behind the News*. Brookside Publishers, 1993.

———. "Why the Amish Can Live Without Television." In Scott Savage, ed. *The Plain Reader*. Ballantine, 1998.

Weaver-Zercher, David. *The Amish in the American Imagination*. Johns Hopkins University Press, 2001.

Yoder, John Howard, trans. and ed. *The Schleitheim Confession*. Herald Press, 1977.

Yoder, Paton. *Tradition and Transition: Amish Mennonites and Old Order Amish, 1800–1900*. Herald Press, 1991.

Yoder, Stephen L. *My Beloved Brethren*. Evangel Press, 1992.

Acknowledgments

I would first of all like to thank the many Old Order Amish who took the time to speak with me, often inviting me into their homes to do so, and also those who earlier cooperated with the production of the documentary *The Devil's Playground*. Most of the Amish had never before spoken at length with outsiders to their communities, certainly not to "English" with notebooks or video recorders in hand. Longtime observers of the Amish who helped educate me and whom I also thank include Elam and Barbie Beiler; Jonas and LeVale Beiler of the Family Resource and Counseling Center; Diane DeRue, Rob Schlegel, and Jennifer Yoder of the Counseling Center of Wayne and Holmes Counties; Donald Kraybill and the staff of the Young Center for Anabaptist and Pietist Studies; Alvin Miller; Emma Miller; Dr. Holmes Morton and Caroline Morton and the staff of the Clinic for Special Children; Daniel Riehl; various presenters and attendees of the Enhancing the Health and Well-Being of Plain Communities conference of June 2004 at Elizabethtown College; and others who did not wish to be identified.

My research was aided by volunteers and staff at the Pequea Bruderschaft Library in Gordonville, Pennsylvania; the Mennonite Society Library in Lancaster, Pennsylvania; the Menno-Hof Center in Shipshewana, Indiana; the Scoville Library in Salisbury, Connecticut; and the New York Public Library. I also thank the NYPL for the use of its Wertheim Room.

I owe a debt of gratitude to those who assisted me by commenting on early drafts of various chapters. They include Richard Grossman, Rich Hodupp, Ed Kerr, Donald Kraybill, Macey Levin, Alvin Miller, Edward Nickerson, Tony Perrottet, Noah Shachtman, Harriet Shelare, and Dr. Robert I. Simon. Various denizens, board members, and staff of The Writers Room provided encouragement to me over the several years of research and writing.

This book benefited from the judicious editing of Paul Elie, Ayesha Pande,

Rebecca Saletan, and the staff of North Point Press, and from the insights of my agent, Mel Berger, and of Daniel Laikind and Steven Cantor of Stick Figure Productions.

These individuals' and institutions' help and contributions notwithstanding, all errors that remain in the book are mine.